Get
Off the
Fence!

Get Off the Fence!

10+1 Steps to Help You Make That Big Decision

RHODA MAKOFF, PH.D. AND JEFFREY MAKOFF, ESQ.

Health Communications, Inc.
Deerfield Beach, Florida
www.hci-online.com

The information in this book is general and does not constitute advice on any reader's specific situation. Readers are advised to consult with their own advisors on important decisions. The authors disclaim a professional relationship with readers and the general public.

Library of Congress Cataloging-in-Publication Data

Makoff, Rhoda, 1937-
   Get off the fence! : 10+1 steps to help you make that big decision / Rhoda Makoff and Jeffrey Makoff.
      p. cm.
   Includes index
   ISBN 0-7573-0051-0 (tp)
   1. Decision making. I. Makoff, Jeffrey, 1961- II. Title.

BF448.M35 2003
153.8—dc21

2002192179

Publisher: Health Communications, Inc.
         3201 S.W. 15th Street
         Deerfield Beach, FL 33442-8190

Cover design by Lisa Camp
Inside book design by Dawn Von Strolley Grove

A day dawns, quite like other days; in it, a single hour comes, quite like other hours; but in that day and in that hour the chance of a lifetime faces us.

—Maltbie Babcock

Contents

Acknowledgments

This book is made possible only by the contributions of many individuals.

We warmly acknowledge the contributions of the people who shared with us the intimate, often painful, crossroads in their lives. Their honesty is priceless.

In addition, for their valuable comments, expert insights and contacts, we acknowledge the contribution of our friends, colleagues and advisors: Ellen Ruth Fenichel, Esq., Andrew Ross, Esq., Bill and Luann Pack, Andy Hirschberg, Sharon Thom, Barri Kaplan Bonapart, Esq., C. E. James, R. Bruce Ricks, Dean and Lori Hartwell, Joseph Bloom, Hisako Farmer, Michael Stallman, Esq., Dakota Kingston and David Fishman of Strategic Decisions Group in Menlo Park.

The research and administrative assistance of Adriane McConaughey was crucial.

We thank Aaron Daru and Doug Wade of Poetic Media, Inc., for their financial and moral support.

We acknowledge the relentless support of Nick Holly of the Buchwald & Associates agency in Los Angeles, and Lisa Hamilton and Alan Nevins of Artists Management Group in Beverly Hills.

We thank our husband/father Dwight L. Makoff, M.D., and our wife/daughter-in-law, Charlotte N. Makoff, Esq., for their patience during the long path from concept to publication. We also appreciate and acknowledge the diverse insights of the members of our ever-growing family, Karen Makoff and Michael Chin, Greg and Eileen Makoff, and Tim and Eve Newhart. Of course, we take sole responsibility for the contents of this book.

We are grateful for the support and wise counsel of editors Susan Tobias and Lisa Drucker of Health Communications, Inc.

A Note About the People Involved in Our True Stories

The feature stories at the end of each chapter are true. Except where the subject consented to the disclosure of his or her actual identity, the names, geographical information and other identifying facts were changed to protect the privacy of the people involved. The types of decisions treated in this book are extremely common, and most readers will know someone who was involved in a similar or "almost identical" situation. Please don't assume that any person you know is connected with this book. You should assume that any resemblance of our subjects to people you know is merely a coincidence.

We appreciate the remarkable diversity of the individuals who shared their personal stories with us and our readers. The story contributors did not participate in selecting the other stories or in writing this book. Our readers should not presume that our story contributors agree with the people featured in *other* stories, share the same values or would have made the same decisions. Each story stands on its own. Likewise, the stories necessarily are told from the perspective of the subject we interviewed—the person who *made* the decision that is featured. The subject's values and recollection of the facts may differ from those of other participants in the same events.

The true stories are not always "perfect" illustrations of the points made in the chapter before each story. The reason for this is simple: Major life decisions tend to be complex. Given the choice between heavily editing the stories, so they appear to fit perfectly, and preserving their true complexity and tension, we opted for reality.

Introduction

If you have a big personal or business decision to make, or know somebody who does, you've picked up the right book. *Get Off the Fence!* shows you *how* to make a "Big Decision." Examples of Big Decisions include:

Do you move in with someone? Move out?

Do you quit school? Go back to school?

How do you make a life-support decision for a loved one?

If you can't find a marriage partner, do you become a single parent?

Should you leave a steady job to start a new business?

Should you buy a house? Buy a second house?

Should you commit your business to a new strategy that could rocket or ruin it?

Do you stage an intervention to stop a friend's or family member's substance abuse?

Do you bring a coworker's illegal activity to your employer's or the authorities' attention?

Should you give someone a marriage ultimatum? How do you respond to one?

Do you marry out of your faith (or race) if your parents object?

Do you fire someone you like?

Do you come out as gay or lesbian? When?

Our method is called the "10+1 Steps." The "10 Steps" are straightforward tactics to move a major decision to resolution. The "+1" is devoted to the important question of what to do with gut instincts: what your "heart tells you to do" and the other, almost metaphysical, hard-to-articulate intuitions that quite often accompany a Big Decision.

You'll look at tough personal and business decisions differently after reading *Get Off the Fence!* You'll approach your major decisions, now and in the future, with confidence. You'll learn the strategies that successful people and wise advisors throughout history have used to work through Big Decisions. You'll lose that feeling of isolation, frustration and confusion that exists when you have a problem, but no approach to solving it. You'll have the tools you need to move your life past any major dilemma—no matter how huge, intimidating and emotional.

You'll benefit directly and immediately from the 10+1 Steps. Bad decisions result in deferred dreams and lost opportunities. Bad decisions can lead you to neglect positive relationships, while negative relationships fester. Bad decisions can cause lifelong regrets and self-recrimination. Strong decision skills will empower you to be more effective and happy. You'll achieve greater goals with fewer regrets. You'll waste less time, move past roadblocks and expend more of your energy to pursue the best possible life. When you look back on your lifetime of decisions, you want to feel that you made the right choices at each opportunity, especially at the major crossroads.

Each chapter is followed by a true story—an often unsettling example of a difficult decision that was made by the subject. *Get Off the Fence!* gives you a powerful approach to resolving decisions about love and marriage, career and business, illness, child rearing, and other situations where tough choices abound. As we explore the concepts involved in strong decision-making, we'll always take you back to real life where we all have to function. Several of the true stories address subjects that are rarely discussed after the painful decision has been made.

Your decisions are the ultimate expression of your individuality and freedom. Your choices inevitably reflect your values and desires: what is important to you, and what you hold to be true and right. This book does not tell you what moral, ethical or religious beliefs or values to hold. We try to present the 10+1 Steps in a way that works with your values, whatever they may be. *Our goal is to teach judgment, not to pass judgment.* The principles described in *Get Off the Fence!* have been applied by wise counselors, operating from diverse perspectives and beliefs, throughout human history.

RHODA MAKOFF, PH.D.
JEFFREY MAKOFF, ESQ.

Get Fired Up: The Good News Is That You Have a Choice

This book is about how to make *Big* Decisions. People often talk about Big Decisions in a negative way as "agonizing choices," "painful dilemmas," "serious problems" and, of course, "pickles."[1] We all know somebody who has tossed and turned, maybe for years, over a major choice. Perhaps you have. Perhaps you are doing so right now. Big Decisions are associated with anxiety, fear, depression, frustration, pain, obsession and that unpleasant set of feelings called "pressure." Big personal decisions relate to dramatic and important life events: love and marriage, childbirth, child rearing, health, education, work, finances and death. Major business decisions often involve the birth, survival or death of an enterprise, the decision-maker's reputation or lots of money.

Some people are skilled at evading Big Decisions. Nobody escapes all of them forever. If you're serious about improving your life, whether through career advancement, resolving a specific personal or business problem, or "changing your life direction," you must be able to identify and make difficult choices. Before we introduce you to the 10+1 Steps to help you make those Big Decisions, we'll use the first chapter to put your decisions in

---

[1] A "pickle" is a food preserved in brine or vinegar or, more relevantly, "an unpleasant or difficult situation or condition: plight, predicament or trouble." *Webster's New Third International Dictionary,* 3rd ed. (Springfield, Mass.: Merriam-Webster, Inc., 1997).

context. The message is that your difficult choices define your life—past, present and future. Fearing a choice that will define your life is a natural response. Nonetheless, your first decision must be to challenge your fears and go confidently forward to make any Big Decision that you face.

Big Decisions Come from Your Freedom to Make a Choice

To improve your life, you must embrace your freedom to make choices. All of your Big Decisions emanate from the freedom to choose, even when you're forced to select between "bad" options. When a situation's outcome is certain, you deal with it. If the outcome is bad, you *cope.* Coping is not big decision-making. Coping is how you adapt to something that you can't change much. This book shows you how to make *choices* that will bring about change, not how to adapt to what can't be changed.

So much for abstractions. Let's look at how choices lead to some typical Big Decisions that you, a friend or a family member may face.

Marriage. In vast parts of the world, marriages are arranged by the parents of the bride and groom (sometimes with a professional matchmaker's assistance). Arranged marriage is still practiced in parts of Asia, Africa and Eastern Europe. The basis for the arrangement is not love, but rather social compatibility, sometimes dowry (property exchanged for a daughter's hand) or other factors that the parents deem important. In some cases, the couple meet for the first time on, or close to, their wedding day. In the United States, Western Europe, and other parts of Asia and Africa, we have "love marriages" (to use the terminology of arranged-marriage societies). With the freedom of love marriages comes the burden to find a person to love, to figure out whether we love that person enough to marry him or her, and to decide what to do if we no longer are compatible with that person. Knowing that millions of people in the world participate in arranged marriages doesn't make decisions about marriage any easier. Hard choices often flow from the freedom we're given to succeed or fail based on our own judgments.

Illness. In 1937, actress Jean Harlow died from a kidney condition at the age of twenty-six. Her death not only was premature, but it was horrifyingly gruesome. While on the set of her last film, *Saratoga* with Clark Gable, Harlow reportedly began to puff up and smell of the waste that her failing kidneys could not process. After Harlow was hospitalized, according to David Stenn's account in *Bombshell: The Life and Death of Jean Harlow,* her friends and family watched helplessly and prayed for a miracle as Harlow deteriorated. Clinically successful artificial kidney machines were not invented until the 1940s, and they were not in general use until the 1960s. The first successful U.S. kidney transplant took place in 1954. Today, a kidney-disease patient (and his or her family) has a host of treatment decisions to make—over the *decades* that the kidney-disease patient is expected to survive after the diagnosis. The same is true of cancer, diabetes, HIV/AIDS and countless other serious illnesses.

Career. Nothing has changed more over the past two hundred years than how we make a living. In the early 1800s, most Americans and Europeans farmed at the subsistence level or engaged in local agriculture-related services or trade. By 1900, farmers made up around 35 percent of the U.S. labor force. A devastating drought forced millions of people to abandon their farms in the 1930s and relocate their lives and livelihoods to other parts of the United States (especially the West). In the twenty-first century, most Americans and Western Europeans have nonagricultural jobs, primarily in the industrial and service sectors. While the weather has minimal impact on careers, individual career decisions have a huge impact. The freedom to manage a career is a great gift, and it carries the burden of sometimes difficult career decisions.

Business. The nearly worldwide free-enterprise system offers a huge palette of business opportunities: large and small, corporate and entrepreneurial, manufacturing and service, local and international, new and mature, profit-driven and nonprofit. Business is more competitive, faster, *potentially* more lucrative and complex than ever before. Some managers master and benefit directly from the factors that make contemporary business so demanding. Others do not meet the challenges and fall by the wayside. The most valuable asset in business today is a management team or manager who has excellent judgment. A manager who merely toes the line and can't exercise sound judgment adds little to an enterprise.

Keep in mind the ultimate source of your Big Decisions: You're alive, and you have choices. General Omar N. Bradley, who led the D-Day invasion of Normandy that marked the turning point of World War II in Europe, said, "This is as true in everyday life as it is in battle: We are given one life, and the decision is ours whether to wait for circumstances to make up our mind or whether to act and, in acting, to live." By seizing an active role in your own major decisions, you affirm your values and control your destiny. Important decisions begin with your freedom and power to choose. Be glad you have that discretion. Hold onto it and learn to use it wisely.

Big Decisions Will Transform You

A Big Decision is one that will change you, and you know it. A Big Decision may alter the course of your life for months, years or a lifetime. Moreover, *how* you make a Big Decision may affect you as much as the decision itself. The reason is that you not only experience the consequences of the decisions you make, but you also learn about (and adjust) your decision-making process as a result of past decisions.

Think about how your own decision process has developed. Perhaps you asked your parents for advice on an important decision early in life—a career or school decision, for example. If the advice proved to be good and it worked out, you were more inclined to ask your parents about your next big career or school decision. If you asked your parents for advice and a nasty argument followed in which you obtained little helpful information or perspective, you were less inclined to consult your parents the next time. Perhaps you concluded that your parents were out of touch or that you didn't need their advice. What if your parents' advice was well-intentioned, but ultimately not helpful? In that case, you might have decided to consult your parents the next time, but you put less weight on their opinions. Your experience of this early career or school decision may affect how you involve your parents in other decisions, even on unrelated subjects, for many years or a lifetime.

Now imagine a pregnant fifteen-year-old girl's decision whether to keep the baby, give the baby up for adoption or terminate the pregnancy through an abortion.[2] The young woman's decision will determine whether as a teenager she raises a child, which undeniably will have a major impact on her life (and certainly on the life of the yet-unborn fetus). If the young woman or her parents have strong views on abortion, a decision to have an abortion could

---

[2] The examples we use in this book show how the 10+1 Steps apply to important decisions that people make every day. For that reason, you'll find lots of examples about marriage and relationships, health, death, substance abuse, child rearing and other issues at the crucible of contemporary life. Although you may feel strongly that there is "no choice" in abortion, drug abuse, homosexuality or euthanasia, you probably would agree that, justified or not, millions of people each year have painful dilemmas surrounding these events. This book addresses the *process* of making decisions, not the personal values of decision-makers.

have serious emotional and social repercussions. The process of making a childbirth/abortion decision without her parents' help, with her parents' help or over the objection of her parents may change the way she relates to her parents for a very long time, perhaps a lifetime. The young woman's Big Decision may have a long-term impact on her *decision process,* no matter what she decides.

Experienced business managers recognize the importance of process in business decision-making. Strong managers spend nearly as much time considering how to decide an issue as what to decide. *Who should be at the meeting to make sure the right input is obtained? Are outside advisors needed? Should they be at the meeting, on the phone or consulted beforehand? What advance preparation is expected of each meeting participant? Are written materials needed? Will the group need communications facilities to bring people in?* The *process* considerations go on and on. You can bet that a manager's past experience making Big Decisions influences the manager's approach to the major decision that is on the table today.

A major decision—even a tough, painful or sorrowful one—presents an opportunity for you to define, refine and express your individual approach to life. You *won't* revel in every decision—especially the Big Decisions. Yet you *will* grow immensely from each experience.

Your Values Are the Core of Every Decision

The 10+1 Steps may be applied to any major decision that arises in your personal or business life. How is that possible? Because we don't tell you what is right for you. It's simply not our role. We know that a great decision for one person may be an extremely poor decision for another. A thousand people with different values, resources and circumstances following our 10+1 Steps could reach totally different conclusions about what to do. They all could be correct. The methods in this book help you discover, analyze and apply your own values to the particular circumstances of your life.

We aren't writing as theologians, philosophers, spiritual advisors or professional ethicists. Having worked through many Big Decisions in our personal and professional lives, involving people who come from a variety of cultural, religious and family backgrounds, we know that the shaping of personal values starts in the family and develops as each individual participates in the community and workplace. While we have personal views on issues of ethics and values, we have chosen to write on the decision-making process and how to make decisions using methods that to a large extent transcend individual values. (If our values show through, please remember that they may not be the same as yours.)

Our approach is based on the notion, admittedly a value of ours, that it's best to make important life decisions deliberately. Because the world is so complex, with few reliable safety nets or parachutes, you'll best serve your family, your community and yourself when you make decisions with care. Don't thrash about in confusion or become decision-disabled by paralysis. The deliberate approach maximizes the chance that you'll survive, thrive and achieve all of your important personal, financial, social and spiritual goals.

Sometimes your values are clear when you start to make a decision. Other times, you must discover, explore and test your values. For example, if your value system holds that "abortion is murder," unplanned pregnancy may present a decision to keep the baby or adopt it out; having an abortion is out of the question for you. What if you find yourself pregnant and have no strong feelings about abortion? Perhaps you've never thought much about it because it wasn't your issue. Now it is. For you, the decision-making process must include finding and exploring your values. If you have no settled values on abortion, you must search for them. This book does not tell you what values you'll find, but it shows you how to *apply* what you find through a process that is comfortable.

Align "Who You Are" with "Who You Want to Be": Build a Path with Your Choices

Everyone who works with highly successful people discovers that the "right moves" take many people quite far in life despite a lack of natural ability and other resources. Likewise, an individual's poor decisions can nullify just about any natural or circumstantial advantage. None of us controls our genetically inherited qualities (not yet, at least!). We can't change our family background, where we were born and raised, or our first language. In our youth, we had little control over many aspects of our lives. Our parents, siblings and teachers were more or less issued to us. The people who were issued to us (or, in the case of parents, who issued us) might even have tried to choose our friends. Yet, where we started is just that: where we started. Beyond what we can't change, we can control a great deal by making the right decisions and following through with our actions.

The steps we introduce in the next eleven chapters help you navigate the turning points and divergent roads in life. Unless you've put yourself in a position of extreme responsibility, you probably won't find yourself at a crossroads every day. You may go for three, five or even ten years between Big Decisions. Those Big Decisions, however, will transform you and define your future choices. Be ready.

We start with Step 1, which shows you how to identify and confront head-on the Big Decision you have to make to move your life forward.

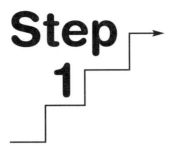

Step 1

Make the Real Decision and Dump the Decoys

A problem well-stated is a problem half-solved.

—Charles F. Kettering

Start your Big Decision by figuring out exactly what you need to decide. It seems obvious. Would it surprise you to learn that many people don't know what their decision is? For largely psychological reasons, the important decision that will transform your life is often hidden from you. Who's hiding it? In most cases, you're hiding it from yourself. In other cases, another person is hiding the decision from you. Step 1 requires you to confront the *real* Big Decision, the one that will move you forward, and to discard the decoys that distract you.

What is a decoy? A decoy looks like a decision and may be a decision, but it's not the Big Decision. A decoy won't transform your life, nor will it solve the important problem. A decoy saps your time and energy while you wrestle with it, leaving you (like the poor duck) to miss the issue for too long. If you pursue the decoy too far, you'll find yourself in the crosshairs of an unsympathetic

1

hunter's weapon—with unattractive options. If that sounds too dramatic, don't forget that in a Big Decision, your life *is* the issue.

Consider these common situations in which a decoy steals attention from the real issue:

- Mark fights with his wife about whether she should make a minor purchase, when the real problem is that Mark is frustrated and dissatisfied at work and wants to make a career change. While money is an issue in both cases, Mark wastes time debating the small purchase when he should concentrate on his career options.

- Jill, the supervisor of a graphics department, deliberates for weeks about what tasks to give an underperforming employee whose poor attitude is hurting morale. Jill knows this employee isn't working out, and another person should be hired to fill the position. Because Jill dislikes terminating employees, she fruitlessly tries to scare up some function that this employee will handle well. Jill is distracting herself with a decoy that will only prolong everyone's pain and frustrate Jill's other employees.

- Cynthia agonizes over whether to break up a relationship with Pete that was dead long ago. Cynthia is certain that a breakup would be messy, so she avoids the discomfort by agonizing endlessly over the decision whether she should stay with Pete. If the relationship truly has no future, Cynthia should be focusing on *how* to finish the dead-end relationship that is holding her back, not on the decoy of whether to end it.

A decoy looks, walks and quacks like a Big Decision. A decoy is not an obvious fake. A decoy may even have a genuine element; perhaps it really *isn't* prudent to buy that little item. Perhaps you *should* try again to reconcile with a spouse or significant other. Maybe you *should* give an underperforming employee (or employer) another chance. Explore these issues, but be careful. The appearance of genuineness is what makes decoys so dangerous. When you address a decoy while leaving the major issue unresolved, your forward progress grinds to a halt. Resolving the decoy chews up your time and energy, interfering with your ability to make the decision that will take you past the problem. A decoy bogs you down as opportunities to make true progress go right past you.

The first step toward strong decision-making is to separate the real decisions from the decoys, and then focus your energy on the important choice.

Why Big Decisions Hide Behind Decoys, and Why You Fall for the Decoys

We all gravitate—mentally and physically—toward what feels good and away from unpleasantness, pain and uncertainty. Big Decisions often present uncomfortable, intimidating and unfamiliar choices. High-stakes, life-or-death, make-or-break, bet-your-company decisions bring out all sorts of fears, paranoia and defense mechanisms. Decoys start out innocently as a way for us to avoid or cope with pain; focusing on the decoy sidesteps the tough issue and directs our attention to a less daunting matter. In many cases, we prefer to be bogged down by a decoy rather than stressed-out by a Big Decision. The problem with self-imposed decoys is that we borrow from the future to avoid confronting a tough issue today. The price is high: the future.

Not all decoys come from our own fertile, imaginative and pain-phobic psyches. Many times, someone else who has a vested interest in defining the scope of our decision presents the decoy. Fred, a credit manager at your company, walks in and says, "The reason the business is low on cash is that our customer, XYZ

Corporation, is eight months behind in payment. We need to decide whether to stop shipping product to XYZ." It's true that you *might* gain something by not selling more products to XYZ Corporation. Is there a bigger problem in this picture? If Fred is a poor credit manager, who negligently allowed XYZ to believe it could get away with a slow-pay strategy, you can be sure that Fred won't identify the bigger problem: Fred's job performance. Fred will try hard to focus all of your attention on XYZ Corporation, but you need to make sure Fred's not allowing twenty more XYZ situations to develop in the future.

Manipulating choices certainly is not limited to the business context. In which of the following three situations is one person foisting a decoy?

- Teen Boy to Teen Girl: "I really love you, and you love me, right? People who love each other should make love. Let's figure out the perfect time and place."
- Father to Daughter: "My drinking is none of your business. Your choice is to accept me as I am or leave my house."
- Husband to Wife: "I want our children to be raised properly. They need a good mother. You've got to leave your career and raise the kids."

The answer, of course, is all of them. In a manipulation decoy, one side says, in effect, "Think about the choice I am presenting so you don't spend too much time on the real issue. If you think about the real issue, you might not choose to do what I want."

In the first example, the boy slides right by the issue of whether the girl should have sex. He tries to pressure her by making it seem as if she already made the decision to have sex, and now it's just a matter of when and where. In the second example, the father wants to make the daughter's options look black and white. The daughter can pursue lots of other strategies. Father doesn't want her to think about them, though, so he frames a horrendous choice. Her real choice is whether to accept her father as he is, or to challenge his drinking habit and try to create a better life and relationship for both of them. The third example is from the perspective of a husband who does not want his wife to work after they have children. (The context assumes that she wants to work.) By pitting his impression of good motherhood against career, the husband deflects the discussion away from alternative choices that his wife might have, such as part-time work, a "mommy track," full-time work with help at home or perhaps the same job at a less demanding company. If his wife is skilled at identifying decoys and *disagrees* with her husband, she'll say, "This isn't about whether I'll be a good mother. I will be a good mother no matter what we do. This is about whether I am ready to leave my career right now. We need to take a look at each of my options." Of course, if the wife *agrees* with her husband on the issue, he probably hasn't used a decoy at all—in fact, there isn't much of a Big Decision.

Whether the decoys are self-imposed or someone else's attempts at manipulation, you must identify and eliminate the decoys before they lead you astray. At best, decoys waste time and other resources. At worst, decoys distract you for so long that executing the right choice once you finally identify the real issue becomes impossible.

How to Identify the Real Issue
and Eliminate the Decoys

"Eliminate the decoys!" is easier said than done. Our protective minds cleverly camouflage decoys or they are strategically selected and disguised by other people who want to influence our choices. Decoys thrive in major decisions because the stakes—emotional, financial, physical and otherwise—are high. Begin by saying to yourself, *I have reached a decision point. Yet what is grabbing my attention may not be the real issue. If I do not address the real issue, I will only defer an important decision. Is the issue presented to me the real problem, or is it just a decoy? What is the root of this problem?*

Talking to yourself, of course, may not be enough. In many cases, the real decision is painful to identify, especially in personal relationships. The extreme is reached in physically or emotionally abusive relationships. The victim may have so much fear that she or he is incapable of seeing that whether to stop the abuse or whether to leave the relationship are decisions that can be made. Such decisions appear to carry new sources of pain. The abused person may be fearful that ending the relationship will lead to more abuse—perhaps serious bodily injury, stalking or death. In other cases, the abused person may blame herself for the abuse and focus on her own shortcomings rather than on abuse that should not be tolerated. Financial fear may be a factor. The victim's attention is drawn to decoys that do not lead to a decision about ending the abuse or the relationship. By avoiding the real issue, the victim deals only with problems that she believes can be addressed without creating potential *new* sources of physical or emotional pain. The consequence is that the victim may be paralyzed in a life of abuse, putting tiny bandages on a hemorrhage, and miss the Big Decision. In such cases, third-party intervention may be required to break the barriers.

If you sense that barriers make it hard for you to identify your real choices, you must take steps to break past those barriers before you'll be able to see the Big Decision. One technique is to ask yourself what decision you would make today "in a perfect world"—a world where you have no emotional, physical or financial limitations or fears. While using a fantasy world to identify the real decision may seem strange, the perfect-world scenario helps you find the decoys by transporting you to a place where you don't need to protect yourself so much. Returning to the example of an abuse victim, the victim might ask what she would do if she and her loved ones were surrounded by a totally secure (even soundproof) shield that allows her to do or say whatever she wants, without any fear of physical or emotional abuse or retribution by her abuser. Suddenly, the victim's choices may look a whole lot different. Without the fear of harm, some victims will jump to leave the relationship. The decoys fall when the barrier of fear evaporates: The real issue isn't whether to leave, but rather how to leave without getting hurt. Still not simple . . . but much more clear.

Nobody actually makes decisions in a perfect world. We all make our decisions in the flawed, scary, imperfect world in which people sometimes seek revenge, act irrationally, stalk, punish, abuse, torment and attack. Fears of all kinds may be very rational and well-founded. In the end, you may permit a well-founded fear to influence your decision, its timing and how you carry it out. You should not, however, allow fear to obscure the decision before you. Only when you identify the real decision can you develop a strategy that moves you toward the choice that can change your life. Thinking about what you would do in a perfect world will start you toward a better decision in the real world.

Next, learn to apply the technique of active skepticism. Challenge supposed alternatives that are presented to you. *Why do I have to decide whether to stop supplying XYZ Corporation? What got me into this situation? Perhaps XYZ is behind, and perhaps they should be cut off—but wasn't it Fred's job to establish sound credit practices and to follow up on receivables before they got both huge and old?* When someone says, "The whole problem is . . . ," your mental response should be, *Is it? Really? Is that the whole problem? Maybe the problem is something else.* When someone says, "You have only two choices," come up with a few more. Express this skepticism (in a diplomatic way, of course) to the person who is trying to define your choices. The other person's reaction may be informative.

Call it paranoia if you like, but always remember that some people will frame *your* choices in the way that's best for *them.* Be skeptical about how others frame your decisions, especially when their own interests are involved. What's in it for them? You and your dependents will bear the consequences of your Big Decision. Set the agenda.

The Big Decision is the decision that solves the real problem and moves you forward. Discard the decoys until you find the duck. If you succeed, you've taken a huge step toward advancing your decision process because you're making the decision that actually matters. When you've identified the true Big Decision and set the decoys aside, move to Step 2. Step 2 shows you how to break down even the most complex problem into bite-size pieces that you are able to handle.

We leave Step 1 with the following points to remember about beating the decoys:

- If you don't beat the decoys, you'll waste time, resources and energy while the real decision that can advance your life will remain unresolved.
- Try the perfect-world scenario and develop an active skepticism toward choices that are presented to you. If fears and worries are interfering with your ability to make a decision, isolate the barriers that hold you back and identify the choice that matters.

End-of-Life: A Twenty-Four-Year-Old Woman Finds That a Life-Support Decision Is More About Knowing Her Father Than Bringing Him Back

Katherine Conley knew that her father would not want to live with a mind that was devastated by a massive stroke.

The late-night telephone call was not a total surprise to Katherine Conley.[3] Katherine had dreaded the moment for as long as she could remember, ever since she was a very young girl:

My father had always been overweight, always had heart problems and always had high blood pressure. For as long as I could remember, my greatest fear was that my father would have a heart attack. I dreaded it. I played it out over and over in my mind whenever he was late to pick me up. If he was fifteen minutes late, I'd be annoyed. Half an hour, I'd be worried. After forty-five minutes, I'd be panicked.

Katherine finished college in 1987 and made her first major adult choice. She decided to move from the West Coast to the East Coast for her first job out of school. Katherine was an only child and wasn't sure she was ready to move so far away. Yet Katherine also felt it was time to become independent, and her parents agreed. She wanted to do arts administration. She applied for a job at an East Coast nonprofit organization. She got the job.

A couple of nights before Katherine left, she broke down in tears about the impending move:

My dad said, 'You know, this doesn't have to be permanent. If you don't like it, you can always come home.' It was the safety net I needed to be able to go, knowing somebody was always behind

---

[3] A pseudonym.

me and that I could always come home. That gave me the confidence to do it. I felt so taken care of and safe with my father there for me.

Katherine moved and started work. She and a roommate shared an attic apartment in a university professor's home. Everything was going great—Katherine's job, her living situation and her social life. Three largely uneventful years passed. Katherine spoke regularly with her parents on the telephone, and she visited as often as she could.

The middle-of-the-night call from Katherine's mother lasted less than two minutes, and Katherine didn't receive much information. The basics were terrifyingly clear, however. Katherine's father was in the hospital, it was major, and Katherine should come home at once:

I got the call at three A.M. or so. I called the airline and tried to get the first flight out. I'd never had to call for an emergency flight. I was on a budget and usually made tickets twenty-one days in advance. This was an unfamiliar experience. Everything that happened for the next two months was a first. I was completely hysterical on the phone with the airline. I couldn't get the words out. I somehow had to convey information and figure out what to do. Money was an issue. I had never heard of bereavement fares. I remember the woman from the airline being kind and dealing with me well. I got out the next morning on the earliest flight. It was the worst trip. I had no idea what to expect. I was out of contact. I remember being on the plane and literally wanting to jump out of my skin. I felt trapped. In this situation, you're sitting there and you don't want to think about it. That flight was the longest six hours of my life.

Friends of the family met Katherine at the airport and drove her straight to the hospital. All Katherine could think was that her greatest fear had been realized. Katherine's father was the most important person in her life. Even Katherine's mom knew it. "I was a total daddy's girl," Katherine recollects. Her parents married late for the era and waited thirteen years to have a child. When Katherine was born in 1965, her father was thirty-seven and her mother was forty-one. They weren't old then, but flash forward to April 1990: Katherine was only twenty-four, but her father was sixty-two, and her mother was sixty-six.

Katherine's father hadn't wanted children. He was concerned about the enormous responsibility. Katherine's mother eventually wore her husband down, and he agreed to have a child. Katherine recalls:

I never felt unloved or unwanted by my father. Once he made a decision to have me, he thought it was joyful. My father was not very interested in me as a baby, but as I learned to talk he realized he had this little person he could reason with and show the world to. We did so much together. I have clear memories of running errands with my father. He taught me how to reason and how to approach problems. We thought the same way. We were that close.

The waiting room of an intensive-care unit is a strange scene. You're thrown together with other people who, by fate, now coexist in crisis. The ICU itself is a large room with hospital beds, medical monitors, emergency equipment and institutional furniture. Under the ICU rules of the hospital where Katherine's father had been taken, visitors were allowed only fifteen minutes per hour with a patient. The visitors spent the rest of the time in the waiting room, sitting, waiting and exchanging status reports with the other visitors. A high-school girl's boyfriend had shot her in the head in a jealous rage, then shot himself. They were in the ICU. Her family was in the ICU waiting room. Another woman in her thirties had been in a head-on collision in a minivan. Her two small children, also in the van, were fine. The woman had severe brain damage. She was in the ICU. Her parents and husband were in the ICU waiting room. Katherine Conley was in the ICU waiting room. Her father had suffered a brain hemorrhage and was in a coma. Katherine recalls:

You develop strange alliances with the people in the waiting room. These were my compatriots. You exchange information with each other. You wait. And wait. And wait some more. You wouldn't know the other people if you didn't find yourselves together because of some crisis.

Katherine learned more about what happened to her father from her father's doctors. Katherine's father had been on a common prescription blood-thinning drug, which was supposed to prevent him from having a stroke caused by a blood clot. In the unlikely event of a stroke, however, the blood-thinning drug could cause a more severe hemorrhage. For most people, including Katherine's father, the benefits of blood thinners are believed to outweigh the risks. Katherine's father suffered an unexpected neurovascular event that, she was told, the blood thinners appeared to have aggravated.

The doctors described Katherine's father's hemorrhage as "massive." It wasn't localized. Before Katherine arrived, a neurosurgeon had implanted a shunt in her father's head in an attempt to drain fluid from the areas surrounding the brain. Her father later had a second surgery. Waiting—lots of waiting—accompanied each step. "Wait and see" was both the doctors' instruction for Katherine and her mother and the prognosis for Katherine's father:

If there's one thing all the shows on TV don't show, it's the interminable waiting. On TV, it all happens in a neat sixty-minute package. In reality, you wait to see the doctor, you wait for something to happen, then you wait more. I hated the phrase "wait and see." My mom is not very good at asking questions, so I asked the doctors all the questions. They wouldn't tell me anything definitive. I was always suspicious that there was something they weren't telling me.

Katherine slept at her parents' home as her father's hospitalization extended from days to weeks. Each day, Katherine would wake up early, drive to the hospital and sit with her father for as long as the hospital allowed. Katherine's mother wasn't handling the situation well:

The nurses told us to talk to my father during the three weeks he was in the ICU. The idea was to stimulate his mind, to try to get a response. I was allowed in for fifteen minutes each hour, then the nurses would shuttle me out. The rest of the time I would wait. I wanted to be with him. I talked to him and told him what was going on. My parents were both avid readers. They always read before they went to bed. I got the book my dad had in process when he had his stroke. I started right where the bookmark was and finished it. Sometimes I read the paper. I skipped stories that I thought would upset him. There was no reaction, but I kept going. You've got to do something. My mother would stare at him and not talk, or she would talk to him like he wasn't a person. It was painful for me to watch. She was shut down. She couldn't talk about it at all with me.

Katherine's father had two neurosurgeons. From Katherine's perspective, one was warm and communicative and the other simply didn't want to deal with patients' families. One day, Katherine was in the ICU and didn't understand something about anesthesia that her father would receive during his second surgery. She caught the latter neurosurgeon on his way out of the ICU and tried to stop him. He was brusque and acted bothered by Katherine. By her own admission, Katherine "threw a fit":

He gave me this look, as if I was wasting his time. I blew up. I said, "You will stay here and answer all my questions. You're not going to do this to me. I need you to answer my questions. This is my father's life." My father had taken care of me for so many years. It was my responsibility to take care of him. My dad would have done anything to protect me and keep me safe. It was my turn.

After three weeks in the ICU, the hospital moved Katherine's father to a regular room at the same facility. He remained in a coma, without any apparent cognitive ability or improvement. He was breathing without a machine, but he was being fed through a tube. After a few days, he was transported to a different hospital. The physicians told Katherine that even if her father regained consciousness, his brain had been damaged. He certainly had lost much of his cognitive ability—forever. The new hospital scheduled a meeting with Katherine, her mother and a hospital employee called an "ombudsman" (now the position would be called an "ombudsperson" or a "patient advocate").

The ombudsman's office was a tiny room, no bigger than a small examining room. Katherine was in uncharted territory. "We're going to talk about some choices you have to make," the ombudsman said.

Katherine looked over at her mother. Her mother was looking at her. Katherine knew she was going to have to make the choices. Katherine recalls:

The ombudsman pointed out that my father's condition had been the same for a while. She said we needed to start thinking about long-term care outside the hospital. She said that the hospital would keep my father only for a limited amount of time, and the limit was approaching. Maybe we'd have two weeks. Long-term, outside care meant a convalescent home. He couldn't live at our house in his condition. I was horrified about putting my father into a nursing home. My dad hated those places. There was no part of him that would ever want to be in a home. My mom and I had looked at some convalescent homes. The local home was considered pretty good, but we just couldn't imagine my father being there. The ombudsman talked about the cost of long-term critical care. It's not cheap. A lot of the cost would end up coming out of my parents' savings, the savings that would have to support my mother. It was clear my father was not improving. There was no improvement in his function or cognition. The objective of long-term care would be to keep my father comfortable, but in a coma, for an indefinite period.

Katherine had expected the ombudsman to raise the issue of long-term care. What happened next caught Katherine off guard. After the discussion of long-term care, the ombudsman told Katherine and her mother, "You also have to make some decisions about resuscitation orders, medication, and food and water sustenance." Katherine recalls her reaction:

I remember the ombudsperson slid a check-the-box form across the table. The form basically had three decisions to be made on it. One, should the hospital resuscitate my father if he stopped breathing or his heart stopped? Two, should the hospital withhold medication from my father? Three, should the hospital withhold sustenance, which we were told would mean no food or water? I remember looking at my mother, but there was no help over there. She was totally shut down. She was looking to me to make this decision. My father didn't have a durable power of attorney for health care. I wasn't prepared for this at all. I had never spoken with my father about his attitude toward death or life support. I'd never made a decision about anyone else's life before. This was my father, the person who I cared about most in the entire world.

Katherine didn't want to lose her father. Every emotion in her body, her whole life, screamed, "Keep him alive!" Staring at Katherine on that table was a death order. It was then that Katherine recognized the true nature of what she would be required to decide:

I realized that this decision wasn't about what I wanted. What I wanted was to bring him back. But the best information I had was that, in the best-case scenario, I'd be bringing him back to a life he'd detest. He was relying on me and on our relationship to speak for what he would want and do what he would want done. He took care of me and made me feel safe. He taught me and raised me. He trusted me. I wasn't acting for Katherine in that room. I was acting for my father. I was making decisions that he couldn't make anymore. I knew my father well. We didn't talk about death in my family, but I knew how he felt about nursing homes. He hated the idea of being put in a home. He was such a mental person, so cerebral. I knew that if he wasn't going to have full mental function, he wouldn't be interested in life anymore. We'd been told that the chance of my father regaining his mental function was low. There's always something that says, "Maybe he'll get better." It's hard to give up hope. But even if he'd improved some, which hadn't happened at all in six weeks, he wouldn't have been comfortable living without full mental function.

Katherine made the following choices, and her mother went along with them and signed the form:

Do Not Resuscitate	Yes
Withhold Medication	Yes
Withhold Sustenance	No

Katherine knew that her father wouldn't want to be resuscitated or medicated to keep him alive in a coma. She just couldn't withhold food and water. "I knew he didn't want to be kept alive any longer in that state, but for some reason I could not withhold food and water. It was so basic. I was comfortable with no extraordinary intervention."

In accordance with the decisions made in the ombudsman's office, no further medication was given to Katherine's father. He died two weeks after the meeting.

Postscript: In Katherine's Own Words

I think about my father all the time. I have no regrets about the decisions I made. I've followed the same process ever since. I do my best with the information I have at the time. Then I let go. My father wouldn't have expected any more of me. The medical prognosis was getting less and less hopeful. It was clear my father wasn't going to regain the happy, cerebral life he wanted.

When I reflect on how I handled that time in the hospital, I often go back to the incident when I yelled at the neurosurgeon. I'd been taught to be pretty deferential with people. Yelling at a doctor, telling him that he couldn't walk away, was very much out of character. I felt so responsible. I owed it to my father to do the absolute best I could because he had always taken care of me. I was fighting for my father. I did things I wouldn't usually do.

My parents should have had more conversations with me about death. The only time it really came up was two years before my father died. I was living on the East Coast. My parents went out one day and bought burial plots, including a plot for me. My father called me after they bought the gravesites. He told me, "I'm sure you'll get married and have kids, so feel free to sell your plot if you don't need it. I just wanted you to always have someplace to go." It was a classic example of Dad taking care of me right up until the end. It's the kind of foresight and protection that he gave me during my whole life.

I kept having to make first-time decisions after my father died. My father was the family organizer and event planner. He threw my graduation party and did most of the cooking. I inherited that role. I planned his funeral. The whole time I thought about how people make all these incredible decisions, and you end up practicing on the most important people first. Children make death-related decisions for their parents in a vacuum. We don't talk much about death in our society. We're so isolated, and everything's so clinical.

Dad would have wanted his funeral to be respectful and understated. I made sure it was.

Step 2

Break a Big Problem into Small Pieces

Divide each difficulty into as many parts as is feasible and necessary to resolve it.

—René Descartes

Some Big Decisions are overwhelming because so many factors are involved. You know, "If I do this, that will happen. But if I do that, something else will happen. Then there's the impact on. . . ." Decisions with lots of moving parts must be broken into small, manageable pieces. The fact that you must break a complex question into simple ones shouldn't embarrass you. You want to take the right step. Don't try to make hard choices. Try to turn hard choices into easy choices.

Each day, medical doctors, lawyers, accountants, psychologists and other professionals go through a process of breaking down complex issues. Frustrated clients and patients plop down before such professionals and relate lengthy, complicated histories of problems, personal interactions, emotions, circumstances and symptoms. The situation has become so overwhelming and

19

unmanageable that the client or patient finally took time to seek help. The first step that a professional takes to resolve a complex problem is to develop a clear understanding of the facts and to break the problem into the smaller pieces that combine to create the problem.

While you certainly might need a professional's assistance at some point, you too can learn and practice the skills that professionals use to break down a Big Decision. Step 2 shows you the sorting and grouping skills required to break down a Big Decision.

How to Break Down a Problem and "Group Your Cards"— An Introduction to Sorting Skills

Most of us fell for 52-Card Pickup once—and only once!—during our childhoods. An unkind friend or sibling smilingly appeared with a deck of cards and asked whether we'd like to play a game of 52-Card Pickup. We cheerfully accepted, only to have the friend or sibling eject all the cards onto the floor with a shuffle maneuver and dissolve in laughter with a malicious "Your turn!" Similarly, a complex decision may create the feeling that your options are strewn on the floor, face down, twisted, unshuffled and random.

Now that you've identified the real issue in Step 1, if the decision has any complexity you'll have to break the decision into its pieces and organize them. Pieces of a decision generally fall into these categories: wants, concerns and practical factors. A "want" is something you seek to obtain (or retain) as a result of the decision: "I want a more creative job in graphic arts"; "I want a more tranquil domestic relationship"; "I want to live in this city"; "I want my son to have a sibling"; "I want my mother to be free from pain"; "I want my business to break even so I don't have to raise capital this year"; "I want to be known as a person of integrity and compassion."

A want may be a goal, but the word "goal" often doesn't fit well for decisions that lack a competitive element. What is the goal when your father is dying? "Goal" also has an unrealistic singularity about it. Your Big Decision probably doesn't involve a single goal. You probably have a bunch of goals that rise and fall in importance on a day-to-day basis. If you try to narrow your decision to a single goal, you'll wind up too general to move forward. We can all agree that "The goal is to be happy" or "The goal is to pay the bills" or "The goal is to be spiritually fulfilled." To make a Big Decision, your thought process must take your objectives to a more specific level. *What* makes you happy? *What* makes you unhappy? *What* job do you want to pay all the bills? *What* kinds of activities fulfill you spiritually? For this reason, we encourage you not to think about the goal, but rather to consider the wide variety of goals and objectives you want to advance through your decision.

A "concern" is a risk that you believe may flow from a certain course of action. You can spot concerns by how you describe or feel about your choices: "I'm concerned that if I do this, that will happen"; "I'm bothered by how Judy may respond"; "I'm afraid I may never find another job"; "I'm worried that staying in this business will put me into bankruptcy." Concerns are those situations that raise worry, fear and other negative feelings when you think about a decision.

"Practical factors" are the facts and circumstances that a situation hands you. These can't be changed, or can only be changed by incurring high costs or risks. Consider the following practical factors:

"My business has only $5,000 in cash and a $10,000 attorneys' bill on the table."

"My employer has a strict policy of terminating employees who moonlight for a competitor."

"To get married within the next three years, I have to take steps now to develop a serious relationship."

"I don't have the grades to get into medical school."

"I have the grades to get into *any* medical school."

"To get name recognition for our product among college students, we will have to spend $250,000."

"I have been diagnosed with cancer and will require treatment that may affect my ability to work at the current pace."

Sometimes challenging the rules, even at high risk or great cost, makes sense morally, financially or otherwise. Until a practical factor is changed, though, so long as it may affect your decision, it should be considered.

Practical factors can be major or minor, and dozens of them may exist. To make a strong decision, step out of the habit of marshaling practical factors to "make a case." A host of practical reasons are always available to do, or not do, just about anything. Samuel Johnson said, "Nothing will ever be attempted if all possible objections must first be overcome." If each pebble in your path becomes a wall, you'll spend your life running into walls. Likewise, you won't make a good decision if you consider only the positive factors.

How to Isolate Your Wants, Concerns and Practical Factors: Start with a Piece of Paper

Step 2 is where we suggest that you do something too simplistic: Write it down. The notes, list or whatever you write will not make your Big Decision for you. Nonetheless, you need to keep track of what you discover as you proceed toward your decision.

Notes are a proven method. Doctors, lawyers, accountants, money managers and many other professional advisors always have a pen and a piece of paper at hand. In the first week at work, advisor trainees are told by their supervisors, "Never show up at a meeting without a pen and paper. It will just delay things when you inevitably have to run out and get them." Notes and lists serve many purposes for a professional advisor. Notes allow the advisor to recall what was said at a meeting. Notes help an advisor isolate key issues as a meeting progresses. Some advisors use forms with checklists to ensure the bases are covered.

The notes that professional advisors take are not limited to what is said at the meeting. While a patient describes a series of symptoms, the physician may be writing shorthand notes such as "RO CAD" ("rule out coronary artery disease") and "Get CBC" ("get complete blood count"). A client sitting in a lawyer's office often will recite a lengthy story, filled with names and events that mean little to the lawyer in the first meeting. The lawyer will write down the basic facts that appear to be relevant, often probing the client with questions. The lawyer also will write notations such as "SL issue?" ("Is there a statute of limitations issue?") or "Fd or St Ct?" ("Should a case be filed in federal or state court?"). The meeting yields notes about the facts and the advisor's first impressions of the issues. After a meeting, many advisors review and annotate the notes.

The habits of professional advisors carry a lesson: Before you go too far in your decision, pick up a pen and paper. Notes have no magic format. Some people use rigid columns or lists; others prefer free-form notes or even prose. In this era of omnipresent business software, you may be most comfortable using spreadsheets, PowerPoint or other applications. What's important is that you notate and organize. Grouping the issues as "wants," "concerns" and "practical factors" may help, but it's not essential. The point is to give structure and expression to your thoughts near the beginning of your decision process, then build it out as you go forward.

If there's a place where you feel especially comfortable, such as a favorite coffeehouse, a certain room or an outdoor location, consider working on your decision notes at that place. Chapels, woods, lakes, mountains, beaches, gardens, shrines, parks, cafes, libraries and a "special conference room" are classic places to pull your thoughts and facts together. The combination of light exercise (walking, hiking) interspersed with note-taking can work really well.

What If You Prefer Graphical or Pictorial Notes?

Writing text notes is awkward for some people who feel they are more "visual" than "textual." When people are asked to write down the basic facts about a decision, some write pages of prose. Others write outlines and lists. Others write less than a page and claim the whole exercise was a waste. This variation is proven every day in courtrooms and classrooms. Sitting through the same presentation, with an identical duty, some jurors and students take meticulous notes, some write down key points, others doodle and others ignore their pads entirely. How much you write down, and how you write it down, are determined by your attitudes, aptitudes, training and habits. The important point to remember is that you may need access later to your thoughts and research.

Decision notes don't have to be words. Bill Pack made his career as an advertising photographer in San Francisco. He's a heavily visual person who rarely reduces his thoughts to text. Pack grabs pen and paper for a decision, but he creates a sketch:

I've never made a "1, 2, 3, 4 . . ." list for a decision. A list wouldn't articulate anything better than what's in my mind. When I make a decision, the concerns and issues become images. Each image has its own emotion. Some are positive; others create a feeling of conflict. The images may never develop into words, even in my thoughts. When I chose my studio, I sat in the studio for an hour to think about whether I could see myself shooting in the space. When it was time to see if it made sense financially, I sketched a rough graph of my income based on past invoices. A picture is more complete than a list. It presents the whole situation in one view and shows how things interwork. When I'm developing a business concept, it becomes a series of boxes. I use marks to show how the boxes relate. There might be one word connected with each box to signify what the box represents. I organize my thoughts by organizing the picture, not text. It definitely was harder for me in school. In school, text symbols are the "normal" way of thinking. This is changing slowly over time. Visual thinking is becoming recognized by society as a major asset.

Bill Pack is an organized decision-maker. He has learned to use his image-driven mind to, quite literally, "see the big picture" when he makes an important decision. His mind adapted his decision-making process to work around his aversion to text symbols; instead, he uses the symbols with which his mind feels comfortable. As anyone would, Pack sees certain concerns as "positive" and others as "negative," but he links the various values to pictures, not to text. Pack still uses pen and paper to organize his thoughts in the form of images.

If you respond better to visual symbols, find or create the graphical representations you need. Many computer programs offer a variety of "views" of numerical data—pie charts, bar graphs, line graphs and other tools—to help you analyze the data. Some investment firms routinely supplement portfolio reports with graphical charts.[4]

---

[4] Other businesses and services *should* offer alternate views. For example, if health-care providers wish to improve the educational function of blood-lipid tests (e.g., cholesterol screenings) for everyone, they should consider a graphical presentation of the patient's results in relation to "the norm." For many people, even information about their own blood has less impact when presented as a number on a list with a little "H" (for "High") next to it. To show a patient that his cholesterol is off the charts, start by showing him "the chart"!

On occasion, concerns about privacy and confidentiality must influence what you'll write down. Jennifer is a visual thinker. When Jennifer decided whether to do a substance-abuse intervention for her mother, she saw the entire situation as a series of pictures, but didn't write down her thoughts. Jennifer feared that her notes would be found:

> When I weighed it, I thought that the worst-case scenario was that she would die. I pictured being told that my mother was dead. Eyes closed on a hospital bed. I pictured her ashes and where we sprinkled them. I pictured her house, without her there. She's never coming back. I pictured people asking about my mother and I am saying, "My mother is dead." I pictured these situations while I was making my decision. I didn't write anything down. I worried that someone would find my notes.

Jennifer's cautiousness was understandable. The images she brought to mind would translate into highly explicit notes about her mother! As important as it is to take notes, practicality must prevail. While most professional advisory firms have security procedures to preserve the confidentiality of client or patient communications, you may not. Be careful where you leave your notes (both physical and electronic), and with whom you share them. Learn how to password-protect your files. It is easier than ever to lose control of information.

Now you have the modest tools you need to break down a complex problem: pen and paper (or lap and laptop). Let's move to how you break a complex problem into pieces. We introduce the process of breaking a decision into wants, concerns and practical factors with a manager's decision whether to report a fraud committed by his supervisor.

Robert's Decision: Whether to Report a Fraud Committed by His Supervisor at Work

Each day, workplace frauds are committed at sites around the world. Most frauds are not completely secret, and many require the participation (or acquiescence) of several individuals. Quite often, at some point, workplace fraud comes to the attention of an employee who wants to stop it. Yet most managers will tell you that coworker or supervisor fraud is rarely reported. Many employees have a don't-rock-the-boat mentality because they don't want to put their own jobs at risk. The loss of a job can be devastating to an employee and his family, especially in a down economy. A whistle-blower's worry about future employability, especially in the same industry, is a rational fear. The law generally imposes few affirmative duties upon employees to become involved.

We use a corporate-fraud example precisely because the situation is so difficult for many employees. It would be nice to say, "Of course, if you're a good, moral person, you will report wrongdoing for the benefit of the company, its owners, the greater good and your conscience." That isn't what typically happens! The following example shows how an employee who wants to do the right thing—and keep his job—might break down his dilemma.

Robert's Original Thought Process About Whether to Report His Supervisor's Fraud

Why does Dan have to lie on his monthly sales reports? I'm very uncomfortable with the situation, and Dan is getting more and more aggressive each month. Eventually, the whole thing is going to come out. I have my moral standards. I want to do the right thing and definitely not break the law, but I need to keep this job. It's a good job, and my daughter just started private school. I can't lose my job. No way. I've heard that what Dan does is common, especially in this industry. I've got visions of the whole thing falling down. Dan will be canned, then someone will ask if I knew about it. If I say yes, I'm dead. If I say no, I'm just another liar. They'll find out I knew. Then I'm dead. Am I committing a crime if I do nothing? How would I go about reporting Dan, if I decide to? I don't trust Dan's supervisor. He's getting a bigger bonus because of Dan's bogus numbers. I think a couple of major customers are involved, too. Maybe I should talk to a lawyer. That will cost a fortune. I'm not the whistle-blower type. My dad always told me to keep my head down. Ratting on my supervisor is not exactly keeping my head down. What if I lose my job and it gets around that I'm a troublemaker? I won't be able to work in the industry. Maybe I'm more protected if I do tell. Maybe I'm not. All I want is to do an honest job and get an honest paycheck. Why do I have to deal with this at all? I haven't been able to concentrate lately. . . .

Robert has hit all the right issues, but he's bogged down in their apparent complexity. In a matter of minutes, Robert's Big Decision could be sorted and grouped, simply by plucking the wants, concerns and practical factors out of Robert's rambling, anxious thoughts:

Robert's Issues Sorted Out

Robert's Wants (No Particular Order)

Robert wants to "do the right thing."

Robert wants to keep his job.

Robert wants to protect his reputation and employability.

Robert's Concerns (No Particular Order)

Robert is concerned that he will be implicated in a fraud that may cost him his job and reputation if he does not report Dan.

Robert is concerned that he will become known as a "troublemaker" if he reports Dan.

Robert is concerned that he might be committing a crime by doing nothing about Dan.

Practical Factors (No Particular Order)

Dan is getting more aggressive, and a disaster may be approaching fast.

Robert doesn't know the right way to report Dan.

Robert needs his job for financial reasons.

It may be expensive for Robert to consult a lawyer.

Although Robert's decision is not *made* by the sorting process, a "cleanness" already has developed. This cleanness will make it easier for Robert to progress to Step 3, which involves identifying and answering certain target questions before he can make his Big Decision. Quite clearly, Robert's **wants** raise two questions: (1) Will Robert lose his job if he reports Dan's fraud? and (2) Will Robert become unemployable if he reports Dan's fraud? Robert knows that "doing the right thing" means reporting the fraud, so that's not a question Robert needs to answer.

Robert's **concerns** raise two additional questions: (3) Is Robert committing a crime if he doesn't report Dan? and (4) How will each alternative course of action affect Robert's reputation and employability (the decision has a "damned-if-I-do, damned-if-I-don't" aspect)?

Robert's **practical factors** raise two further questions: (5) What would it cost for Robert to talk to a lawyer? and (6) How should Robert go about reporting Dan, if he decides to do it?

The thoughts that run through our minds before and after we sort are quite different. Before we sort, the considerations, emotions, pros and cons, and so on swim through our heads almost at random. That's what happened to Robert, and it was making him pretty nervous! After we sort a problem, our thoughts focus on specific questions. The goal of Step 2 is to bring better clarity of mind and precision to a decision. We'll come back to Robert's situation in Step 3 and determine how Robert should approach his target questions.

Advanced Sorting Skills:
How to Sort Complex Wants,
Concerns and Practical Factors

Robert's decision whether to report Dan is not simple. Nonetheless, the process of identifying and ordering wants, concerns and practical factors may be far more complex than what Robert faced. To make a complex decision, you often need to take sorting to a deeper level. Use the following approach for complex decisions:

Separate "Driving" Wants, Concerns and Practical Factors from the "Tag-Alongs"

After you've identified the wants, concerns and practical factors in your decision, separate the "driving" (major) ones from the "tag-alongs" (secondary or less important ones). For your wants, separate what *must* come out of the decision from what would merely be a nice additional benefit if things work out. You may want to make ten thousand dollars more in salary next year. Will this want drive the decision, or would you forego the ten thousand dollars to satisfy another objective, such as a better job title, more responsibility, your choice of offices, more time with your family or some other benefit? Separating the driving wants from the tag-alongs may require enormous thought, soul-searching and investigation. At the end of it, however, you'll have a much clearer picture of what will influence your decision and what is merely noise. Even if you "want it all," each step toward having it all requires you to prioritize what you want to obtain sooner and what can wait.

Similarly, you must separate what *strongly* concerns you from concerns you can live with. For example, you may be concerned about what your friends will think if you make a certain decision. Is this a driving concern or can you accept some negative feedback from your friends, if that's what it takes? If public opinion doesn't matter much to you, it's a tag-along. This step also may require soul-searching. Everyone wants validation, affirmation, confirmation and all the other good "-ations" from friends, colleagues and loved ones. In Big Decisions, some -ations will end up as tag-along concerns, for the time being, if you are committed to your driving wants.

Do the same with your practical factors. Separate the major realities and rules of the game from the minor ones. Major practical factors are unlikely to be changed, and they are likely to affect in a significant way the decision's success or failure. A major positive practical factor in deciding whether to start a business might be a rich uncle who will pay your mortgage if your business fails. A major negative practical factor is that your uncle has told you that you must first raise twenty-five thousand dollars in start-up capital from someone else. Minor practical factors might be: "I will have to use part of my home as an office for awhile" or "I will need to give up evenings and weekends until I can hire help." (Of course, if evening soccer league is the most important activity in your life, working evenings may be a driving practical factor.)

You see that sorting is not a purely mechanical process. It helps you make a Big Decision by forcing you to compare your wants and values with competing wants and values. By asking "How important really is this to me?" you head toward a comfortable balance.

Now Where Are You?

Do all of your driving wants, concerns and practical factors point to the same decision? Don't agonize endlessly over tag-along issues. Pinch your cheek if a dozen major wants and concerns say yes, and a couple tag-along issues hold you back. In Step 10, we talk about actively managing the downsides that accompany most Big Decisions. Minor concerns and practical factors often can be managed. Your Big Decision might offend someone. You might incur a financial cost. Your decision might steal a weekend, or a week or maybe even a year. You might have to explain yourself to some people. You may have to ride out some temporary embarrassment. Mere inconveniences shouldn't cause you to avoid a decision that serves your driving wants and concerns. The price you pay to address minor issues is the normal cost of a tough choice.

In truly tough decisions, some important wants are advanced by a decision to go in one direction, while other important wants are advanced only if you make a different choice. Similarly, one choice may trigger (or solve) some concerns, while another choice may influence other concerns. Practical factors may loom large. You may leave your job to start a new company, but you may go bankrupt in two years if the new business doesn't take off and you run out of money. You may accept an experimental treatment that provides hope for an illness, but your life may be on the line if it doesn't work. Big Decisions typically involve hard choices. Don't be paralyzed by the prospect of losing any benefit or avoiding any pain, no matter how minor. Think about what you're missing, losing and suffering while you're stuck because you can't separate the driving wants, concerns and practical factors from the tag-alongs.

An Example of Breaking Down an Extremely Complex Issue: Whether to Become a Single Mother

Let's look at a decision that a number of single women (and some men) in their forties are making: whether to become a single parent. For many people, this decision is extraordinarily complex. Megan decided to become a single mother using an anonymous male sperm donor. Here is the list of Megan's wants, concerns and practical factors—not yet grouped or ordered, but as they circulated in Megan's head:

Megan's Wants (No Particular Order)

I want to experience the love, nurturing and personal growth of parenthood.

I won't be content having neither a mate nor a child. I want a family of some kind.

I want a child who is compatible with me—physically, mentally, emotionally and genetically.

I want to have someone who cares for me during the end stages of my life.

Megan's Concerns (No Particular Order)

I am concerned about what my family will think, insofar as it might affect the child.

I wonder whether bringing a child into the world without a male role model at home is fair.

I am concerned about my ability to raise a child on a single income.

What would be the impact on my work?

I am concerned about what would happen to the child if I die or become disabled. Is that a fair burden to put on my parents and siblings?

How would the child feel about having a "donor father"? What if other kids found out? Would they tease my kid?

Could I handle a child with special needs (if necessary), personally, financially and career-wise?

Would the child be well-rounded with no role model at home other than me? My child's immediate family will be very small.

I am concerned if I don't do something that I'll regret missing the experience of parenthood in future years.

I am concerned about going through the late stages of pregnancy and childbirth alone. I don't have a strong support group where I live at the current time.

Megan's Practical Factors (No Particular Order)

I am in my early forties. I will be unable to have a child if I wait much longer.

The fertility-treatment process is expensive, and none of it is covered by my insurance.

I will need full-time child care if I have a child, especially if I want to work.

Bouncing around in Megan's head, the competing factors made the decision seem intractable. Some days, Megan was consumed by the desire for parenthood. Some days, she thought about her desire for a husband. Other days, Megan worried about what her father would say if she showed up at Thanksgiving, pregnant with no spouse. These swings were influenced by the people Megan spoke with on a particular day. Her sources of assistance—friends, family, coworkers and a spiritual advisor—had different approaches to the decision, all expressed with great conviction! Here is how Megan separated the driving and secondary (tag-along) issues in her decision:

Megan's Two Driving Wants and Why

Megan's Driving Want #1:

"I won't be content having neither a mate nor a child. I want a family of some kind."

Why? "Family is so important to me. I could accept a husband but no child, or a child but no husband. I value the love and shared experience of family life. My choice is whether to be alone or whether to share my life with someone. I feel very strongly that I want to share it. This is pushing my decision."

Megan's Driving Want #2:

"I want to experience the love, nurturing and personal growth of parenthood."

Why? "This is closely related to my need for family, but it's not 100 percent the same. There are lessons that I know I'll learn through parenthood—things my child will teach me. There are many things I will teach my child. It's different from 'family.' It's a one-to-one experience of teaching someone you love about life and learning from the child."

Megan's Three Driving Concerns and Why

Megan's Driving Concern #1:

"I am concerned that if I don't do something, I'll regret missing the experience of parenthood in future years."

Why? "The window is already closing. My chances of having a baby with one of my own eggs is low and getting lower by the day.

Who knows what will happen with my health in the future? I don't want to look back on life and say, 'I missed it. I could have been a parent, but I didn't do it while I could have.' Such regrets could be very painful for me."

Megan's Driving Concern #2:

"I wonder whether bringing a child into the world without a male role model is fair."

Why? "I am very much my father's daughter. I can't imagine him not in my life. So much of what I am came from my father. Even today, my father is my first phone call when I need advice. There's no guarantee that a male will come into my life, so there is a very real possibility that my child won't have a male figure. This definitely makes me stop and think. It is a very important problem."

Megan's Driving Concern #3:

"I am concerned about what my family will think, insofar as it might affect the child."

Why? "I have huge concern that my child will be disowned by my family. My child won't have family from the father's side, so my family is all the child will have. I love my parents dearly, but they are very, very old school. I have a real concern that they'll reject the child. Then what does the child have? If something happened to me, the child could have nobody in the entire world."

Megan's Driving Practical Factor and Why

Megan's Driving Practical Factor:

"I am in my early forties. I will be unable to have a child if I wait much longer."

Why? "I'm learning how it would feel to be too late. I've been to doctors, and read books and articles. The bottom line is that time is running out, at best. It's now or never."

That took a lot of work! What did Megan accomplish? By one rough measure, you might conclude that she made her decision more than twice as easy. She started with seventeen wants, concerns and practical factors, each taking up space and time in her mental computer. Now she has six driving wants, concerns and practical factors with which to work. Megan's decision is not made, but the direction is clearer, and her thoughts are more focused.

Before we move to the next step, let's take a minute to examine Megan's reasoning process—why certain wants, concerns and practical factors became tag-alongs. Remember that your own reasoning and values might be different, even faced with the same situation. For example, many people have strong moral objections to single parenthood through "artificial" methods.

Why Certain of Megan's Wants, Concerns and Practical Factors Became Tag-Alongs

None of the issues Megan raises is petty. We explored with Megan why certain issues didn't make it to the driving-issue category. We wanted to know why these "tag-alongs" won't make the difference to Megan. Following are Megan's comments on the issues that won't drive her decision, arranged in order of importance to Megan:

Megan's Tag-Along Want #1:

"I want a child who is compatible with me—physically, mentally, emotionally and genetically."

Why? "Plenty of natural parents have incompatibilities of all kinds with their kids. How much does any woman know about her mate's gene pool? The anonymous donor process provides a lot more genetic information about a donor than most women get from a husband. This issue goes more to how I'll choose a donor."

Megan's Tag-Along Want #2:

"I want to have someone who cares for me during the end stages of my life."

Why? "There's no guarantee. I might have a child who takes great care of me when I'm old, but I could also outlive my child, live in a different place or not be on speaking terms. It's too remote, too far down the road for this to be a factor."

Megan's Tag-Along Concern #1:

"Would the child be well-rounded with no role model other than me? My child's immediate family will be very small."

Why? "It's my job to do the best I can to expose my child to beliefs other than my own, as well as other people and places. I'll do my best to travel with my child and experience different things. It may not be ideal to have a tiny family with just me and the child, but I'm aware of the issue and we'll create as big a community as we can."

Megan's Tag-Along Concern #2:

"How would the child feel about having a 'donor father'? What if other kids found out? Would they tease my kid?"

Why? "Donor fathers are becoming more and more common. If this is an issue, there will be many others who are dealing with it as well and we'll figure it out. Some groups have organized to track donors. It won't be as bad if I have two children. Kids are teased for all kinds of things. If it happens, we'll deal with it."

Megan's Tag-Along Concern #3:

"What would be the impact on my work?"

Why? "Work is very important to me, but I am confident I'll be able to manage both work and a child. People have been juggling careers and kids for a long time. It won't be simple, and it will cost money. That just goes with parenthood."

Megan's Tag-Along Concern #4:

"I am concerned about what would happen to the child if I die or become disabled. Is that a fair burden to put on my parents and siblings?"

Why? "I can't control the future. These things happen. Any kid can be orphaned. I am in good health, and I have been for my whole life. I'll do my best to plan for a disaster, but I'm not making my parenthood decision on the assumption that everything will go disastrously wrong at some time in the future."

Megan's Tag-Along Concern #5:

"Could I handle a child with special needs (if necessary), personally, financially and career-wise?"

Why? "It definitely would be tougher to be a single parent of a child with special needs. But I'd find a way if I am put in that situation. People who have special-needs children seem to make it work. It may require special schools and, possibly, more help at home."

Megan's Tag-Along Concern #6:

"I am concerned about going through the late stages of pregnancy and childbirth alone. I don't have a strong support group where I live at the current time."

Why? "Pregnancy and childbirth are temporary. I'll hire someone. I'll get by."

Megan's Tag-Along Concern #7:

"I am concerned about my ability to raise a child on a single income."

Why? "I am a freelancer, so there's definitely a concern. I do have some other resources. My grandmother left some funds that pay income to me. It's not a huge amount, but it gives me a small income that helps support me when business gets slow."

Megan's Tag-Along Practical Factor #1:

"I will need full-time child care if I have a child, especially if I want to work."

Why? "I'll make it work."

Megan's Tag-Along Practical Factor #2:

"The fertility-treatment process is expensive, and none of it is covered by my insurance."

Why? "I'll make it work."

You'll note that even the tag-along issues are very important in a decision of this magnitude. You aren't dismissing an issue when you label it a tag-along. You're saying that other issues will dominate when making a difficult choice in which you can't have everything.

Megan ultimately decided to become a single parent. On balance, her driving wants, concerns and practical factors supported that choice. We asked whether she ever thought that becoming a single parent would make it harder to find a mate in the future. This concern is often voiced in discussions about the subject. Megan dismissed the concern. "In my age group, a child could be a plus as much as a minus. A man who wants to get married also might be happy that family comes along with it. With an anonymous donor, I would bring a child but no ex. That just wasn't a concern of mine."

No sooner did Megan make the decision than she found herself with a string of other decisions:

When you first make the decision, there's a sense of relief. Then you say, "Oh, my God, that was just the tiniest decision." The hard decisions just keep coming. Some of the ones that come later are harder. Once I decided to be a single parent, I thought I'd just go and get pregnant somehow. When it didn't happen, there were so many issues related to pregnancy. Donor sperm? Donor egg? Then there's the hardest one of all: when to let go. When do you admit this just isn't going to happen? I've learned a lot about the adoption process, too. When I started out, I thought, *Well, if pregnancy doesn't work, I'll just adopt a child.* In fact, a single woman, over forty, with no children and a freelance job isn't a great candidate. There is a very real chance this just isn't going to happen for me.

The weakness in the process of breaking down your decision into its pieces is that the approach is only as good as you are at identifying and narrowing the issues. If you're unable to accurately identify your wants, concerns and practical factors, your analysis will be flawed. If your analysis is flawed, your decision stands a good chance of being flawed. In this area, conversations with friends and advisors can help. Nobody can make the decision for you and, as we discuss at length in Step 4, even your most trusted allies may have biases. Nonetheless, if your cards are spilled on the floor, don't hesitate to call upon all of your available resources to help sort the issues.

We leave Step 2 with the following points to remember about breaking down a problem:

- Challenge the feeling that you're "swimming" in a complex decision that has too many parts. In many cases, a complex decision is made up of much simpler pieces.
- Break down a decision into its component pieces: your wants, concerns and practical factors. Make notes along the way.
- The essence of breaking down a complex decision is to identify the parts of the decision and prioritize them as driving wants, concerns and practical factors or tag-alongs.
- Remember that decisions are choices. You'll need to let go of some of your minor wants, and move past smaller concerns and practical factors, to make the best overall choice.

Career: It's One Thing to Leave a Job You Can't Stand, but It's Always Tough to Leave a Really Great Job

Ed Lloyd leaves his prominent position at a leading U.S. non-profit corporation for the "psychic income" offered by UNICEF.

In April 2001, Ed Lloyd was fifty-six years old, and in his fourteenth year as the executive vice president and chief financial officer of Local Initiatives Support Corporation (LISC). LISC is a highly effective nonprofit corporation and the largest financial promoter of low-income housing in the United States. Established by the Ford Foundation in 1979, LISC provides grants, technical assistance and below-market loans to community development corporations (CDCs) to develop low-income housing in nearly forty major U.S. cities. LISC also brings shopping centers and other businesses to inner-city neighborhoods. Over the years, LISC has developed into a sophisticated, multifaceted entity and the recognized leader in U.S. community economic-development strategies.

Ed's career blossomed at LISC, and his talent, in turn, helped make LISC what it is:

I was never interested in the private sector for my personal career. There are plenty of good people working in the private sector. I always wanted to work in nonprofits. Before LISC, I was with the United Negro College Fund. I moved over to LISC in 1979. LISC grew immensely when I was there. The transactions we did became larger and more complex each year. I grew enormously in the job, as LISC itself grew. I was working on a daily basis with the top leaders in the country. I had a job for as long as I wanted it. Until April 2001, I'd never thought of leaving LISC.

In April 2001, Ed received an unsolicited call from an executive search firm. The search firm told Ed that the U.S. Fund for UNICEF was looking for a new senior manager. UNICEF is the United Nations Children's Fund. Organized in 1946, UNICEF works in more than 160 countries and territories to provide health care, clean water and improved nutrition to millions of children in Africa, Asia, Europe, Latin America and the Middle East.

Ed had been identified as someone who could handle the job at UNICEF, but he put off the discussion. LISC was in the middle of some important projects. Ed didn't want to be distracted. But it started him thinking. The search firm persisted, and Ed found himself with an interview. He began to explore mentally where his career stood in relation to his major life goals:

I had often said to my wife that, when I retire, I want to work with children. When the UNICEF approach came, I told her, "Maybe this job with the U.S. Fund for UNICEF would be a chance to work with children now. We can work in the areas we read about every day, but which very few people, certainly few middle-class African-Americans, really understand. It seemed like a chance to get involved in the problems of children in Africa, Latin America and Asia. I knew that UNICEF could benefit from the skills I'd built over the past thirty-five years. For the first time since I joined LISC, I looked at another job and said, "Hey, I might give this a shot."

When Ed interviewed with the U.S. Fund executive team, he knew the position was a good fit. This meeting started a series of serious discussions among Ed, his wife and his son Jason. Family consultation about major job choices is a practice that Ed established many years earlier:

Work is very, very important to me. I'm originally from North Carolina. My first job as a four-year-old boy was picking cotton with my mother and my father. We were poor. I know what it's like to put cardboard in the bottom of my shoes to cover up a hole. When the seasons changed, we'd go out and pick cotton, tobacco, beans or whatever else was in season. Work choices affect the whole family. I always thought that when I married and had a family I'd try to involve my family in decisions that affect all of us. I also felt it was important for me, as an African-American man, to make sure that my son understood how important work was, and what the responsibility of work was for him and in relation to family.

In 1989, when Ed had considered whether to leave his job with the United Negro College Fund to go to LISC, he'd taken Jason to lunch for a father/son talk. Ed wanted Jason to be involved in Ed's decision whether to leave the United Negro College Fund for LISC. Jason was twelve then and for years had been around Ed's colleagues at the United Negro College Fund. Jason was part of the office family, and the office was part of Jason's family.

At lunch, Ed and Jason talked about what it meant to leave their friends at the United Negro College Fund and why Ed was thinking about LISC. Ed talked Jason through the importance of work, how much work meant to Ed, how much it should mean to Jason. Ed made a point of talking to Jason about all the benefits that the United Negro College Fund job had provided to the Lloyd family's standard of living over the years and the importance of the United Negro College Fund's education funding work for African-Americans. Regardless of where Ed's career went, he emphasized, the Lloyd family would always support the United Negro College Fund. Ed's biggest concern was that Jason wouldn't understand why Ed would leave the United Negro College Fund when its work was so important and the people at the United Negro College Fund had become such good friends of the Lloyds. Yet, Jason said something that Ed never forgot. He said, "Daddy, I've noticed that lately when you come home you're not quite as happy as you used to be. So maybe it is time to move on."

Thirteen years later, when Jason was twenty-five and living outside of the Lloyd home, Ed talked to Jason about possibly leaving LISC. They talked about the extraordinary contribution LISC had made to the inner-city neighborhoods. They talked about Ed's pride at having been associated with LISC and how much the position at LISC had benefited the Lloyd family. The talk then turned to what Ed and the Lloyd family could do for children around the world with UNICEF. The discussion centered on their desire to be generous with their skills and experience, and on where UNICEF fit in with Christian beliefs. It was a discussion in which values were thoroughly weighed. They agreed that Ed should look seriously at an opportunity to apply his skills to child poverty in the world.

Ed would have to take a pay cut to take the U.S. Fund for UNICEF job, although not a major one. In the end, though, Ed's decision whether to leave LISC wasn't being driven by salary compensation. Rather, "it was about enriching myself by learning more about different problems in the world." To learn about new problems, however, Ed would be leaving a very prominent position that addressed problems that were closer to home:

There were a lot of people who said to me, "Why are you leaving for an area where the problems are huge and most people in this country won't see the benefits?" At LISC we made the agenda. We were setting the direction in which inner-city development would go. You could see the good we were doing in the inner cities. Former Treasury Secretary Robert E. Rubin was the chairman of the board of LISC. Marc Shapiro, who is the vice chairman of J.P. Morgan Chase, was the chairman of LISC's investment committee and audit committee. We had a really high-powered group of people who were involved in the organization. We were working with the largest, most powerful foundations and corporations in the country. There was a lot of prestige. We had a huge impact. I could call important people, and my calls would get returned. When we went to cities we met with major CEOs. People said, "Ed, why would you leave this?"

Ed had no pattern of leaving jobs. Feelings of loyalty and concerns about a difficult transition of a complex job to a successor at LISC held him back more than anything:

I always hoped my staff would take "ownership" of their positions. I tried to instill in people a sense that they owned their jobs, that they weren't just working in them. I owned my job at LISC, almost to a fault. I'm sure there were a lot of opportunities I let get by because I was so committed to LISC. When the U.S. Fund for UNICEF approached me, I wasn't thinking about leaving. We worked with CDCs around the country. For me, it all worked. A lot of the relationships and knowledge were in my head. When I thought about leaving, I was very concerned about a transition. Nobody was asking me to leave.

Ed agonized over the decision enormously. In the end it came down to fulfilling a lifelong dream of directly improving the condition of children, especially in Africa, versus his loyalty to LISC and ability to continue the important work that LISC does every day. In early September 2001, Charles Lyons, president of the U.S. Fund for UNICEF, made Ed an offer for the U.S. Fund for UNICEF job. Then things got complicated.

On September 11, 2001, Ed's offer from the U.S. Fund for UNICEF was on the table. The day after the attacks on the World Trade Center and Pentagon, Ed went to visit Charles Lyons and told him he should feel free to take Ed's offer off the table, that Ed would understand. Ed thought Lyons would be concerned that donations to UNICEF would drop after the September 11 events. Would that, as well as any related economic and political effects, raise doubts about whether it was the right time to bring on someone who might be perceived as "too high-powered" for UNICEF's budget?

Ed wanted to give the U.S. Fund for UNICEF an out. Lyons responded in a flash: "I thought about it, Ed. I need you now more than ever." Ed Lloyd accepted the job offer.

In November 2001, Ed left LISC and began his new job at the U.S. Fund for UNICEF. Ed Lloyd, now fifty-seven, is the senior vice president for systems and operations and chief financial officer of the U.S. Fund for UNICEF. He's one of three members of a top management team for the U.S. Fund. Ed is responsible for all of the financial operations and accounting for the fund, information systems, human resources, compensation, processing of all revenues, accountability of the financial books and records, and working with boards and committees throughout the United States.

Postscript: In Ed's Own Words

When I resigned from LISC, I got a lot of different reactions. Many people came up and congratulated me. Others seemed to feel betrayed or something, and didn't say much. They knew how happy I was at LISC. I had a complicated job, and I'm sure there was concern at LISC that the transition to my successor would be a challenge.

I had moved very high in the nonprofit world. There aren't many African-Americans who had reached such a senior level. I had gotten through the glass ceiling, which seems to exist as much on the nonprofit side as on the for-profit side. At meetings, people often couldn't believe that LISC had an African-American chief financial officer. I am sure some people believe I abandoned LISC. Everyone was surprised. Other people had left, though. I could leave, too.

After September 11, I expressed to my wife that, now more than ever, we need to understand why some people in other parts of the world dislike us so much. What can we do to influence people in this country to be more curious about why others feel this way? I know a lot of the CEOs of major corporations who are black. Like most businesspeople, that group knows little about what is going on outside of their businesses. Part of my new job is to educate African-Americans about the plight of other people in the world, especially in Africa.

Part of my orientation process at the U.S. Fund was to visit a UNICEF country. So I went to Ghana in July 2002. I spent a week there. What I saw on the trip angered me, but it also rejuvenated my spirit and confidence in the ingenuity of black people. Our visit to the Slave Castles on the Cape Coast and to villages in Ghana forever changed my life.

The Slave Castles are huge buildings, built by the European slave traders in the late 1400s to hold slaves who were to be exported by ship. They are in beautiful locations on the coast, but the feeling inside the castles is eerie. You can practically hear the screams and smell the death. The slave traders put hundreds of people in tiny rooms. Groups of slaves would live there for weeks until they were put on ships. There was no sanitation. There was a yellow mark on the walls a couple of feet high. That was the level to which human waste had piled up. There are terrible dungeons in the Slave Castles. There were two "special cells," one for women and one for men. They were for slaves who absolutely rebelled. The one for women had holes for air. The one for men had three doors to the final chamber. The final chamber had no light or holes for air. People died there.

I didn't understand how anyone could treat another person like that. Later on in the tour, I went back to the death cell. I looked around. I cried. I went back to the tour, but then returned for a third time. This time I closed the door, just to see what it was like with no light and no air. It was like a lightning bolt went through me. My mind made a connection with my job. I knew I'd made the right choice. I was in a country I'd never been in, but where my roots were. I was going to be able to do something for the people in this country, the people who had been stored and killed in Slave Castles.

We visited some important urban projects of UNICEF, then went to the northern part of Ghana. This part is mostly Muslim and very poor. There I saw at work the money that UNICEF gives. I saw two high-pressure pumps that had reduced one kind of disease by 70 percent and microlending programs that helped women work. I saw immunization programs, education/vocational programs and electric-power programs. We visited five villages. It was important for me to see how the money was being spent and how much the people in the villages were doing with whatever support they received. In one village, the villagers had hooked up a power line from a source four miles away. What was attached to the end of the line? A single computer that the village used to teach its girls computer skills.

The trip brought home that there are lots of folks who could do my job. The prisons are full of people who, if the right person or after-school program had been there, would be doing what I am doing. I'm not special. I'm just fortunate. There are lots of young kids in those African, Indian and other villages who have brilliant minds. It's just a matter of getting them a break. It's my responsibility to share my knowledge and good fortune.

I thought on the plane back to the United States that I have a responsibility to communicate what I've seen to people in the United States. I need to go to people in my social set and get them to the Slave Castles and the villages. I know I made the right job decision. This is psychic income that no other job ever gave me. I'm where I need to be.

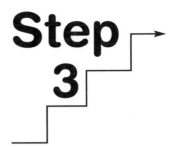

Step 3

Face the Target Questions and Admit What You Don't Know

I was gratified to be able to answer promptly, and I did. I said I didn't know.

—Mark Twain

It is better to ask some of the questions than to know all the answers.

—James Thurber

You've now identified the real decision to be made, and sorted and prioritized the issues. It's a huge step to move from a jumble of facts and concerns to a Big Decision that has structure.

In Step 3, you'll identify the unknown questions you must investigate before you make the decision. These questions are your target questions. A target question may be as simple as

"Does a nursing home in my town have an Alzheimer's care center that fits within my parents' health-care budget?" or as complex as "How will a noncompete clause in our contract with XYZ Corporation be interpreted under Venezuelan commercial law?" A target question may be laden with emotional issues ("Is my husband having an affair?") or even danger ("Was my son involved in a drug-related gang killing?"). If a Big Decision is emotionally troublesome, perhaps you're afraid to answer the target questions. Unless you answer your target questions, your decision has little chance of being correct.

Your task now is to take each of your wants, concerns and practical factors and determine what information you must know to move forward. These elements form your target questions. If you have anxiety about making a Big Decision, mentally explore whether a major part of your anxiety is caused by a lack of solid information on an important issue. In many cases, investigating your target questions to resolve the unknowns makes the decision easier. Step 3 is where you identify the target questions to investigate.

Your Target Questions: Back to Robert's Decision Whether to Report Dan

In Step 2, we introduced you to Robert's decision whether to report his supervisor, Dan, for fraudulently inflating his sales numbers. Robert's wants, concerns and practical factors raised six questions:

1. Will Robert lose his job if he reports Dan's fraud?
2. Will Robert become unemployable if he reports Dan's fraud?
3. Is Robert committing a crime if he doesn't report Dan's fraud?
4. How will Robert's whistle-blower decision (either way) affect Robert's reputation?

5. What would it cost for Robert to talk to a lawyer?

6. How should Robert go about reporting Dan if Robert decides to do it?

All of these are possible target questions. Now determine whether some of them should be addressed before others, in case the answer to one will render other questions moot (i.e., unnecessary to resolve).

In Robert's case, answering the questions in the following order makes good sense: (5); (3); (1); (2) and (4) together, because they raise essentially the same issue, which is the impact on Robert's reputation; then (6).

Here is Robert's reordered list, with an explanation of each question's place:

1. *What would it cost for Robert to talk to a lawyer?* If he can afford it, Robert should seek independent legal advice. A lot is at stake, and some issues are clearly legal. For all Robert knows, he may be courting criminal liability. Even if an hour with a lawyer costs Robert a couple of hundred dollars, the consultation will clarify the situation. Indeed, a qualified lawyer should be able to answer some or all of Robert's other target questions. Determining the cost of an hour with a lawyer is not difficult, so why delay?

2. *Is Robert committing a crime if he doesn't report Dan's fraud?* This point is a material one for Robert. Not sticking his neck out is one thing; going to jail is another. Robert needs to have an accurate picture of his legal liability, given what he knows about Dan and whether any of Robert's conduct arguably could make Robert an accessory. Other questions may look different to Robert if criminal liability is a danger for him.

3. *Will Robert lose his job if he reports Dan's fraud?* Robert will want to investigate, as much as possible, the attitude of his superiors to the kind of activity in which Dan is engaged.

Robert may well be doing his company a big favor by reporting Dan, but Robert will need to judge how high he has to go
until he reaches a sympathetic person. In some cases, fraud
extends all the way to the CEO or even the board of directors.
If Robert is concerned about his job, he needs a handle on
who is his best audience.

4. *Will Robert become unemployable if he reports Dan's fraud?
   How will Robert's reputation be affected if he reports Dan?
   What if he does not report Dan?* These questions are hard to
   answer, but Robert should do what he can. Robert can infer
   that he will have trouble going anywhere Dan and his cronies
   have influence if Dan knows Robert reported him. Certainly,
   Robert should investigate whether he can report Dan on a
   confidential basis.

5. *How should Robert go about reporting Dan if Robert decides
   to do it?* Doing the right thing in the wrong way will only
   make a martyr out of Robert. Robert doesn't want to be a
   martyr. Remember, Robert only wants to do an honest job
   and get an honest paycheck. If Robert takes time to investigate how to report company fraud, he will be rewarded with
   a smoother process.

By reordering his target questions, Robert will answer the most
useful, pressing questions first. In so doing, Robert will move efficiently toward his Big Decision. We'll come back later to show how
Robert's target questions might be answered. At this point, it's
sufficient that Robert identified his target questions and put them
in order.

The order in which you answer your target questions is more a
matter of efficiency than anything else. Prioritizing questions
before you know the answers may be hard. After all, a question's
importance sometimes is not known until it's been answered!
Just do your best. One of the hallmarks of an experienced

decision-maker is the ability to prioritize avenues of investigation. Such a skill grows as your experience and confidence develop. You won't lose much if you make a few mistakes along the way. One caution: If you aren't confident in your ability to prioritize the target questions, be sure to answer all the questions before doing anything "final." Don't ignore valuable information because you inadvertently answered a less important question first, then made your decision based solely on that answer.

All of the Things You Do Not Know

Spotting the target questions is much easier if you're honest about what you don't already know. Many people can't admit they lack answers to the questions that affect their lives. We all know an extreme case: the Silver-Tongued Master of All Situations. The Master never is baffled, stumped, stymied, confused, uninformed or out of his league. If you're a Master (and you can admit it), please learn how to say three simple words: *I don't know.* Even if you're not such an extreme case, do you investigate your important decisions as much as you should? Unless you admit what you don't know, you're stuck with what you do know. And you don't know everything, no matter who you are. When a question is crucial to an important decision, it's not enough to guess at the correct answer. Great decision-makers do not make Big Decisions by speculating about important matters. Great decision-makers admit their personal knowledge is limited, and they do their homework. The first step is to admit what you really don't know. Yes, Master of All Situations, find your Inner Ignoramus!

Technology executive C. E. James has been involved in strategic decision-making for twenty years as an entrepreneur and executive. James believes that many businesspeople who can't say "I don't know" fear they will look weak. "In actuality," James observes, "when you can't ask, it's a very trapped position." The one who can't ask is weakened.

New York investment banker Andy Hirschberg works in a highly specialized business niche. Hirschberg matches pharmaceutical companies with products, and helps find and negotiate licensing deals, mergers and acquisitions. Hirschberg's profession brings him into regular contact both with entrepreneurs and long-standing companies. Hirschberg's first piece of advice to entrepreneurs who want to negotiate with the "Big Boys" is simple: "Know what you don't know!" According to Hirschberg, "The biggest mistake an entrepreneur can make is to think that because he (or she) did something extremely well in one area, he can do it everywhere. You may have developed a major product, but that doesn't make you a financial expert or a great negotiator. You can't fake experience."

In some cases, you might not fear the appearance of ignorance. Instead, you may fear the truth. This fear may lead you to avoid and deny the truth. If you can't investigate a critical question because you don't want to hear the truth, you're not in a position to make a decision. You're trying to cope with a situation by hiding from reality. As an immediate coping strategy, avoidance and denial might stave off some pain—temporarily. In decision-making, hiding from the truth has no benefit, now or later.

At the end of Step 3, we tell the true story of Suzanne Farnham's agonizing decision whether to convert to Judaism to overcome a religion conflict with the parents of the man she wished to marry. A key part of Suzanne's decision-making process was her reluctant willingness to read books supplied by a friend who was gung ho on conversion:

> Deciding to read the books was a challenge. When I realized I was resistant to reading the books, I thought, *C'mon, you can't be scared of an idea.* I had to read the books. It can't be offensive to find out more information. I still was resistant to it. I didn't even

bring the books home. I thought David might think the discussion was over, that he'd won. He would think I was going to convert. Early in our relationship, I'd told David that I would never convert.

The books had a pro-conversion slant. They did not convince Suzanne to convert. In the books, however, Suzanne learned that her children could convert to Judaism and be considered Jewish even if Suzanne didn't convert. By not hiding from facts that pertained to her decision, Suzanne discovered a possible solution to the problem.

All of the Things You Assume Without Checking

Everyone makes loads of assumptions in daily personal and business life. We assume other people are basically honest, take them at face value and rarely investigate people's pasts. We don't always count the change. We don't weigh the cereal box to make sure it really is "Net weight 18.2 ounces." We're happy to let law enforcement and investigative journalists root out deception and tell us about it. We believe much of what we read without double-checking it. Why are we comfortable to act on all of these assumptions?

One reason we don't verify everything is that most of our assumptions are *mostly* correct. That's all we need to make unimportant decisions: mostly correct information. Indeed, we know that when we do receive incorrect information, the mistake probably was a careless error and not the result of someone else's dishonesty. In many cases, we'll use the same source again! Another reason we accept so much information at face value is that we want to find people (and institutions) trustworthy, especially spouses, children, parents, friends, business partners, colleagues and well-known companies.

For day-to-day living, relying on a lot of potentially flawed information makes sense. The cost of verifying everything would be high in time, money and aggravation. The benefit of having perfect information on minor matters would not be much higher than the benefit of 75 percent accurate—or possibly even less accurate—information. Restaurant, movie and music critics serve a useful role: We delegate the time and expense of evaluating leisure activities to these professionals. If a reviewer serves us well, we reward the reviewer with our loyalty (which doesn't hurt his or her career and job satisfaction). Our reward is that we improve our lives by making better choices, without personally conducting resource-consuming firsthand investigations of leisure options. In short, on a day-to-day basis, we ignore minor inaccuracies, make effort-saving assumptions and delegate investigation so we can make efficient choices.

Different rules apply to a Big Decision. The cost of making an incorrect Big Decision is higher than the cost of seeing the wrong movie or eating at a lousy restaurant. The benefit of acting on accurate information is much greater, and the burden of finding high-quality information is more justified. In a Big Decision, you must challenge your assumptions about important facts and move as close as possible to the truth. Challenging your assumptions is not always convenient and often creates more work. Nonetheless, the quality of your Big Decisions will skyrocket if you base them on good information.

Don't feel, though, that you must abandon all assumptions when you make a Big Decision. Even when a Big Decision is at hand, you might assume that basic principles of market economics will apply in market economies, except to the extent there is economic regulation.[5] The laws of physics will apply. You don't need to reinvent the wheel, ignore all of your past experience, or investigate trivial and obvious matters. You do need to apply a high

---

[5] In contrast, assuming that a particular person will act in what you believe is in his or her financial self-interest can be a serious mistake. Individuals have a large and complex variety of motives and values, many of which are neither economically driven nor especially apparent.

standard to what you hear, read and otherwise rely upon for the decision.

Learn to Test Your Assumptions When You Make a Big Decision

Overcoming the tendency to make assumptions is not easy. We diligently practice assuming, speculating and jumping to conclusions every day of the year. Here is a simple example of how the practice of piling assumption upon assumption can result in a poor decision:

> Bob liked his company but considered quitting because he felt he needed some new equipment to do his job right. The company didn't have it. When a customer criticized what Bob knew to be inferior work, Bob felt he had to make a decision to stay or quit based on whether the boss would approve the new equipment purchase. Bob discussed the situation with Bill, a coworker at the same level who had been in the company many years and always seemed to know what was going on in the boss's mind. Bill assured Bob that the boss would never order the new equipment. "Too costly. Don't even ask!" Bill implored. As Bill explained, Bob's predecessor asked for that same equipment and the boss ridiculed him.
>
> Bob quit and took another job. When Bob's replacement arrived, he asked for the new equipment. The boss independently had heard negative customer comments in the past year and had no problem approving the new equipment purchase.

Bob made two major assumptions in reaching his decision to quit. First, Bob assumed that Bill had the facts straight about what happened when Bob's predecessor asked for the equipment. Second, Bob assumed that the boss's views (as related by Bill) had not changed and couldn't be changed through further discussion. Because Bill had been an extremely reliable source, Bob might be justified in relying on Bill's information about what happened several years ago. Bob stopped his investigation too soon, though. Bill didn't claim he had any real information on what the boss would think about the issue now. Bill's information was stale, even if it was correct. In fact, Bill's information was so stale that it didn't matter whether it was correct. The information was essentially irrelevant.

Similar flawed approaches play out every day. We believe we know so much about the people with whom we deal on a daily basis that our assumptions become real, even when they are wrong. People change, circumstances change, and another person's attitude toward a major decision may be different from his attitude toward a minor decision. Our assumptions themselves fluctuate, based more on our mood than on the facts. When we feel optimistic, we make optimistic assumptions. When we feel pessimistic, we make pessimistic assumptions. Because assumptions are only tenuously tied to facts, they fall victim to our mind games.

Investigating Assumptions About the Present and the Future

In the previous example, Bob could have investigated Bill's information. Even if the boss was an intimidating person, Bob could have approached the boss with something less than a direct request for the equipment. Plenty of strategies come to mind: a memo to the boss suggesting that the new equipment had some great features and would solve a variety of production problems; information to the boss about a special price available on the equipment; a note passing on feedback from a customer about the problem ("FYI—tell me if you want to know more about this"). Broaching a subject with someone else, especially a higher-up, is not always easy, but often it is quite easy to subtly investigate a person's receptiveness to an idea. Can subtlety and indirectness be inefficient? Of course. Can they help you make a decision by obtaining important information? You bet. Given the boss's actual frame of mind about the equipment, the boss would have taken the bait.

In many cases, confirming whether an important assumption is correct is easy. Many assumptions can be verified with a single telephone call, meeting, e-mail or Web search. That simple step often is not taken because we're programmed on a daily basis to accept less certainty, even when more certainty is available. When a Big Decision is involved, a more rigorous standard must be applied.

We often make assumptions about future events because the future is uncertain and difficult to prove. Rather than cause you to bypass an investigation, a lack of certainty about future events should cause you to do *more* investigation. Investigating the future is possible, but it requires increased effort. Investment decisions illustrate this point. The growth (or shrinkage) of your retirement account will depend on how you invest the funds and how a variety of uncertain future events plays out. Although investment of retirement funds is a very important decision, many investors seem to assume that the financial markets will continue to do whatever they're doing lately. If the market has been going up, people pile in. If the market's been down, people flee. Is either strategy based on a fair assumption? No. Although many approaches to analyzing the financial markets are available, the assumption that where we are today is where we will be three months or ten years from now has no support. If you're going to invest, you need to investigate economic, business and market cycles and behavior, as well as principles of asset and entity valuation, possibly at the level of individual companies, and diversification until you have a clearer picture of how the future is likely to emerge. While there always will be uncertainty, conscientious investing will beat ignorant investing in the long term. If you can't handle the investigation required to be a conscientious investor, find a good money manager.

In general, investigating the future starts with an investigation of what has happened in the past (and why), then moves to a review of how the present circumstances compare with the past, and winds up with an analytical model of how the future can be expected to unfold based on the first two. If you can't (or won't) do this, find help.

Replacing your assumptions with knowledge (or at least a greater sense of the odds) is not cost-free. Investigation is time-consuming and typically leads to far less than clairvoyance. You'll never know exactly how the boss will respond. You can't know precisely what your competition will do. Nobody can predict with certainty what the economy will do (and when), or what political developments will come along and seem to change everything. Events bigger than your Big Decision may interfere and lay waste to your best plans. You might become ill and interfere with your own Big Decision. Uncertainty is for sure. Nonetheless, despite the uncertainties that affect everyone and everything, make your Big Decision with the best information on all important points. If you ultimately have to guess because you can't come close to knowing what will happen, make your guess an educated one. You'll feel better later.

We leave Step 3 with the following points to remember about your target questions:

- Examine each of your wants, concerns and practical factors. What target questions do they raise?
- Be honest about what you know and don't know. Are you

guessing about legal, medical, business or other technical questions? Are you afraid to consult with someone who knows the answer, or are you concerned that you might look bad?

- Don't fear the answers to your target questions. What you don't know *will* hurt you.
- Continue to write down or draw your decision's progress. Give the decision a physical form and organization. Use graphics if you feel more comfortable with them.
- Test your assumptions. When you look at the facts related to your decision, ask what you really know and what you're assuming. Be bold about testing your assumptions. Be prepared to find that an assumption was wrong. Do some investigative work. Talk to someone who can give you the information you need, even if the conversation might be difficult.
- If you've got the luxury of time, set your notes down for a while. Think about the decision periodically over several days and see if you forgot any issues.

Marriage: A Woman's Investigation of Interfaith Conversion Leads to a Painful Compromise and Marriage to the Man She Loves

Suzanne Farnham and David Ross struggled for eight years with starkly conflicting worldviews of fundamentalist Christian and conservative Jewish families.

Suzanne Farnham[6] grew up in the Midwest and South in a strict Southern Baptist home. Her mother worked at the Southern Baptist church, and her father had attended a Southern Baptist seminary. The Farnham

---

[6] The names in this story are pseudonyms.

family was in church at least five nights a week. On Sunday mornings, Suzanne and her siblings attended Sunday school and church. When Suzanne was a teenager, she taught at a mission church on Sundays. Afterward, she went to teen choir and an evening service. Choir also met on Monday night. Wednesday was mission training. Thursday was Bible study. Each summer, Suzanne attended Southern Baptist camps.

Fundamentalist religion was the center of life for Suzanne's parents and the Farnham family. Even when they went out for fast food, the Farnhams prayed at the table before each meal. Suzanne and her sisters weren't allowed to wear shorts or anything else that showed their knees. Wine was not allowed at the church (grape juice was used during services). When Suzanne brought a male friend to the house, Suzanne's father made a point of asking the boy if he had been saved. "My parents firmly believe in all that religion has to offer," Suzanne says. "They firmly believe that if you are not saved, if you do not accept Jesus Christ as your Savior, you will live for eternity in hell."

Suzanne credits her parents for fostering strong family values and moral strength. The Farnhams were vehemently antiracist, even when they lived in communities where racism was common. "I never heard my parents utter a racial slur. My parents believe, politically and religiously, that all people are created equal. They would never refuse to have another person over for dinner because they were of a different race."

Suzanne describes the strong sense of obligation that came with her family's fundamentalism:

You are going to spend your eternity in heaven, and everyone else is living in the dark. This is a great gift, which requires you to conform your entire life to certain standards. You must lead people to Jesus. You must practice your religion publicly so that people can witness your religious faith. I went to evangelism training and mission training. I learned how to go door-to-door for Christ. I tried to convert people at school. There was little difference in our minds between Catholics and Jews. Either you were a true Christian who had been saved or something else. Every evening we did a family devotion. Each kid did a Bible lesson after dinner. Rather than seek out a place where there was a Southern Baptist church, my parents preferred to live in places where there was no church. Where there was no church, they could start a church and convert others.

Suzanne was an A student and a popular young woman. Her parents approved, reluctantly at first, of her joining the high-school cheerleading squad. After high school, Suzanne enrolled at a well-respected Southern Baptist college. Suzanne expected that, at some time during her college career, she would meet a Christian man who would become her husband.

At the Southern Baptist college, Suzanne started to pull away from fundamentalist religion. Suzanne recalls, "I was exposed to a lot of different ideas and people who had rebelled in various ways. I questioned things that I had always just accepted." In college, Suzanne studied the Holocaust and was exposed to the Jewish experience for the first time. She had only known one Jewish person growing up. Her parents' attitude toward Jewish people was positive. As Suzanne put it, "Baptists believe that Jews are in fact God's chosen people. It is heartbreaking to Baptists that the Jews have not 'chosen God back.' My parents wholly believed that we should be trying to convert Jews. They have nothing against Jews at all; they really want the Jews to see the light."

Studying the Holocaust in a college course profoundly affected Suzanne. "It was such an unbelievable turning point for humankind—that we could be so far along and that could happen. It made me more interested in Jewish history and Jewish people. It made me very sympathetic toward Jews and what they have been through as people." A few months into her college education, Suzanne ceased to identify herself as a fundamentalist Christian and rejected the religious practices and beliefs of her family. Significantly, although Suzanne rejected fundamentalism, she "didn't move on to anything else."

When Suzanne visited home during college, she kept her new thoughts about Christian fundamentalism to herself. Suzanne's parents attended Suzanne's graduation from college. She had graduated with high honors and had been accepted into graduate school. Suzanne had a boyfriend and was thinking about marrying him— a Christian who was light on practice. Just before Suzanne started graduate school, she and her boyfriend broke up.

Suzanne met David Ross during her first year in graduate school and recognized immediately that she and David came from "very, very different backgrounds." David was Jewish and raised in a family that strongly identified with Judaism. Some of David's family had barely escaped the Holocaust. The rest perished. The Rosses were not less traditional Reform Jews. They were very traditional Jews who attended a synagogue where the women and men sat separately. Growing up, David didn't know many people who weren't Jewish and certainly didn't know any Southern Baptists. All of David's friends were Jewish. His family's friends were Jewish. None of David's family members had married a non-Jew. David had not made any break from his background. He was firmly in that world.

Religion was not a barrier for David when it came to befriending—or dating—Suzanne. After a year as friends and graduate-school colleagues, Suzanne and David became intimate. Two months into the relationship, Suzanne thought everything was going smoothly until David dropped a bombshell. David told Suzanne rather matter-of-factly that he would never marry someone who wasn't Jewish. *Never.* Suzanne was stunned:

My reaction was just to blurt out, "Well, I would never convert." But I was deeply confused. Before then, I had thought of Jews as the victims of racism and exclusivity. I just didn't understand at all where this was coming from. I knew I could marry a Jewish person, and I definitely thought David might be that person.

This conversation launched eight years of turmoil in Suzanne and David's relationship. David's view on interfaith marriage did not stop his relationship with Suzanne from progressing. Religion aside, their mutual respect, trust and personal compatibility grew and grew. David and Suzanne loved each other. They wanted to stay with each other. Yet the religion issue kept rearing its head and quickly involved their families.

David's parents expressed no serious objection to David dating non-Jewish women. They seemed to assume that a dating relationship would not lead to marriage. When

David's parents realized that he was serious about Suzanne, they told him not to think about marriage. They told David that a marriage to Suzanne would fail, that he would lose his Jewish identity, and that overcoming the child-raising and other issues would be impossible. When Suzanne visited David's parents with David, they were cordial—but not warm. They invited Suzanne to dinner, but not to a show afterward; there just weren't enough tickets. The closer David and Suzanne became, the more obvious it became that their parents' dearest religious and cultural beliefs were on a collision course:

David's parents were concerned not just about this world, but also the future. They believed that Jews should continue to exist in general and in their family. In the Jewish religion, the children are Jewish if the mother is Jewish or she converts. It wasn't about intolerance. It was about worldview. My parents believed eternity was at stake. I would go to heaven because I'd been saved. You can't be unsaved. If my children weren't saved, they wouldn't be in heaven. It came down to going to heaven on the one side and propagation of the faith on the other side.

At the end of graduate school, the relationship between David and Suzanne was stuck in limbo. In the foreground was David's conflict, which was more than a conflict between David and his parents. The conflict was in David's own values. Unlike Suzanne's abandonment of Christian fundamentalism, David never abandoned Judaism. Although David loved Suzanne, he clung to his preference to marry a Jewish woman. David loved Suzanne, though, and he could imagine marrying her and raising children with her.

Suzanne had no problem marrying a Jewish man, and

she wanted to marry David. Suzanne was predisposed against converting to Judaism and, despite what she had told David at the outset, she hadn't made a final decision on conversion. Suzanne knew that her parents would have serious objections if their future grandchildren were not saved into the Southern Baptist church. Their beloved grandchildren would be condemned to an eternity in hell.

For five years after graduate school, Suzanne and David repeatedly broke up and got back together. They lived in different cities at first. They dated other people. They pursued their own careers. Yet as time marched on, their lives always came back to two points: They wanted to get married, and marriage created enormous family problems on both sides.

By the eighth year of their relationship, both David and Suzanne had reached their thirties. Time was becoming a factor for Suzanne. Suzanne wanted to have children, and she needed to know whether she would marry David or find another husband:

I had to decide what to do about this religion situation because I was at the point where I wanted to get married, and he was, too, but we had this issue standing in our way. If we were going to get married, we had to come to a compromise. David would not propose until this was worked out. We discussed marriage all the time. This was not a relationship where there is a proposal and a decision. We had discussed marriage for years.

Suzanne and David agreed that Suzanne would take a leave of absence from her job and move in with David. They would give it six months. By the end, they would get engaged or break up. Suzanne's decision to move in with David created a crisis with her parents. It was a harbinger of problems to come. Suzanne recalls her mother's initial reaction:

First there was silence, then sobbing. She couldn't believe this had happened to her child. She told me I was a failure, and I had rejected everything the family stood for. She said I was going to have to face God. All my childhood we had heard it was a sin to live together before marriage. We weren't allowed to watch Three's Company. *David and I had tried to put on a façade for a short while, but it didn't work. Finally, I just came clean. I was absolutely devastated by my mother's utter rejection of me. She never called me at home when we lived together. She only called me on my cell phone, even if she knew I was home. My dad didn't approve either, but his role as a father seemed to trump everything else. He was disapproving, but less judgmental and less harsh. It was much harder than I expected.*

Suzanne's decision to spend six months resolving her relationship with David was pivotal. On David's side, the main issue was whether he would marry a non-Jew against his family's wishes. On Suzanne's side, the main issue was whether she would convert to Judaism. They agreed that if they could move past the religion issue, they would marry.

The first subject to come up during the six months was whether Suzanne would convert to Judaism:

Converting would have made everything easy. I'd get past the issue with David. But if I converted, I would do more than reject my family's religion. I would be accepting someone else's religion. It would kill my parents. Converting would be an egregious slap in the face. I didn't feel like it would be an honest decision. I respect the Jewish religion deeply, but I don't believe in it. My conversion would cheapen the religion to the people who really subscribe to it. I also was worried that converting would send the message to David's parents that they had "won." I was concerned that this would set a bad precedent in the relationship.

I had a good friend who was exploring conversion at the same time. She had all these books about people's experience with conversion. I read all the books. They didn't make me want to convert. I was pretty close-minded when I read them, though. It didn't seem like conversion instantly made people accepted by other Jews. A lot of the people who converted were not accepted right away.

My feelings were reinforced by some materials I read online. I read recommendations by some rabbis about why non-Jews should not be invited to Jewish events. This was very unlike how I was raised. We wanted to bring non-Baptists into our house. The exclusivity bothered me. There were values I had about inclusiveness that may have started in my upbringing, but survived my rejection of the Baptist religion.

Suzanne decided that she would not convert. Now it was David's turn to make a decision. Were there any conditions under which David would marry Suzanne absent conversion? For eight years, Suzanne and David had assumed that Suzanne would have to convert for their children to be considered Jews. While Suzanne was researching conversion, she learned something new: The children of a non-Jewish mother can be converted to Judaism at birth, even if the non-Jewish mother never converts. This was an epiphany to Suzanne. It was important information in an impasse that had pitted Suzanne and David's love against strong family religious values for eight years. Suzanne knew that she could accept converting her children at birth and raising them Jewish if she didn't have to convert.

Suzanne proposed a compromise to David: Suzanne

would not be Jewish, and the children would be. That situation would not make David's parents completely happy, but it would address their main concern: that Judaism should propagate down to future generations. The compromise would offer nothing to Suzanne's parents. If David accepted the compromise, Suzanne knew she'd have to face uncertain consequences with her parents.

David accepted. Eight years after they met, Suzanne and David were engaged. The engagement was not the end of the discussion about religion in the family; it was only the end of the first chapter. In the months before the wedding, Suzanne and David hammered out a precise vision of what it meant to raise their children Jewish, while respecting the different beliefs of Suzanne's parents. The details were endless: When do they go to temple? To church? What holidays do they spend with each family? What is the family position on Christmas? How about Christmas trees? One item on which they agreed was that "our kids will not be told that it is better to marry a Jew than a non-Jew." This point was extremely important to Suzanne, and David went along.

David and Suzanne married in a ceremony performed by a rabbi in May 1998.

Postscript: In Suzanne's Own Words

My parents were happy when I was engaged. I think they thought that eventually they would convert David. They explained that, of course, the marriage would only be for this world, because David wouldn't be joining me in heaven. For my parents, the problem was with the children. When I told my mother that we would raise the kids Jewish, my mother told me she could not imagine loving grandchildren who would be unable to be with them in heaven. My parents believe they'll be heartbroken for eternity because their grandchildren won't join them in heaven. At first, my parents said they weren't coming to the wedding, but they did. Every decision was very, very difficult—more and more alienating to our family. My parents tell me I have rejected my entire history and my entire family.

David and I sort of set our future in motion, but it came at enormous cost to my family and me. David felt he really compromised, but I still feel it was so little compared to what I've done. I've entirely altered my relationship with my family and caused them pain every day. It causes them pain to think about my kids, to talk about my kids, to wonder where they went wrong. It's a decision that has enormously grave consequences. I didn't fully appreciate the consequences when I made the decision. I don't think there's anything else I could have done—any other way to resolve it for me. When I took my parents out of the equation, everything else felt right. But it's hard to take your parents out of the equation. I know you can't make decisions for your parents. I can't live out their lives. But I just wish there had been some other way. I don't think there is. I explored all kinds of different options. I didn't find anything that helped me to deal with my parents.

I know this compromise barely worked. It didn't work for my parents. I was concerned that everyone in my family would be Jewish but me. Yet I had a very strong match with David. He was the right person. Although these other issues were important, we knew we would make it work. A mother is attached to her children.

I don't regret the decision because it enabled me to marry David and move forward with that. I am optimistic about my marriage. But I'm that kind of person. I look at a glass that's half full and say, "What do you mean it's half full? It's full!"

Maybe I'm overly optimistic.

AUTHORS' NOTE: Suzanne Farnham's true story is an opportunity to remind our readers that each true story is told from the perspective of a single featured decision-maker. Other parties to each of the stories might have quite different perspectives on the decision, and certainly there is enormous room for differences in values.

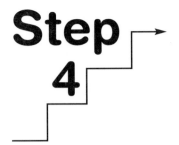

Step 4

Parents, Friends, Lovers, Lawyers and TV: Find Your Best Sources and Advisors

Read not to contradict and confute, nor to believe and take for granted, nor to find talk and discourse, but to weigh and consider.

—Francis Bacon

When you investigate your target questions, you'll find lots of information that is incomplete, biased, falsified and exaggerated. Bad information leads directly to bad decisions. Unfortunately, bad information is everywhere. People offer you advice on subjects about which they have little useful knowledge. Printed material may be very pretty—and totally inaccurate. Bad information does not emanate only from bad people. Even the most well-meaning, reputable sources of information may hire a sloppy researcher.

Third-party misinformation is not the only hurdle to overcome as you investigate your target questions. Personal biases are entrenched thought patterns and prejudices that may undermine your decision. Personal biases often are cloaked in the guise of common sense. Albert Einstein observed, "Common sense is the collection of prejudices acquired by age eighteen." Even poor decision-makers believe their decisions are supported by common sense! Unless you examine yourself at least as closely as you examine outside sources, you'll find that you are your own biggest source of misinformation.

One of the most serious decision-making errors is to jump too quickly to what you think "must be" the right conclusion, then seek out only information that supports your conclusion. Don't think of your role as making a case. Your role is to discover the facts that are needed to make a decision and to weigh them. Let facts influence your decision. Do not let your decision alter the facts. By analogy, if your Big Decisions were being made in a courtroom, you would be the judge, not one of the lawyers.

In Step 4, you examine your information sources, especially on the target questions, to determine your most reliable sources and jettison sources of bad information. The starting point for Step 4 is to acknowledge that virtually all information is biased. The success of your Big Decision depends heavily on your ability to manage biased information.

What Is a Fact? When Is a Fact Not a Fact? When Does an Opinion Masquerade as a Fact?

Everyone has some feel for the distinction between a fact and an opinion. A fact is observable or can be proven true. An opinion is a belief one holds, but which is not proven. In contrast to facts, which we expect to be constant, opinions vary from person to person and depend upon the opinion holder's values, perceptions and beliefs.

Fact and opinion become blurred in many areas. Professional advice is one area. When a physician tells you, "You have low blood sugar" or "Your biopsy is positive," you feel she has communicated a fact. Somewhere in a pathology lab, a technician probably exercised judgment in analyzing the test, but the technician's discretion is supposed to be so limited that the information you're being given is treated as a fact.

When the physician tells you, "We'll have to run some further tests on your mother, but I suspect that the problem is hormonal," the physician is giving you an opinion based on facts he learned in his training and experience. If the physician were to say, "Given your financial means, you owe it to your mother to get her the best medical care available in the world. Money is no object . . . ," this statement is an opinion; the relationship, if any, between the son's or daughter's financial means and the amount of money to spend on a parent's medical care implicates the physician's own values.

The fact/opinion distinction also comes up in commercial transactions. When a salesperson tells you, "This car goes from zero to sixty in 4.5 seconds," he is telling you a fact. The same is true when the salesperson tells you, "*Consumer Reports* gave this car the highest score in safety of any car last year" or "I just bought this car for my wife's thirty-fifth birthday." When the salesperson tells you, "This is a great car—the best buy on the lot right now," you're hearing an opinion. The concept of "best buy" reflects a value judgment about the trade-off between price and quality. In contrast, a statement that the car has the "lowest price on the lot" is a statement of fact. It's true or false, without resorting to anyone's values.

To become a skilled decision-maker, you must learn to separate facts from opinions because an opinion is only as good as the beliefs that are behind it. If you accept another person's opinion as a fact, your decision based on that "fact" may advance the other person's values and objectives. If yours are different, you may be making a mistake.

Finding Opinions and Biases
That Are Hidden in the "Facts"

Even when information is presented as a "fact," you must determine whether the information reflects the methods, opinions and biases of the source. A newspaper reporter may be a totally honest journalist, but not a thorough one. Because of a journalist's deficient methods, you may receive only part of the story. A real-estate brochure may list ten great features of a house for sale, including five undoctored photographs of the outside and inside of the house, but fail to mention a noisy neighbor next door. Whether the omission was intentional or sloppy, the impact is to deny you information you need to make a decision. The brochure is "factual," but not complete.

Much of what is offered as factual information—polls, tests, surveys and other data—is not the product of statistically reliable work. Many polls and surveys are published with (or without!) a disclaimer that says, in effect, "Sorry, this isn't real public-opinion data. We just asked whoever happened to be watching at 10:00 P.M. to call and tell us what they all thought. Then we tallied it up."

Why are we bombarded with unreliable data? Public-opinion data is often entertaining. It adds "color" to dry subjects. While rigorous factual analysis is a questionable moneymaker, entertainment is a proven moneymaker. An increasingly blurry line has developed between product promotion, entertainment, and news and information. When you're shown the results of an unscientific poll, you aren't being informed of a fact. Even the source often admits it's not scientific. You're being entertained. Misinformation is fun! That is, until you invest all of your retirement money based on it.

Should you trust a movie review on a Web site that is owned by a movie-production company? What influences operate on the people who decide which genocide gets covered, which lost child is news, and which social and political reforms are most needed? Time will tell whether a single business can analyze, communicate, entertain, advise and make gobs of money at the same time. To some extent, these functions seem to require mutually exclusive values and priorities. Good analysis often is neither entertaining nor profitable. The heart and soul of a news company's value as an information source is its ability to report the truth, even if it doesn't further vested interests.

Bill O'Reilly is the host of a television talk show called *The O'Reilly Factor* and author of an interesting and popular book called *The No-Spin Zone.* O'Reilly's journalistic thesis is that the world contains too much self-serving disinformation and not enough straight talk. O'Reilly argues that people shouldn't tolerate disinformation or "spin."

Having proclaimed himself the vanguard of spinless journalism, one would hardly expect O'Reilly to spin his own academic background. Yet a chummy interview with fellow commentator Tim Russert undid O'Reilly. In an effort to establish plausible kinship with a blue-collar audience, O'Reilly put an outlandish spin on why he attended the blue-blood—not blue-collar—John F. Kennedy School of Government at Harvard.

Here is the "No-Spin Man" spinning one:[7]

> RUSSERT: You did go to Harvard for a master's degree.
> O'REILLY: But late . . .
> RUSSERT: Late in your life. Did that change you at all? Did it refine you? Did it round off those rough edges?
> O'REILLY: Come on, those Harvard pinheads. The only reason I went there is so I could get into the Harvard Club and have lunch over here, and you can't get in unless you have a degree. So I said, "Jeez, I mean, it's right around the corner. I got to get in there," so I—look, first of all, I was stunned when they actually accepted me. It was a mid-career program, so there were geezers like me in the

---

[7] CNBC interview between Tim Russert and Bill O'Reilly, October 27, 2001 (transcript prepared by Burelle's Information Services ©CNBC).

program, and I had pretty good grades, I guess you'd call them, in—from Boston U. and my graduate school. But I went there for—really, I went there for sociological reasons. I wanted to see how the other half lived 'cause I never had seen that. And I got an eyeful. Because people who go to Harvard and who are that—they're usually the elite, and they're—they're given a lot of things by their parents. They're usually very monied; they're usually very cultured —the total opposite of me. And I wanted to see the attitude, and I learned a tremendous amount at the Kennedy School at Harvard, tremendous.

O'Reilly's attempt to portray himself as some kind of social weapons inspector for less-privileged classes was pure spin—about O'Reilly's own credentials, no less. Harvard is more selective than that. Did the Harvard admissions committee mess up and grant admission to a person whose main goal was to check the attitude of rich students and eat at the Harvard Club? Did O'Reilly spin the Russert interview or his Harvard application? Probably both. Even the words of a spin-free man must be scrutinized.

Before you accept a published fact as true for a Big Decision, figure out who is stating the fact and why. Be cautious of sources that are caught up in entertainment showmanship, where "public image" may lead to shtick-driven positions on important issues. Remember that sources don't always disclose conflicts of interest. If you discover a conflict that a source has not disclosed, treat that failure accordingly.

How Do You Know What Information Is Reliable?

How do you decide what information to believe and what to ignore as you investigate your target questions? Let's look at the principles of credibility that U.S. courts have applied for more than a hundred years. Whether it's a routine case, a death-penalty trial or a billion-dollar claim, juries and judges evaluate information using these factors:

- If you've received information from a person, what is the person's demeanor? In other words, ask yourself whether the person behaves the way truthful people behave. If the source is an entity, such as a business or a publication, do its representatives act how you'd expect truthful, reliable representatives to act?
- Is the information of a sound character and quality? Is it well-reasoned? Well-supported? Is it based upon sources that are regarded as reliable?
- What is the relationship between the person who provides the information and the information itself? Did the source personally see or hear the facts it reports? If the source relies on other sources, how reliable are the other sources?
- Does the information source have a bias, interest or other motive? Will the source make or lose money because of the information, directly or indirectly? Take a broad view. If the source is an organization, does it rely on membership fees from members who have a particular agenda? If the source is a person, who is paying the person? If the source is a business, how will the information advance or hinder the business's position in the market? Sources also may have nonfinancial agendas that affect the quality of its statements, including political, moral, social and other objectives.
- Has the source previously said things that are inconsistent with what it is now saying?
- Has the source said something that you know is not factual? If so, you should wonder how much the source has misrepresented the truth about other facts.
- Has the source been shown to be false or incorrect in the past?

Has the source's reliability been sufficiently tested for you to form a view on its reliability? Give "unknown quantities" the benefit of the doubt only at your peril.

• What is the source's reputation for honesty and accuracy based upon past conduct?

• Does the source rely on questionable information when more reliable information is available? Plenty of so-called "data" is around to support all kinds of positions. An information source that twists and turns data is suspect.

Courts deem these factors to be more reliable than a lie-detector test. These factors help to evaluate information from any person or organization.

How Much Investigation Is Enough?

How do you know when you've investigated the facts enough? This issue is especially bothersome to people who don't do fact research very often. A major part of the training of professional advisors and decision-makers involves learning protocols that define adequate investigation. The goal, of course, is to investigate until you have the answer, or until you find a controversy about the answer and you understand the controversy well enough to conclude that you're comfortable basing your decision on a particular approach. The fact is, many times you won't be 100 percent sure of at least one important fact when you make a Big Decision.

One sign that you're investigating well is that you see the same information in a number of places. In other words, when a lot of different approaches and sources lead to the same piece of information, you're probably on the right track—unless everyone's wrong. Be cautious, though. In a wired world, twenty Web sites can have the same information—all of which originated from a single source. Twenty thinkers haven't reached the same conclusion; one thinker's conclusion has been repeated twenty times! If the thinker is a poor thinker, you're seeing one person's poor thinking twenty times. If you find that several different, current and highly credible sources agree on a fact, and you find no persuasive school of contrary thought, you might ultimately conclude, "If they all base their reputations on this fact, I'm willing to do the same thing. If they are all wrong, I did my best."

Another caution: If twenty different sources have the same bias, those sources may independently reach the same biased conclusion. The fact that all of the sources reached the same conclusion proves little, except perhaps that similar bias leads to similar conclusions. Is it surprising that thousands of Wall Street analysts, whose firms collectively made billions of dollars from technology stock trading and investment banking, pumped the same stocks during the late 1990s' market boom? The naysayers could barely get media coverage, and sometimes they lost their jobs. Putting aside whether the analysts acted with integrity, a massive failure occurred on the part of investors and some of the business media to accurately assess the enormous impact of industrywide bias on investment analysis.

Your Advisors: The "Caring Biases" of Parents, Friends and Relatives

Parents, friends, spouses, siblings and others who are close to you can be crucial resources. These people know you, and their interests typically are more closely aligned with yours than with the interests of other people out in the cruel world. If you and Sandra are both vying for the same job at your office, your friends and family would vote for you to be promoted over Sandra every single time. In fact, they'd vote for you without knowing the first thing about Sandra.

Many people can't imagine making a Big Decision without consulting family or friends. Life would be very tough without the people who help us "deal"—the confidantes, listeners, sympathizers, huggers, comfort givers and flower senders who are there when we suffer a loss, experience a trauma or face a Big Decision. Family members and friends often fall into this group.

Does this mean that family members and friends are categorically the best source of advice on a Big Decision? Not necessarily. So far, we've talked about biases that arise when someone seeks to advance his own interests by distorting the information that you receive. Not all biases are ill-intentioned. In giving advice on a Big Decision, someone who wants only the best for you may be as biased as someone you don't know, or even more biased. Bias is not necessarily evil. You must consider the "caring biases" when you make a Big Decision.

Most parents desperately want to protect their children from harm of all types. Parents are often extremely risk-averse advisors who may discourage a child from taking a risk that even the parent would readily take (or actually took in the past). Parenting style may play a part. Some parents allow children to "make their own mistakes" and are reluctant to say or do anything that could be regarded as pressure or interference. Other parents feel that they know best because of age and experience, and that they short-change their children if they fail to guide them in the right direction on decisions. Some parents are deeply offended if a child appears not to be under their control. Some parents find great joy in encouraging their children "to fly." Parenting styles may persist into the child's adult years. When evaluating the input of parents, think about how *they* see their role and how that affects their advice.

Close friends bring similar dynamics to a decision. Most of us like to talk to our friends about a Big Decision. This communication can be extremely useful. Friends offer a supportive audience for our ideas. Friends help us grapple with our values and emotions, without passing the harsh judgments that certain family members might be prone to offer. Friends who have relevant personal experience or professional expertise offer the benefits of their background at a bargain price. At work, professional friends can help us navigate business and political issues that we are ill-equipped to handle.

For all the benefits friends bring, you must remember that friends also have biases. A very close friend, just like a family member, wants you to be happy, feel comfortable and avoid all types of harm. If your friend believes that a good friend should support you no matter what, you'll only hear what the friend thinks you want to hear, which leads to very biased advice and information. What you *want* to hear and what you *should* hear may be two different things. A close personal friend's well-intentioned "blind" support actually may encourage you to make a bad decision. Work friends run the gamut from Blind Supporters (anything goes), to Golden Mentors (sound advice, great support), to Trojan Horses (watch out!). Each has a bias worth considering.

In most cases, close friends and family members don't want to act as your lawyer, physician or career counselor. They want to support you. Unless your friend or family member has the background to double as an expert, the crucial role of friends and family is to empower you emotionally and spiritually to make decisions that you find difficult. Big Decisions require courage, commitment and sometimes the ability to sustain physical, emotional or financial pain, peer pressure and other significant consequences. Supportive friends and family can help you make your decision and carry it out, which are wonderful benefits of the relationship. The challenge of friend and family advice is easily illustrated in the job context:

Carla has been an accountant at Lockwood & Courier for three years. She makes a good living, and the accounting business is extremely steady. Carla's boss has told Carla that she will become a partner after two more years. Partnership is tenure at the firm—"a job for life." Carla tolerates her work, but finds herself unchallenged (bored) by certain tasks. Through her work, Carla has become close to a new client of the firm. The client's president has asked Carla to leave Lockwood & Courier and become the first Vice President, Finance of the business. Having worked with the client for eight months, Carla believes the business is on the way up. Carla would have a chance to break out of the outside advisor mold and "become a player." On the other hand, Carla has seen new businesses come and go. The job would offer none of the long-term stability of Lockwood & Courier. When Carla thinks about the opportunity, she is excited, flattered and terrified.

Carla has a classic choice: stability or start-up. How do her family and friends react?

Father (accountant): "Stay right where you are. The accounting business will always take care of you. Clients come and go. I've seen my share of client bankruptcies. You don't know if Lockwood & Courier will take you back. Why ruin a good thing? Is this about money?"

Mother (homemaker): "I don't know, Carla. It sounds exciting. Maybe it's more excitement than you need. How will you manage a high-powered company job and a family? You do want a family, right? Accounting is nice and predictable. It allowed us to raise you in this neighborhood. Next thing you know, the new company will want you to move far away. You know how our corporate neighbors come and go. Lockwood & Courier won't do that."

Best Friend (corporate employee): "Go for it, Carla. I know you'll do great there. How many times does this kind of opportunity come along? If it doesn't work out, look at the experience you'll get. Once-in-a-lifetime. You're always saying you're bored. They'll always take you back at Lockwood. They love you there. If you work for the client, the client's relationship with Lockwood will be stronger. Lockwood will love you for that, too. You'll be CEO one day anyway, and you won't have to go back to Lockwood. Do it!"

Father, Mother and Best Friend are all well-meaning people who want Carla to make the right choice. Are the interests of any of them the same as Carla's interests? Probably not. They also don't have much information about Carla's prospective employer (or Lockwood & Courier), outside what Carla has told them and what Father knows from his own experience in the accounting profession. Carla's parents want Carla to be stable and cared for, emotionally and financially. They definitely don't want her to leave town. Carla's parents are not looking to maximize Carla's career potential; they're focused on the personal costs and risks. They believe Carla's doing fine, and keeping everything the same can't hurt. Best Friend wants to be supportive. She's reacting more to what she thinks Carla wants to do than to anything Best Friend has analyzed. Best Friend sets herself up as the opposite of Carla's parents in this case. While the parents express their love by being overly cautious (perhaps), Best Friend expresses friendship by giving voice to Carla's grandest hopes and aspirations. Everyone in the picture cares about Carla, but each one's relationship with Carla brings a different flavor of caring bias to Carla's decision.

In the previous example, Mother, Father and Best Friend seem to fall into certain stereotypes. Accountant Father is cautious; home-maker Mother is protective and family-focused; Best Friend is a cheerleader. Clearly, each family is different. Some parents scream "Go for it!" Some friends are negative. When you ask experienced advisors, however, you don't hear a lot of talk about how every one of their clients has a unique decision style. What you hear is that people's decision styles often are dictated by some very stereo-typical perceptions of their own roles. We aren't saying that all mothers should be homemakers or that all homemakers are con-servative, family-oriented people. We are saying that a mother who chose to be a homemaker and is satisfied with that choice is likely to raise home- and family-related concerns in response to a child's decision. A mother who is a chief financial officer of a major corporation might look entirely differently at Carla's decision, depending on whether the mother is satisifed with—or regretful about—her own career and family choices.

In the end, Carla may decide that she doesn't want to quit a very steady job and take a high-pressured, speculative job. Much of what Carla's parents say may appeal to Carla's values. On the other hand, Carla may see the risks of leaving Lockwood & Courier as truly limited. Accountants are always in demand, and Carla has proven herself professionally. Even if Carla largely discredits Best Friend's blind importuning, the core of what Best Friend says has merit; the risk of Carla failing is limited. Carla most likely can try out a new career at the client's company and, if it doesn't work, not skip a meal.

Provided you consider the biases, the advice of parents, siblings and friends can be extremely valuable. They are unlikely to intentionally mislead you, and they want your decisions to turn out well. A parent or friend who is an expert in a field can be a ready source of dependable information within that field—and you can't beat the price. Parents and friends can be helpful contacts. Word-of-mouth recommendations and references from people you trust often are the most helpful. Finally, don't lose sight of the fact that age and experience do beget wisdom. Your parents and other senior mentors are the most accessible source of real-life experience.

We haven't addressed the biases of a spouse. The true story at the end of this chapter is about Ken Anderson's decision whether to donate a kidney to his brother. In making this decision, Anderson consulted only with his spouse, God and his physicians. Others' opinions were merely of passing interest, and they had no impact on

Anderson's decision. This limited approach to input on truly major decisions is common, especially in medical decisions. While we feel comfortable making some generalizations about the caring biases of parents and friends, such a wide variety of decision dynamics occurs between spouses that we simply won't generalize here.

Unlike friendships, marital relationships may go through periods where they're barely voluntary. Marital decision-making is subject to legal factors that aren't present in a friendship (nor are they typically present between a parent and a grown child). In certain situations, not consulting with a spouse or acting without a spouse's consent may even be unlawful. What's the bias of a spouse who's having an affair on a decision whether to buy a house? What's the bias of a seriously ill spouse on an end-of-life decision you might have to make for your parent? You can see the complexity. It's surely a topic for another day.

How to Handle the Opinions of Destructive Family Members and Friends with Issues

So far we've treated friends and family members as positive, though biased, forces. The world is not always so pretty. Some parents, stepparents, siblings, and other kith, kin and acquaintances may have a truly destructive attitude toward you and your objectives. Just as supportive words from a family member or friend can be a huge shot in the arm, a few negative words from a parent or other trusted person can be enormously deflating.

A family member whose attitude toward you is generally positive may have a problem in his own life that makes it difficult for him to give you good advice. A family member who has a substance-abuse problem, for example, may have so much turmoil—or chemicals—in her own psyche that her judgments about you are impaired. A parent who has seriously abused you physically or mentally has betrayed your trust and is not a reliable resource for you. When a family member has problems that make it impossible for him or her to help you make sound decisions about your life, that person should play a limited role in your decisions. In such cases, you should seek a mentor, counselor or other guide so you aren't alone in making important decisions, especially if you're young and a parent is impaired.

Unlike relatives, you choose your friends. Unfortunately, friends also may have problems that affect you. Some friends will have a love/hate relationship with the prospect that you will succeed. In an ideal world, a friend is not jealous, envious or critical of your progress. In some cases, though, a friend may have a deep-rooted fear that, if things work out too well, you no longer will want the friendship. Other friends may be so caught up in their own dilemmas and personal issues that they can't attend to your Big Decision. Others simply may not have the experience, skill or confidence to help you make a Big Decision. If a friend has severe issues or personal limitations, remember that this circumstance will affect the quality of that friend's advice and information. Go ahead and listen respectfully to these friends, but consider their limits.

Your Advisors: Teachers, Strategy Mentors and Support Mentors

To generalize about advice from the wide variety of teachers, counselors, spiritual advisors and other mentors who may take a special interest in your decisions is difficult. Mentors have a profound—and often very positive—influence upon many people's lives, especially on Big Decisions.[8] The benefits of a mentor are

---

[8] Of course the rules that apply to parents and friends "with issues" also would apply to a mentor whose own problems make him or her ill-suited as a trustworthy source of advice for you. When a relationship of trust exists, harmful comments or conduct by supposed mentors can be extremely damaging.

greatest when the mentor has both the desire to help you and the skill and experience to do it.

When weighing the advice of a teacher or other mentor on a Big Decision, consider whether the mentor is acting mostly as a Strategy Mentor or a Support Mentor. The difference is key. A Strategy Mentor positions herself as your captain in navigating difficult waters. She tells you what decision will best move you toward a goal that you and the mentor agree you should attain. A Strategy Mentor basically tells you what to do, even if her instructions are couched as "suggestions," "hints" or "advice." If you contravene a Strategy Mentor's instructions, you risk imperiling the relationship. If the Strategy Mentor believes that your interests are served only when you follow her advice, she may believe the relationship has become pointless if you feel free to disregard her directions. A Strategy Mentor gives advice in the form of "Your next move is to . . ." and "This is how you handle it. . . ." Your relationship with a Strategy Mentor remains smooth as long as you and the mentor accept that the mentor knows best. While you occasionally may agree to disagree on some matter, even the disagreement is done by mutual consent and is respectful.

A Support Mentor is more of a "warm authority" who encourages you and uses the dignity of his higher position to aid you. In contrast to a Strategy Mentor, a Support Mentor fundamentally wants you to choose your path. The Support Mentor smoothes your way. Joseph Bloom was an accomplished concert pianist who now is a sought-after accompanist for young musicians. Bloom is a passionate musician who, by his own admission, "never forced a major decision" in his life. He pursued his love of music wherever it took him, largely without regard to financial or social consequences. Bloom was literally raised at Carnegie Hall; his father was the executive director there. Bloom's father never pressured Bloom to go into music, but passion carried Bloom there as a teenager, and he quit college to be a career musician:

> It's hard as a teenager to know that your passion is different from anybody else's passion about music, or anything else—or whether or not other people have passions. There are pieces of music that would absolutely work volcanic eruptions inside of me. There are pieces that were so beautiful I could not bear it—literally, physically, could not bear it. . . . Some of the most transcendent experiences I've ever had in my life, where time almost stops flowing altogether, where consciousness is so present that I don't even know how to describe it, come from music.

Bloom refuses to make decisions for his musician-students, some of whom must choose between studying music and traditional academics. The reason, Bloom admits, is that music "means too much" to him. Bloom sees himself as a Support Mentor for serious students who face a choice between a career in art and other options. Here's how Bloom describes his mentor role:

> If I really believe in a person's talent, I will say, "Regardless of anything else, as long as I am alive you will have my 110 percent support in this. I will be there for you in any way you need me—whether it's career advice or connections. I will give you all of that." I tell my students about people I know who earned a good living in a music-related career down the line. I might mention people like a psychiatrist friend of mine who went into music and later did very well in other kinds of work. I would not tell a student what decision to make. I am not so presumptuous to think I know. . . . I would say to the student, "You are wonderful. I believe in you. Be confident." It's so important for the student to know I believe in him or her. It's so much more important to do this than to make the decision. I have no divine insight.

Strategy Mentors and Support Mentors are unquestionably important. Nonetheless, as you might suspect, your mentors have biases. Consider the biases of your mentors in the same way you'd consider the caring biases of friends and family members. A

Strategy Mentor wants you to achieve the goal that you and she agreed was the basis for the mentoring relationship. The company vice president who took you under her wing might be a good source of advice on whether to accept an offer to become a division head in Puerto Rico. Might this Strategy Mentor be biased when you ask her whether you should leave work early every Thursday to coach your son's basketball team? Yup.

Consider another example: Let's say the vice president, your Strategy Mentor, made her career in the manufacturing division, and you are her protégé. The chief operating officer notices your speaking skill at a meeting and hints that you may want to apply for a position in the corporate communications office. If you get the communications job, you'll have to leave the manufacturing division, and you will no longer report to your Strategy Mentor. The situation has just moved from professional to personal for your mentor. The opportunity in communications may strengthen your relationship with your mentor, or it may destroy it. The outcome will depend on her objectives and your objectives, and how you each perceive the impact of the new position. Don't assume, however, that the mentor who guided you up the ladder to be her protégé will give you unbiased advice about whether to leave her division. Maybe she can; maybe she can't. . . .

A Support Mentor wants to keep you happy, energized, confident and, of course, feeling supported. Support Mentors are most valuable when you have a better chance to achieve your goal if you feel supported. Undoubtedly, this proposition is true in creative and athletic pursuits, but it's also true in academics, careers and even diets. A Support Mentor's biases are similar to the biases of a close friend. The difference is that a Support Mentor often has a better sense of reality than a friend. If the mentor is a teacher, an expert in the field or has other background, the Support Mentor may have a very clear picture of your actual chances of success or failure. That perspective doesn't mean the Support Mentor will tell you the truth, the whole truth and nothing but the truth. Support Mentors routinely hide opinions that aren't supportive—and tell white lies on occasion—to make sure you feel supported. Is it wrong for a Support Mentor to tell a white lie?

Consider this example:

What's Inside the Teacher's Head: Teddy is so bright. If only his family weren't messed up. It kills me to see a kid with this much potential have to fight for enough peace and quiet just to do his homework. He should go to college one day. Nobody at home cares a bit. When I told his mother that Teddy was bright, she just started talking about problems with his dad. His dad won't even come to meetings. I hear he's in and out of jail. Probably a drug problem. I just don't know if Teddy can overcome all these obstacles. I have a lot of doubt that he can.

What the Teacher Tells Teddy: Listen, Teddy, you've got a gift— a first-class mind. You're a special one-in-a-thousand kid. I know it's tough at home and in the neighborhood. I don't know how you do it, but your work is very strong. We have to focus on your future. If you want to be somebody, Teddy—if you want to move out of that neighborhood—we've got to keep you on a college track. I know you can do it, Teddy. I am going to be there. We're going to show that nothing can stop you.

That teacher wasn't exactly honest, but he knew that without support and encouragement, Teddy could easily lapse into frustration, discouragement and apathy. Most of us would agree that the teacher's bias is a good, healthy bias; motivating Teddy is a noble task and may help him achieve what the teacher doubts can be done. In this example, Teddy may be far better served by encouragement than by a totally honest opinion. The example does illustrate, however, the frailty of Support Mentors as sources of reliable opinions.

Your Advisors: When Do You Need an "Expert Opinion"?

In some cases, you'll find that making a decision requires expertise—special knowledge that comes from skill, training and experience in a field that's beyond your own knowledge. If you lack the skill, training and experience to anticipate how a Big Decision will play out, consider finding someone who knows the area. In decisions that involve medicine, law, accounting and financial planning, early consultation with an expert often is the most important step you'll take. In our complex world, the need for expertise goes far beyond the traditional "learned professions." Experts can provide valuable advice on virtually every subject. The difficulty is in determining what kind of expert you need, separating the competent experts from the charlatans and receiving quality advice without blowing your budget.

An expert advisor can help you do the following:

- Clarify the specific facts you need to make your decision and isolate the target questions
- Sort through conflicting opinions of friends, family members and others
- Give you confidence that you've "done your homework"
- Advise you on what decision to make, in the form of a professional opinion

How do you recognize when you'd benefit from an expert consultation? For many people, this step isn't easy—for the same reason a person will drive for hours, lost, and refuse to ask directions. Aside from the fact that expert advice often isn't cheap, it also isn't always convenient, and seeking advice goes against a common "I'll-figure-it-out-myself" mentality. If pride of authorship makes writers resent help with their work, what might be called "pride of accomplishment" makes many individuals reluctant to enlist an expert. They want to win on their own. Pride of accomplishment can lead to inefficiency, waste and sometimes failure. You may be a fantastic parent, but a poor teacher. You may be a fantastic teacher, but a poor parent. You may know plenty about packaging a product, but nothing about managing a sales force. You may be a great businessperson who knows nothing about a legal issue that faces your business. Conversely, you may be a great lawyer who knows nothing about a business decision. Believing that your skill in one field translates into omniscience is a huge mistake!

Half the battle is over when you admit that someone else might be able to help you. The clue that you need expert advice is the same clue that surfaces when you can't find your driving destination: You have that lost or "out-of-my-league" feeling. The feeling is hard to describe in words, but we all know it. Some would describe it as "confusion," but you can be very lost without being confused. Good indicators that you're lost in a Big Decision are that you don't know what to do, and you don't have a sense of "the rules." Logic gets you nowhere, as is true when you're driving in an unfamiliar neighborhood without a map. While you certainly might find your destination by driving around, if each left turn or right turn is a guess, you'll succeed only by luck.

When you find yourself guessing about the direction your decision should take, and also guessing about your options and the odds of success, you probably need an expert. Some illustrations:

- Your company needs investors. You've never raised money, would not know what to say to investors, don't know what paperwork is required, don't know what investors would look for and don't know where to find them. Find an expert . . . or be eaten alive.
- Your child is depressed and won't talk to you. You know something is wrong, but you can't even have a discussion because your child won't talk.

- Your relationship with your spouse has deteriorated. You don't know whether it can be fixed or how to fix it yourself. You don't know what to do next.
- Something came up at work that is too big to handle (perhaps you've discovered a fraud, a crime or a potentially harmful defect in a product). You don't know what to do, and you are afraid of doing nothing.
- You want to purchase something that you've never purchased before, and you don't know exactly what to look for, how to negotiate or what's a fair price.
- You're applying to an educational institution. You have to complete a lengthy application, including an essay. You have very little idea how the admissions committee will analyze your application. You don't know who's on the committee or what the process is. All you know is that you're applying for one out of a few hundred spots—along with fifteen thousand other applicants.
- You're being harassed. You want the harassment to stop, but you don't know how to do it.

If you feel out of your league in a Big Decision, an expert who has vast experience wants to help you. The expert can tell you what your obligations and choices are and suggest strategies to approach the decision. An expert can tell you how things worked out for 150 other clients who had a similar problem. With the guidance of a good expert, your chances of becoming more lost and wandering into quicksand are greatly reduced. The odds you'll make the right decision and achieve your objectives will rise.

What's the catch? In many cases, expertise costs money, possibly a lot. Appendix A to this book is entitled "A Guide to Finding and Managing Attorneys, Physicians and Other Expert Advisors." Read it if you need to find an expert. For free advice, don't forget the Internet. The Internet is the world's most comprehensive repository of helpful, honest and accurate low-cost expert advice. Unfortunately, the Internet is also the world's largest repository of unhelpful, false, outdated and inaccurate expert advice. If you use the Internet with extreme care and sufficient skill, it's a powerful resource.

Organizational Influences, Organizational Bias and the Advice of Coworkers

Organizations provide much of the information and advice with which we all make Big Decisions:

- Our health-care options (including the standard of care for medical screening, testing and treatment) are heavily influenced by the policy determinations of government bodies and medical-specialist associations.
- Our next job may be determined, in large part, by what our current employer says about us.
- Our children are educated according to curricula and practices that are established by policy-making bodies, boards and other organizations.
- We receive our news through sources that are owned by huge commercial organizations, whose interests go far beyond news reporting.
- The vast bulk of retirement-planning information is provided by organizations that have strong vested interests in the financial markets.

Organizations have interests and biases, just as individuals have interests and biases. Many organizations are skilled at delivering their message in a highly credible package. Billions of dollars are spent on packaging, publicizing and otherwise promoting products, services and concepts. Needless to say, when making a

Big Decision you need to penetrate the gloss, the rhetoric and the highfalutin endorsements to reach the substance. You haven't fully analyzed information unless you have determined the precise connection between the interests of the information provider and the information itself.

The Organization Man (and Woman) in the New Millennium

In his 1956 classic *The Organization Man,* William H. Whyte commented on the tendency of modern man to yield so much individual discretion to "beneficent" organizations (principally large corporations) that provide material wealth and emotional distraction. The remarkable aspect, Whyte observed, is that the end of individualism was not brought about by tyrannical rulers using force; we simply traded it away. Individualism was not stolen from us. We exchanged it for "stuff."

A decade after Whyte's book, of course, the United States went through an extreme period in which old institutions, including government, family and business, were questioned. Nevertheless, nearly fifty years after *The Organization Man,* we find ourselves as organizationally dominated as ever. Virtually every aspect of our lives is intertwined with one or another organization. If individuality was threatened in 1956, it arguably is nearly extinct in the new millennium. *The Organization Man* was republished in 2002. One has to marvel at how relevant *The Organization Man* remains.

Organizational influences surround you and are embedded in your thought processes. Peer pressure is real, and it is magnified when brought to bear by large groups of peers. You must understand how organizational dynamics affect your decisions so you can harness the powerful resources of organizations and resist unhelpful pressures.

The following example illustrates the impact of organizational influence on an individual:

> George knew that StarGazing Corp.[9] was a good company from his first interview. George and the StarGazing recruiter spent as much time talking about George's hobbies as his job qualifications. When George started work, he was astonished by the intense camaraderie at StarGazing, which was not what George expected at such a big company. People in the halls smiled when George passed by. Friendly competition was encouraged in George's department through prize-type incentives, but teamwork was placed above everything else in the corporate culture. When George's daughter was in the hospital, flowers came to the hospital: "Get Well Soon, From All Your Friends at StarGazing." Over time, George became one of StarGazing's biggest boosters. George couldn't imagine leaving StarGazing—definitely not for one of its competitors, which George saw as places that did not take care of their employees. In his mind, George owed it all to StarGazing. George wanted to succeed at StarGazing and be one of the top executives that he admired—the ones whose accomplishments were legends at the company. As George's career progressed, job recruiters began to call, seeking to interest George in positions outside StarGazing. George refused these calls, telling the recruiters that he was "not looking and wouldn't be looking—please don't call me again."

The management of StarGazing Corp. is doing a lot right. George is a very loyal employee who presumably gives his all at work. By fostering a collegial and humane work environment, StarGazing has achieved a level of commitment that mere money can't buy. This loyalty undoubtedly translates into productivity, creativity, a good reputation and other benefits for the company. What about George? George has been extremely well-treated by StarGazing. So long as StarGazing remains the same, George is sitting pretty at his job.

The problem is George's seemingly blind loyalty to StarGazing. George's unwillingness to learn about different job opportunities

---

[9] A fictitious name.

weakens rather than strengthens him. He doesn't know where he stands in the world outside StarGazing. George probably should allow himself the distraction of telephone calls from recruiters (even if George simply uses the calls as a way to elicit information about the job market). Things may change one day. What if a new, less civilized management comes into StarGazing Corp.? What if a superior at StarGazing asks George to do something illegal, unethical or dangerous? George probably will be better off, in the long run, if he quietly maintains a more arm's-length relationship with StarGazing. Like the people who make up an organization, organizations don't last forever. They change, too.

When you make a decision that relates to an organization in your life, be it a workplace or other organization, step back and ask how the organization influences your decision. Would your decision be the same if the organization changed? It *will* change one day. What are the decisions that the organization prefers that you make? How has the organization directed you toward that decision? What do you receive when you make the decision the organization wants you to make? Is it worth what you must give up? Are there risks in going with the flow? Does your risk increase over time as your future becomes more tied to the organization? Is the organization pressuring you to do something that makes you uncomfortable? If so, what's next? If your decision is based on information that the organization supplied, how do the organization's interests affect the information? Is the organization communicating with you or selling you on something? To what extent do you share, or not share, the organization's system of values?

How Much Weight Do You Give Coworkers and Others in Your Organization When You Make a Decision?

When evaluating the views of coworkers, superiors or other members of an organization, always identify and consider your sources' position and biases. The oft-cited axiom of public policy-making behavior is, "Where you stand depends on where you sit." A person's position is an uncanny predictor of opinion. The relationship between someone's personal and organizational interests and advice is not limited to politics. If the boss wants you around, the job offer from another company is "the biggest mistake in the world." If the boss wants to get rid of you, the job offer is "a great opportunity." Likewise, self-interest may taint the advice and opinions of a colleague, even when the advice is from a colleague whom you regard as a friend.

If this discussion seems overly cynical, keep in mind that we're not telling you to ignore what your coworkers have to say. Just be sure to consider where your colleagues "sit." In a Big Decision, you're much more likely to fail because of your naïveté than your cynicism. It's sad, but true.

Organizational Behavior in Smaller Organizations

Organizational behavior is not limited to large organizations. A one-person office is lonely, a two-person office is company, and a three-person office is . . . office politics. In fact, anyone who's had a business partner can tell you that even a two-person office can have plenty of politics. While some small-time office politics may not fall strictly into the category of "organizational behavior," much of it does. The pressures and alliances in a small organization can extend beyond the boundaries of the organization and involve advisors, suppliers, referral sources, customers and even family members.

Consider organizational pressures and biases whenever your decision involves a group, large or small.

We leave Step 4 with the following points to remember about facts, opinions, advisors and organizations:

- The more important your decision is, the more careful you should be to determine the true facts and obtain opinions from well-qualified sources.
- You should examine the credibility and biases of all sources, not just sources that are unknown or hostile. Consider the credibility and biases of parents, friends, teachers, mentors and other well-meaning people.
- Recognize when you need expert advice and take steps to find a competent expert in the field.
- Think about the impact of organizational behavior. Are you making this decision for yourself or because you are tied to an organization that is trying to define your choices?

Living Organ Donation: A Man Listens Only to His Wife, God and His Soul When He Decides to Give a Kidney to His Ailing Brother

Ken Anderson answered the question "Am I my brother's keeper?" by giving his little brother a "small part of me."

Like virtually all human beings, Ken Anderson was born with two kidneys. Kidneys process and eliminate liquid waste from the body. While the kidneys certainly are vital organs, a human can live a completely healthy life with a single kidney. In other words, God gave us a spare. Because kidneys are subject to a variety of diseases, our spare kidney may be a gift of life (as the National Kidney Foundation calls it) for ourselves, if we lose one kidney, or for another person to whom we may donate a kidney during life or after we die. With advances in medical science during the twentieth century, humans can stay alive with no kidneys at all—using an artificial kidney machine that cleanses the blood ("dialysis"), as a kidney would do. Life on dialysis is challenging, though. Dialysis patients are literally tied to the machine three or more times each week for treatments that last for hours. Many resources are available to assist dialysis patients, but the impact on a patient's quality of life is huge. Dialysis is a life-saving procedure that offers both hope and great burdens.

In 1993, Ken Anderson learned that his younger brother Mike had developed end-stage renal disease (ESRD) at the age of thirty-four. ESRD is the end result of progressive, irreversible deterioration of the kidneys. The inevitable consequence of ESRD is the need for dialysis or a kidney transplant. Without treatment, death will occur; it's just a matter of time. In 1993, Ken was a healthy thirty-nine-year-old, married to Lori with five young children. Ken was the oldest in a family of nine children—eight grown brothers and one grown sister. Mike's doctors told Mike that he soon would start lifelong dialysis unless he could obtain a kidney transplant. To obtain a transplant, Mike would have to wait on a very long list for a cadaver kidney (one from a person who donates a kidney after death) or receive a kidney from a living donor. Siblings are genetically the best living donors.

Not every sibling may donate a kidney. The organ has to be an acceptable match so the transplanted kidney is less likely to be rejected by the recipient's body. The matching process starts by ensuring that the blood type of the donor and recipient are suitable, then proceeds to an analysis of various other genetic factors based upon blood tests and tissue matches. Ken and his eight siblings each had eleven tubes of blood drawn for the testing process. At the end of the tests, Ken heard the news: He was a perfect match for Mike. A perfect match makes the chance of an excellent result very likely. The decision was now Ken's:

It's hard to describe how I felt. I felt very good that I might be able to do something meaningful in life, yet I hadn't really discussed the reality of this whole thing with the most important person in my life, my wife of sixteen years. A stay in the hospital was the last thing I wanted to do this summer. When the doctors tell you that you are A-number-one healthy and you must stay in the hospital for up to a week and have your side cut open, it changes your mood a little. I still had many questions. How do my kids feel about this? Also, as the owner of a small business that employs twelve, I must wear many hats. What will I do to replace myself temporarily at the office? Who will cut my lawn? Who will cut and split the firewood? What will the long-term consequences be for my health?[10]

Ken was prepared emotionally to give up his kidney. He recalls, "I saw a person, my brother, slowly deteriorating to an early death—I could help to stop that. My gut feeling was that I had to do it, no matter what it took." Not everyone agreed that Ken should give his ailing brother a kidney. Others expressed a different view of donating a vital organ:

It was both encouraging and sad to experience the reactions of various people when they heard I was donating one of my kidneys

---

[10] The quotes in this piece are taken from interviews and Ken Anderson's account of his transplant in a book entitled *A Small Part of Me* (Boston: The Boston University Office of Publications, 1995, 1999). A copy of the book may be ordered through *home.attbi.com/~kennethanderson.*

to my brother. Most people thought it was a commendable thing to do and offered their complete help and support, while many said they couldn't or wouldn't donate an organ, even for someone very close to them. One neighbor asked my wife at the bus stop one morning if she had any say in my decision and said he thought I was being very uncaring to my immediate family. What if I died during the operation? What kind of life would my wife and kids have without a husband and father? Suppose my remaining kidney were to fail—then what would we go through for the rest of my life? During the seven months of preoperative testing I was on an emotional roller coaster—but I always remained positive, even if deep inside I had some nagging negatives.

In the end, Ken made the decision with his wife, with his own Maker and nobody else. Ken believes that more opinions would only have confused the issue. "My wife told me that it was a wonderful thing to do and that she would support me 100 percent if it was what I really wanted to do. The kids showed some concern but trusted I would make the correct decision." Ken's belief in God also helped him confront his major decision:

I say a few prayers every day, and I know in my past forty-eight years that many have been answered—some in ways that were not what I expected, but with great results. I asked God to take over my mind and let me make the correct decision, because no human wants to subject himself to unnecessary suffering and pain. I look back on it now and all the decisions and procedures seemed to flow nicely and easily.

In August 1993, after extensive preoperative testing and preparation, Ken Anderson and his brother were sedated in side-by-side operating rooms at the Boston University Medical Center. Ken's left kidney was removed, and he was sewn up. During the next hour, Ken's kidney was installed in Mike's body. (Mike still has his old, damaged kidneys as well.) After five days, both Ken and Mike Anderson left the hospital. The postoperative recovery process took many weeks, but soon it was just a memory.

Postscript: In Ken's Own Words

I have no regrets at all about my decision. We knew from the start that the kidney could reject hours, days or months after the transplant, but there was only one way to find out. Nine years now, and it's still going strong for Mike.

I am my own person. When I have my mind set on doing something, nobody can influence me otherwise. If my wife hadn't supported me, I'd have talked about it with her—to try to get her to see it my way. That wasn't going to happen, though. She's not the kind of person who would have been against what I was doing.

The negative people were just crazy, to my mind. They didn't have any influence. If someone thinks that giving a kidney to a person whose kidneys are failing is wrong, he needs a major mind adjustment. He was brought up wrong. I come from a large family. We didn't have many financial resources growing up. My mother was always baking something for a sick person or doing something for a less fortunate person, and my father was always working to support her efforts. That sticks with you.

It was interesting to listen to opinions after I knew I was going to proceed with the donation. None of them, whether positive or negative, changed my mind in the least. The negative comments never depressed me. They made me more determined to proceed.

Postscript: In Lori Anderson's Own Words

When we first found out that Mike would need a kidney and a sibling would be his best donor, I somehow knew it would be

Kenny. Call it "woman's intuition," I guess, but I just had a feeling he would be the one. I think that he did, too.

I remember that we went out to eat with a couple of his brothers and their wives, and they were all talking about how they would react if they found out they would be the one to donate. I was very quiet that night because in my heart I could feel that it would be our ordeal. I also knew I would support any decision Kenny would make about donating his kidney to his brother.

Even though I could feel in my heart that Kenny would be the one to donate, when the call came confirming this news it hit me hard. I knew he would have to make a decision. I was afraid something would happen to him if he went through with it, but I also put myself in Mike's wife's place. If Kenny didn't go through with it, at the least Mike would be on dialysis and have the inconvenience and ill effects from it. At the most, Mike's wife would lose her husband, and their children a father. It would affect our whole family. If Kenny decided to donate, I would support him and try to put my fears aside.

Sometimes people seem to forget what Kenny actually did and what a selfless and awesome thing it was. They often ask about Mike and don't think to ask how Kenny is doing. I thank God each day that he is healthy and was able to do such a wonderful thing for someone else. I know if I were ever called upon to give a kidney to my siblings, I wouldn't hesitate for a moment. I am very proud of Kenny and thankful that he and others like him care enough to do something that many would never think of doing.

AUTHORS' NOTE: In the ten years since Ken Anderson's kidney donation, the process of kidney donation has become a bit easier through the use of minimally invasive surgical techniques.

In 1995, the Boston University Office of Publications first published Ken Anderson's detailed account of his experience as a kidney donor, entitled *A Small Part of Me*.

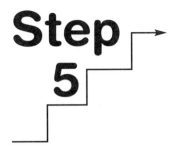

Step 5

Figure Out the Odds, Reduce the Uncertainties and Ditch the Anecdotes

The significant problems we face cannot be solved at the same level of thinking we were at when we created them.

—Albert Einstein

Big Decisions are difficult for two main reasons: (1) They require you to reconcile conflicting values or objectives, and (2) they involve uncertain outcomes. Much of the work you do on values and objectives occurs inside your head, with some advice from friends, family, mentors and sometimes an expert. In contrast, you manage the uncertainties of a Big Decision primarily by obtaining information from outside. Are you convinced that your decision is so unique that nothing out there can help you predict the outcome? If so, you're dead wrong. Don't use a Ouija board when better resources are available. You have to live with the consequences of your Big Decision, so do your homework. You'd be surprised at how much uncertainty you can eliminate with a little investigation.

In investigating your Big Decision, be sure to avoid "anecdote-itis." Anecdote-itis is the common tendency of people to over-generalize from little stories and biographies (anecdotes) about what happened to other people. In many cases, the anecdotes on which we rely are biased, incomplete or just plain false. In Step 5, we explore both the helpful and dangerous uses of anecdotes in making a Big Decision.

When you're done with Step 5, your progress toward the Big Decision will be on solid footing.

Improve the Odds of a Great Decision by Figuring Out the Odds

Here's a familiar situation: A lack of information about how a decision will turn out causes uncertainty. The uncertainty leads you to perceive risk. When you perceive risk, you start to fear negative consequences. To reduce the fear, you take evasive, pro-tective action rather than strong forward steps. If the information you lacked at the outset would have shown, in fact, the presence of little risk, you've basically run away from a third-grader in a ghost costume!

Between the Internet, the library, your friends and mentors who have special knowledge, and occasionally an expert, you can eliminate much of the uncertainty in a Big Decision. The informa-tion you need won't come to you, however. You have to go out and get it.

Here's a simple example using one of the toughest issues of all: whether to do an intervention to stop a friend's (or family mem-ber's) drug, alcohol, gambling or other self-destructive addiction. Let's assume that you feel compelled to do something about the problem because your friend is slowly killing himself. None-theless, you're fearful that an intervention may destroy your friendship or trigger even more self-destructive conduct (such as running away, suicide or violence). You've heard that an intervention may cause your friend or family member to "hit rock bottom." What does that mean? How often do interventions succeed? How can you minimize the chances of a bad outcome? What is the cost? These questions don't represent total unknowns. You just don't have the information yet in your possession.

In two hours, at minimal expense, you can become very knowledgeable about interventions:

- On the Internet, you'll find dozens of Web sites devoted to addiction interventions. Start with the sites that are the most general and sponsored by well-known national organizations, such as the American Council on Alcoholism, Narcotics Anonymous or the National Council on Alcoholism and Drug Dependence. Many reference librarians can help you formulate Internet searches. If neither you nor your library has Web access, a reference librarian can quickly help you find books and other resources.
- Start by learning general information about intervention philosophies and strategies. Don't spend much time on the success stories right now. Look at information from experts who've been involved in hundreds of interventions, as well as surveys by reputable organizations. You'll find very specific information about success rates in interventions. Always be sure to consider the quality and source of any information you find. On an issue such as "What is the success rate of alcoholism interventions?" an important question is how the study defines success. Is it the same as your definition of success?
- Look next at specific information about intervention programs. What resources are there for you? You'll find brochures, "Ask-an-Expert" pages, hotlines, counseling centers, and telephone numbers for residential facilities and every

imaginable resource, many of which provide the information you need at no charge.

- Now take a little time with the success stories and other anecdotes, not to predict how your intervention will unfold, but to explore whether you're ready and to gird yourself for what is to come. You'll learn how nonunique your situation really is. You're not alone.
- If possible, print out pages of the Web sites that contain the information you need for future reference. Web-site content and Web addresses change. You don't know when you'll need to come back to a resource that you found in your initial research. Bookmarking the Web page works only if the Web address doesn't change *and* you control the computer.
- When you've completed your online research, it's time to finish your work offline. Choose a source that appears reliable and available, contact the source and have a conversation with an expert. Voice your fears, concerns and uncertainties. See what you learn. You'll be surprised by how much information you can obtain for free. Many organizations are pleased to speak with you on a confidential basis.
- Find programs in your area so you have a local contact and possibly a place to visit. Many facilities have intervention specialists who offer step-by-step counseling.

Along the way, you'll learn how interventions are orchestrated, how to deal with denials and setbacks, and who can help. If you need motivation as well as information, take time online or in the library stacks to investigate the horrible consequences of addiction. A little research can go a long way toward helping you understand where your decision will lead.

Major business decisions are no different. You want to turn your hunches, concerns and speculation into data, to the extent that the resources of your business permit. You're about to spend forty thousand dollars (or four thousand or forty million dollars) on a promotional campaign. Three different approaches are under consideration. You might want to consider a focus group from your target audience to see which approach works best in the real world. Depending on your budget, the comparatively low cost of doing a focus group may save a lot of money from being spent on a mistake. A focus group involves presenting information to an independent group of people and soliciting their honest comments, often with a professional's assistance. It is a controlled mass "demo" and interview.

If you don't want to use a formal focus group, consider inviting a few friendly customers to lunch, together or separately, to solicit their opinions. Many customers will be flattered (or at least happy to be treated to lunch). If you can't do that, let some outsiders hear your pitch and give feedback. The less they want to butter you up, the better. People you don't know, remote acquaintances and nonemployees often are your best guinea pigs. In large enterprises, market testing is standard. The time you spend on testing, and on small-scale adventures in trial-and-error testing, is almost always worth the cost. A "we-know-best" mentality is dangerous, especially in sales, marketing and other communication functions.

Rarely is there a good reason to guess at something that is knowable, especially if the knowledge is readily available, inexpensive and doesn't cause unreasonable delay. The bottom line: Turn unknowns into known quantities through a thoughtful investigation.

The Power of Anecdotes

We all love anecdotes. Anecdotes are snippet biographies and stories that often are presented to persuade us to feel something, believe something, do (or not do) something, or simply show that a person is good, smart, cool, successful, bad or otherwise attention-worthy and interesting. Anecdotes are powerful and effective communication tools because they reduce abstract concepts to something we all understand: real life. A biographical anecdote seems to prove that something worked or failed outside the laboratory: "If you just do this, look what can *really* happen for you." Testimonial ads and shows, in which real people talk about how well a product or service supposedly worked, sell products. Testimonials therefore are a centerpiece of marketing. The success of many products, including many unapproved health remedies, is based solely on untested, unverified and biased testimonials. The impact of anecdotes is strong even when important decisions are involved. Anecdotes dramatically influence our choices about marriage, health, religion, career, child-raising, education and finances.

Anecdotes are memorable. Rudyard Kipling once observed, "If history were taught in the form of stories, it would never be forgotten." We use a lot of anecdotes in this book. Several of them will stick with you. In contemporary journalism, current events are largely communicated through personal stories. The structure is familiar: An article starts with a description of the macro events (the war, the famine, the coup d'état, the piece of legislation, the leader's speech). Once the generalities are covered, the article's focus turns to the event's impact on some real people. This part of the story brings it home to the reader. The same is true of television: Report the event, then show some comments "from the street." Presidents have joined the party as well. State of the Union speeches and other major policy addresses commonly digress to tell about "Mabel Johnson of Louisville, Kentucky, who supports three children and. . . ." President Ronald Reagan's masterful storytelling won him the nickname "The Great Communicator."

On a personal level, when you make a Big Decision, friends, family and others flood you with anecdotes:

"Look what happened to Sally when she moved in with Gene. . . ."

"I knew someone who had open-heart surgery and. . . ."

"My friend took some of those tablets and never had any pain again. . . ."

"The last time someone made a proposal like that to the marketing department, she was gone in two weeks. . . ."

"Jim got rich when he. . . ."

"Helen lost everything when she. . . ."

"I felt better letting him die with dignity. . . ."

"I felt better doing everything I could to save him. . . ."

"She waited until she was forty and now look. . . ."

And so on!

Anecdotes are powerful communication tools. Nonetheless, if your values or circumstances differ from those of the people in an anecdote, your best decision may be the opposite of what worked in the anecdote. If you have the same values and circumstances, the probable outcome of a course of action still may be different for you. What makes perfect sense for another person may be perfectly senseless for you. The following sections discuss anecdotes and will sensitize you to the limits of anecdotal information in decision-making.

The Problem with Anecdotes

The main problem with using anecdotes to make a Big Decision is that anecdotes can mislead you about the relationship between where the subject of the anecdote began, where she ended and why. Anecdotes about a person who succeeded often seem to affirm all the steps that preceded her success, including steps that did not in any way cause or contribute to it. In the language of logic, this is the fallacy of "affirming the consequent": Let's say we know that if X is true, Y occurs. Can you always say that whenever Y occurs, X is true? No. Here's an example: Assume that "All children like candy." Can you say, "I like candy, therefore I'm a child"? No, because the first fact ("All children like candy") and the second ("I like candy") are not necessarily related. I might be a grown-up who likes candy because it gives me a "sugar rush." (The result would be different if the first statement were "*Only* children like candy.")

Now let's show how to avoid similar false logic in a Big Decision about how to finance a new business, for example: A magazine reports that Jack's business succeeded wildly. The article describes how Jack charged up his personal credit cards to raise start-up money because he had no other resources. Does that mean it was a sound strategy for Jack to raise start-up money by running up his credit cards? Should you do the same thing for your start-up business? No, at least not because of anything in Jack's story. While Jack may not have been able to start his business without credit-card financing, the factors that *caused* Jack's business to succeed likely have nothing to do with the source of his start-up money. The only point "proven" by Jack's story, assuming it's true, is that it's sometimes possible to get a lot of money out of credit-card companies and use the money to take risks. Whether that's a good strategy for you does not depend one bit on Jack's experience. Jack's positive experience with credit-card financing is largely irrelevant to your own financial decision.

In *The Perfect Store: Inside eBay,* author Adam Cohen describes how an eBay public-relations person invented the story that founder Pierre Omidyar created eBay so his fiancée could trade Pez dispensers. According to Cohen, the story was a lie. The management of eBay at the time thought that the truth—a computer programmer desired to create a more efficient marketplace through the Web—was too boring to attract attention from the writers of feature articles. Based on eBay's own public representations, the false story was repeated as true by no less than the *Wall Street Journal, Business Week,* many other newspapers and then–Vice President Al Gore. And eBay got away with it. As a management principle, falsifying facts about your company, whether good for PR or not, is a terrible idea. You can get sued and maybe even land in jail. That eBay got away with it is based on the tenuous, unreliable logic of "all's well that ends well." Does that mean eBay's public-relations strategy should be ignored? No. The reason is that eBay's public-relations scam apparently *did* contribute to eBay's success in building its leading market position. The eBay story therefore does have a valuable lesson: A new company trying to build a position in a market could benefit if it is able to articulate why it is special and interesting (and, in eBay's case, a little fun). It is the responsibility of an ethical management to avoid stepping over the line into dishonesty. The lesson is that when you evaluate anecdotes about other people and businesses, your essential task is to separate facts that *caused* an outcome that is relevant to you from mere *happenstance* that was of no particular consequence to the outcome.

A second problem with anecdotes is that they often are incomplete, biased snippets that create a misleading impression about the facts and circumstances of a decision. You pick up a business magazine at the airport before you catch a flight. You read an article about how Matt and Ann left their steady, high-paying corporate jobs at the peak of their careers, started a new company "on a prayer" and made millions. In the article, Matt and Ann tell you that entrepreneurship is the only way to go, and they swear they'll never go back to a big company again. This piece validates your faith in entrepreneurialism and inspires you. The article is interesting. Is the anecdote useful to you? Perhaps you've been thinking of starting a business. Does Matt and Ann's story mean that you should walk a resignation letter into Mr. Big's office and tell him you're taking the Great Leap?

Most likely, the article tells you little that is relevant to your decision whether to start a business. For starters, the article is about Matt and Ann's business, not the one you have in mind. At least that's obvious. Other facts may not be so obvious. Perhaps Ann had a trust fund or well-to-do parents providing a safety net. Unless Ann mentioned it to the writer, you'll never know that Ann wasn't taking all that much risk. Did Matt and Ann have kids who needed to be put through college in three years, as you might? When Matt left his job, did his manager promise to throw a lot of business his way? Matt might omit that from his press kit! He may want to come across as a cool risk-taker. If the story of Matt and Ann has some relevance, you need to extract it from what is irrelevant. That's virtually impossible, of course, because even if you disregard what's irrelevant in the article, you don't know what never appeared in the article in the first place. The writer might not even know.

Quite often, and for totally legitimate reasons, writers write about the most interesting aspects of a start-up adventure—perhaps "The Dream" the founders pursued. Don't confuse the inspiring parts of someone else's story with what is most important to your Big Decision. Entrepreneurs talk most about "The Dream" at two points: before they've done anything and after they've succeeded. In between, it's primarily sweat, risk, aggravation, frustration and fear. Starting your own business may be a great idea, but not because of Matt and Ann. While Matt and Ann provide good inspiration, their story adds little more to your Big Decision process.

Success stories about businesspeople and celebrities typically combine the subject's carefully managed profile, the spin of skillful public-relations people, and the impressions of a reporter who may lack the time and budget to test the claims and whose main information source is the subject. From 1998 to 2000, thousands of stories appeared about supposedly "hot" companies and executives who ended up bankrupt and discredited within months. Many of the stories were absurdly sympathetic to the subjects, whose businesses often were heavy advertisers in the publications. This period marked a recent low in journalistic integrity and, unfortunately, contributed to the decisions of millions of people to jump into the fool's gold rush now known as the "dot-com bubble." This genre of journalism has been called "business porn." Many of the periodicals that featured this sort of reporting are out of business, just like the companies that served as their subjects.

Be careful not to use anecdotes to figure out the odds. An anecdote is a story about how one situation turned out, usually told after the fact and without the whole picture. Although history can teach a great deal about both good decisions and mistakes, you can't learn from history until you have an accurate picture of what actually happened.

The Bright Side: Anecdotes Can Shape Your Values and Educate You About Your Choices and Strategies

Anecdotes can still be useful tools to help you discover, explore and test your values. This use of anecdotes is well-known to people who teach values, and it is deeply ingrained in religious communication. Parables and fables are common anecdotal and metaphorical teaching tools. A story about a heroic person in *People* magazine may help a reader explore his values, although the story is an anecdote. By pondering questions such as "Would I do that in the same situation?" or "How do I feel about the events in this story?" the reader defines and refines his own values. Even a wholly fictional story may influence a reader's values. An animated fantasy movie or Saturday morning cartoon may influence a viewer's values, as may music lyrics. The song "Family Portrait" by the artist Pink powerfully implores parents to fix marital problems before their children are injured in the crossfire. You know the values in a story are opinion, not facts.

Anecdotes are helpful in another respect. They may expose you to new choices, resources, strategies, and sources of risks and benefits. Another person's decision may have had consequences you hadn't thought about, but should. An anecdote might mention a resource that you didn't know existed, or a new approach or strategy to solve a tough problem. Reputable business magazines are filled with stories that provide useful, current information about trends, innovations and approaches. An anecdote may provide important moral support by combating the feeling that you're alone and going through a unique and isolated experience. Finding online bulletin boards, support groups, magazines, kindred spirits and people in a similar situation, or worse, can be comforting. Who among us hasn't read a posting on an online bulletin board and thought, *Thank goodness I'm not him!* Other people's experiences may help define your decision, and provide courage, ideas and resources as you work through a decision.

Compare and Contrast Success Stories and Other Anecdotes with Your Own Situation

Experienced decision-makers regard success stories with extreme skepticism. Instead of asking, "How am I just like the person in that story?" the experienced decision-maker asks, "How am I different?" and "How is the situation I face different?" The person who put the anecdote together (whether it was the subject, a writer or a filmmaker) often is trying hard to create a positive connection between the subject and the audience. A savvy decision-maker seeks to neutralize such audience-interest bias by seeking out the differences. Does this mean that a story about someone's failure should receive more consideration than a story about a great success? Absolutely. You usually won't make the mistake of assuming that a person who failed did everything wrong. Stories about failure tend to focus on particular mistakes that caused the failure. You rarely read stories that build a case for why John Smith is, and always was destined to be, a failure. Nobody wants to read that. In contrast, so many success stories are unrestrained victory dances, designed to show that the star of the show—the Successful Person—is a Golden Boy or Girl, or a Child of Destiny.

Whether it's a success or failure story, you must compare and contrast anecdotes with your circumstances. Ask whether the people in an anecdote have the same values as you and whether your situation presents the same risks and benefits. Remember that people and companies who profit from a product, or profit by encouraging certain conduct, have a vested interest in telling a story that *fully* supports their pitch. Many publications vastly prefer success stories. Even stories about tragedy tend to show triumph over adversity. Hollywood likes movies with happy endings. Success stories and happy endings are not hard statistics and verifiable data. When you make a Big Decision, anecdotes are suspect. Better data need to win out.

Rumors, Whispers and Rare Events

What about rumors, whispers, on-the-ground intelligence and other information that's not hard data by any stretch, but which might be both correct and timely? Listen to it! Think about it and pursue it. Because this information is anecdotal, it may be unreliable, misleading and incorrect. It also may be the best infor-mation available and an early warning of hard data to follow. Like the villager who lives next to a volcano, disregard rumblings only at your peril.

Consider the source of soft information very carefully. Look for confirmation from a reliable source before you make a Big Decision based on soft, anecdotal information. The disadvantage of rumors and other soft information is that the ultimate source may be impossible to determine, so assessing the source's credi-bility and bias is impossible. The advantage of soft information is that it may not contain the bias and spin that infect "official information."

Anecdotes also serve an important function when you must analyze a unique or rare event. If an event occurs frequently, you need not base your decision on one or two isolated cases; a larger number of cases provides more reliable information. When a unique or rare event occurs, however, the only available informa-tion may be anecdotal, which is one reason that preserving and studying history is critically important, even though history often seems like a compilation of anecdotes. When we face a unique or rare event, historical precedents supply the reference points we use to address it. When Americans needed to put September 11 into perspective, commentators went straight to comparisons and contrasts with Pearl Harbor and the Oklahoma City bombing—two isolated, quite dissimilar events that occurred more than fifty years apart.

Soft anecdotal information must be considered in its entire con-text. Businessman Gouri Shankar describes an experience in which a piece of anecdotal information was what he needed to feel comfortable going forward with a family member's dangerous surgery:

> A close relative of mine was suddenly taken ill with an extremely

serious heart condition. A part of his aorta had ruptured in a very unusual way. We met with the heart surgeon, who was well-known but already had done several surgeries that day. Although the surgeon was willing to do this surgery, too, he was quite concerned about the outcome. He was honest with us. He said, "The surgery will take seven to eight hours. There's a significant chance your [family member] won't survive the operation. I've done around ten thousand surgeries, but I probably operated on only two patients who presented a problem of this specific type." I looked at the surgeon and said, "I am so glad to hear that you've operated on two similar patients. It's far better to have you do this operation than a surgeon who's had none." I grabbed the surgeon's hand and assured him that I had complete confidence.

Perhaps Gouri Shankar should be faulted for placing excessive weight on the surgeon's minimal experience with heart problems of the *particular* type that his family member faced. The complete picture, however, includes the surgeon's other 9,998 or so heart surgeries. The other surgeries may not have been quite as complex or dangerous, but Gouri Shankar's family member certainly was in the hands of a very experienced heart surgeon.

Acceptable Levels of Risk

If you could be certain how your decisions would turn out in all respects, you wouldn't have a Big Decision. You'd simply go down the path that offers the greatest benefit for the cost (financial, spiritual, emotional and otherwise). Many critical decisions, however, require you to place a bet of sorts, to decide even though you aren't sure of the outcome. To make things harder, a decision to pursue one goal (or set of goals) may require you to forego others. The benefits of the path you don't want to take may be more certain than the benefits of the path you prefer. Few people would always be satisfied with the limited rewards offered by the path of greatest certainty. In most cases, the decision to improve your condition requires you to risk some of the benefits you already have or could attain without much risk.

The amount of risk that is acceptable to each person relates back to that person's values, personality, past experience and probably genetics. Risk tolerance has physical, intellectual and emotional elements. Some people are comfortable taking certain kinds of risks, but not other risks—for example, a large financial risk, but only the smallest physical risk. Other people are cautious in just about everything. Others seem to thrive on every kind of risk. No matter what your risk profile, you'll make poor decisions if you fail to investigate the actual risks in a Big Decision. If you're cautious, you won't optimize your decisions if there's too much uncertainty about the risk because your desire to avoid risk may cause you to assume the worst. Likewise, if you can accept high levels of risk, you may minimize unknown risks—which may lead you to take risks beyond what a knowledgeable risk-taker would accept.[11]

The object of Step 5 is to separate which outcomes of each possible choice are certain from which are uncertain and, among the uncertainities, which are probable from which are improbable. With a little investigation, you can know much of what appears to be uncertain at the start. Even if you can't predict the exact outcome, you may be able to predict a range of outcomes and the effect of different outcomes. As your knowledge of the uncertain elements grows, you reduce the actual risk (and also the emotional stress) of your Big Decision. This brings you closer to the decision that is right for you.

---

[11] Steps 9 and 10 address two related points. Step 9 tells you to "Keep the Risks of Failure (and Benefits of Success) in Perspective." In other words, don't exaggerate the risk of failure or benefits of success. Figure out what the real risk is and act on it. If you're cautious, be safe but not paralyzed. If you have a high risk tolerance, take a reasonable chance after you understand the real odds. Step 10 encourages you to actively manage the risks of your decisions, so you can go for the upside. In other words, explore what you can do to move the probability of success in your favor or to reduce the consequences of failure.

We leave Step 5 with the following points to remember about probabilities, risk and anecdotes:

- Determine whether your decision or parts of it are sufficiently commonplace that research will yield important information about the likely outcome. While some features of your decision are undoubtedly unique, many parts are not. Be open-minded about the facts you find. If a fact doesn't support where you want to go with the decision, admit that the fact is against you.
- Do your research. The Information Revolution is tremendously empowering, but it only offers you tools. You must take time to use the tools to make your decision. Research is not as hard as it used to be. Much research can be done in a short time at a low cost.
- Reduce the uncertainties in a decision to avoid overcompensating because of your personal risk profile.
- Anecdotes about what happened to another person are among the poorest form of decision information. They are often incomplete, intentionally misrepresented and biased. Use anecdotes cautiously.

Travel: A Consultant's Advisory Trip to Nigeria Becomes a Lesson in Choosing Destinations and Coping with Peril

David Fishman received an education in respecting credible warnings when he took an assignment in Lagos two weeks before a military coup.

In the fall of 1993, David Fishman was a young professional, twenty-seven years old, at his first job out of Harvard Business School. He was about to ask his girlfriend Julie to marry him. His employer then and now, Strategic Decisions Group (SDG), advises businesses on how to create value through better decision-making and implementation. With a Harvard M.B.A., an economics B.A., a master's in engineering/economic systems from Stanford, and prior investment banking and consulting experience, David was where he wanted to be.

One benefit of being a business consultant, for professionals who like to travel, is that consulting work is often done on-site at a client's offices. Consultants have the opportunity to see the world on business. David already had spent time in several countries. When an oil and gas industry client asked SDG to advise a management group in Lagos, Nigeria, for a few weeks in 1993, David wanted to be on the project. David recalls, "I wanted to go because I'd never been to Africa. It would be a great opportunity to combine business and pleasure. We were going to help the client's Nigerian team improve the quality of a few major decisions, including decisions about several major financial investments."

David mentioned the opportunity to work on an assignment in Nigeria to a senior SDG director:

He told me not to go. I asked, "Why?" The director replied, "Haven't you seen the State Department reports? It's not a particularly safe area. If it were me, I wouldn't go." SDG won't force a consultant to travel to a place the consultant doesn't want to go. I clearly had a choice. But our client was a multinational, had its own compound and had a security detail. Other Westerners were in the country. I discounted information about the danger and rationalized my desire to go. There's always unrest in Nigeria, I thought. You can get mugged in New York City.

Six weeks later, David was in a car threading its way from the Lagos airport through the crowded streets of Nigeria's capital city. The car reached the client's compound, which was a guarded village behind fifteen-foot cinderblock walls. The walls were topped with barbed wire and guarded by armed men. Inside the walls were residential units, office buildings, volleyball courts and everything else the residents needed to live and work. David and his colleagues were taken to a guesthouse in the compound. Everyone was conscious of unrest in the country, but it supposedly was outside the walls. The SDG team started its job of advising and teaching decision skills to the client's Lagos managers.

On November 17, 1993, about halfway through David's assignment, General Sani Abachi seized control of Nigeria after the ruling military leader (General Babangida) annulled a June election. These events soon affected life in the Lagos compound where David and his colleagues lived:

We woke up and noticed that none of the "Westerners" who lived in the compound were wearing ties. It was a business day, and ties were customary among Western businesspeople who lived in Nigeria. I asked someone why nobody was wearing a tie. It was unusual. We were told that the coup could lead to attacks. I was told that if the compound were invaded, the rioters would go after the Westerners. They would identify the Westerners by their ties. I skipped the tie that day.

The crisis worsened as the day developed. Participants in the coup disrupted communications and transportation. There was rioting in the streets. David learned that he and his colleagues would not be able to leave the country. It wasn't clear when they would be able to get out or whether the compound would be attacked. "You couldn't do anything. It was too dangerous to leave the compound." The compound had a satellite phone, so David called his parents and Julie. David made his family and future fiancée nervous, and they made David more nervous in turn. David had no information about what was going on outside the compound, so he couldn't reassure his family. David's parents and Julie only knew what the news reported. The news played up the situation's drama and violence. Nobody connected with David was looking for drama, but David's father did start talking about renting a private plane for a rescue.

David hung up the phone. Now he was panicked. He'd come to Lagos to give advice on decisions. Now his life was on the line. Would he get home? The island of the compound that was supposed to protect the residents and visitors was now floating in a hostile sea. The fact that David had volunteered to come to Lagos didn't make things easier. Totally agitated, David implored of a colleague, "What are we going to do? What can we do? We've got to get out of this place! This is going downhill fast. What's going to happen?"

"We need to stay calm!" David's colleague said. He was twenty years or so older than David and taught decision science at Stanford University. "What?" David snapped back. "Calm down? How can we calm down? We're in the middle of a military coup! We can't get out of here! Our lives are at risk. We can't even wear ties without putting ourselves in danger. We've got to do *something!*"

The colleague remained calm and delivered a piece of advice that David calls "a watershed":

David, the reality is that there are no decisions to make. There's nothing you can do. You're learning the difference between a decision and an uncertainty. You don't have a decision to make right now. You just have a lot of uncertainty to live through. Right now you have to learn to deal with the situation.

David did calm down. He recalls:

I was still very anxious, but what my colleague said made me realize that I didn't have any control over the situation. It was a relief in some respects. I didn't have to figure out what to do. I still had the anxiety of waiting for something to happen to me, but I realized I had to deal with the uncertainties and not try to make choices I didn't have.

Fortunately, the compound wasn't invaded. After a few days, General Abachi opened the Lagos airport to commercial air traffic. A convoy took many of the Western expatriate workers to the airport, where they were put on the first planes to leave. David's meticulously trained mind didn't save him in Lagos. David was just darn lucky.

Postscript: In David's Own Words

I remember that last trip to the airport. There was still unrest in the streets. We were put in an armed jeep. The guard in the front seat had a machine gun, and he kept his finger on the trigger and his elbow on his knee. The roads weren't very good, which made the jeep bounce around a lot. All we could think about was what would happen to the guard's finger if we hit a big bump.

My colleague was right. I had no choice in the compound. No viable choice. I could have gone through the gates on my own, but that would have been insane. I have an action orientation. I went to Nigeria to teach decision skills. I ended up with no choice, in a crisis situation that I had never experienced before in my life.

There are two main lessons I learned from the experience in Nigeria. When coping with a crisis, don't use information to feed your worries. Worrying doesn't help much. Instead, use information to plan what you'll do if and when choice returns. The other lesson is about the word "maturity." Basically, a mature individual can be defined as someone who's comfortable in different situations. During the coup, what it meant to me was that I had to get comfortable with a situation in which I wasn't able to control the outcome.

In our professional practice, we distinguish between good decisions and bad outcomes. A good decision may lead to a bad outcome, and a bad decision may lead to a good outcome. My decision to disregard the State Department warning was a bad choice. Now I check what's coming out of the State Department and The Economist. *These sources have reliable information about what's going on in other countries. I don't dismiss it or rationalize it away as I did before I went to Lagos. I follow official travel warnings now. The government has information that isn't available to the public. It makes warnings for a reason. I'm often invited to go places where there's a warning in effect. If there's a warning, I just won't go.*

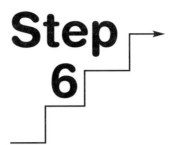

Step 6

Take Your Emotions Along for the Ride

We should take care not to make the intellect our god; it has, of course, powerful muscles, but no personality.

—Albert Einstein

At the constitutional level where we work, 90 percent of any decision is emotional. The rational part of us supplies the reasons for supporting our predilections.

—William O. Douglas

A commonly held belief is that the best decisions are made without emotion, with the cloud of personal feelings cast aside and based only upon the so-called objective facts. Many people accept, as Oscar Wilde facetiously wrote, that "the advantage of the emotions is that they lead us astray." In Step 6, you learn that to ignore or devalue your emotions when making a Big Decision is a huge mistake. In most cases, your emotions are an important positive force in your Big Decision. In the few situations where emotion may be truly detrimental, such as in valuing property, you still should consider your emotions because they *are* a factor.

Human beings are highly emotional animals. Our society would quarantine (or put to death) a dog that got as angry twice a year as some humans in responsible positions become every day.[12] Emotions are all around us, inside of us and inside everyone with whom we deal. "Life does not consist mainly, or even largely, of facts and happenings," Mark Twain observed. "It consists mainly of the storm of thoughts that is forever blowing through one's mind." The thoughts blowing through our minds are driven by our feelings. Considering our feelings when we make a Big Decision is not only rational, but it would be irrational to deny forces that inevitably influence what we choose and determine how comfortably we live with our choices down the line.

Even extremely strong emotions may play an important role in sound decision-making. Love, inspiration, anger, frustration, embarrassment, disillusionment, disgust, rage and fear may propel us to make a decision we've avoided. Sometimes strong emotions bring us to a higher level of objectivity and rationality. Strong feelings may carry a new, clearer picture of a situation and a commitment to make a change. The metaphorical last straw forces us to overcome the inertia of life and deal with something we should have addressed long ago. We've all given the benefit of the doubt to another person for too long, until an incident pushed us to a new assessment, then action. Many Big Decisions start with an emotional bang. Samantha Littlejohn, whose true story is told at the end of Step 10, recalled the extremely strong emotions she felt when she decided to orchestrate a series of addiction interventions:

> I feared that I was losing my mother, and that I was going to lose her for sure if she kept drinking the way she had been. I was

---

[12] We'd judge the dog too dangerous to live among people!

desperate. I thought she was going to die, be killed or kill someone.
. . . I hated her behavior, but I loved her.

At the end of Step 1, we told the story of Katherine Conley's
end-of-life decisions for her father. She reflected on the impact of
emotion on her Big Decisions:

> Rationality and emotion are completely intertwined in this kind
> of decision. It's ridiculous to think you're going to sift through the
> emotion and make an emotionless choice. My decisions weren't
> irrational, but they were totally emotional.

Emotion is vitally important when your Big Decision requires
personal execution. A decision requires personal execution when
you not only must make a choice, but also must carry out that
choice. Most long-term decisions, such as the decision to marry,
go to school, have a child or start a business, are decisions that
require personal execution. What seems sensible on paper when
you make a decision may look very nonsensical after a few
months if you lack the commitment and other emotional qualities
that are required to carry it out. Time and again people set themselves up for failure by arriving at what they think (or are told) is
the "rational" decision, only to fall short in commitment, which is
basically emotional staying power. This result frequently occurs in
career and education decisions. If your decision requires personal
execution, it isn't enough that the decision is what other people
tell you makes sense. There's nothing wrong with doing what
makes sense, but the decision has to make sense *to you,* and you
must be emotionally committed if commitment is required to
succeed.

Business decision-making expert David Fishman, managing
director of Strategic Decisions Group (whose early career travel
story was featured at the end of Step 5), observes:

> Emotion is a two-edged sword. It's wonderful, and it's also dis-
> astrous. When used correctly, emotion is an important part of

decision-making. Emotion is necessary in many cases to drive passion. Passion drives creativity. Passion can also drive a commitment to act. Without action, you end up with decisions that don't go anywhere. We want emotion, but we want to harness it. We don't want emotion to drive destructive coping behaviors or to paralyze people. Emotion should be harnessed to productive decision-making uses.

Putting aside whether major decisions *should be* made with emotion, you won't be given the choice. Big Decisions carry strong emotions with them, whether you like that or not. Indeed, some decisions evoke instinctual forces that are more powerful than mere emotions. Self-preservation is an instinct. If you make a decision that you believe is truly life-or-death, you may have instinctual reactions that you can't completely manage with reason. You can try to fight your self-preservation responses, and you may lose that fight. The same is true of decisions that concern your children. You have parenting practices, viewpoints, opinions and strategies. You also have parenting instincts. Differentiating the strategic parent from the instinctual parent is not always easy. Likewise, you have mating instincts, nesting instincts, grouping instincts and a variety of other natural instincts. Sometimes you should struggle to prevail over these natural forces; never deny they exist.

Step 6 shows that you can make a Big Decision that is both rational and emotional. Remember that the opposite of rational is irrational—not emotional. Don't deny how you feel when you make a Big Decision. Don't deny the emotional nature of others. People are rational, social, instinctual and emotional animals. If you try to base your decision solely on the rational and social elements, you may see your best strategies sink into a quagmire of tears and fears.

The Emotions That Affect Your Big Decisions

We'll start by defining some terms. "Emotion" is not the same as "intuition." In the final chapter, we discuss how to handle the more amorphous influences on your decision. These include intuition, "gut instincts," what your "heart" tells you to do and your doubts—all of which sometimes seem to have a metaphysical impact on a Big Decision. Emotions are the more tangible feelings we all experience, some of which (for example, anxiety, anger, depression, happiness) also may have strong physical manifestations. Emotion is how we feel as we experience the world and events in our lives.

Emotions may affect your decisions even if you don't acknowledge that you feel them. Many people have a hard time acknowledging their emotions, and certain emotions are stigmatized—take fear, as in "Of course I'm not chicken!" Likewise, even when you know you're feeling emotions, it may be difficult to identify how (and how much) an emotion influences a decision. A depressed person may underestimate the likelihood of a good outcome because he thinks, "Nothing ever works out for me." Similarly, a person who's riding an emotional high may see the world through rose-colored glasses and be less cautious. While *public* displays of emotion in business are largely limited to competitive emotions (chest-pounding when a key sale is made, "whipping the competition"), businesspeople are as emotional inside as anyone else, even at work. We use emotion to include a decision-maker's feelings, even if the feelings are internal, unrecognized, denied or misrepresented. If you consider only emotions that are visibly expressed, you'll mislead yourself by ignoring vast internal emotions.

Decision advisor David Fishman observes that many businesspeople avoid the term "emotional":

> "Emotional" is a word that has developed unfortunate connotations. Yet we all have emotions. It's who we are. We are not machines. People need to say to themselves (and others need to

know) that we're personally concerned about the implications of a decision and its possible outcomes. We should celebrate this concern. We're emotional because we care. It's important to care. If we didn't care, we'd be indifferent to the outcome of a decision. Then what would be the point?

There are many different human emotions, which people experience in limitless combinations. We all respond to situations with somewhat different sets of feelings. Nonetheless, some life situations are commonly associated with certain emotional responses:[13]

- Abortion—embarrassment, anger, guilt, disappointment, regret, shame, relief
- Addiction intervention—worry, fear, desperation, frustration, anger, compassion, determination, love
- Coming out as gay—fear, guilt, sense of freedom, relief
- Death of a loved one—shock, anger, sadness, depression, loneliness, isolation
- Desired childbirth/adoption—joy, love, pride, frustration, worry, exhilaration
- Divorce—anger, rage, sadness, feelings of betrayal, relief, guilt, disappointment, pessimism, disillusionment, depression, regret, anxiety, insecurity, confusion, jealousy, fear, sense of futility, shame
- Job loss—fear, betrayal, insecurity, shame, worry, anger, depression, anxiety
- Job promotion—pride, self-confidence, security, anxiety
- Long-distance move—anxiety, sadness, depression, hope, excitement
- Marriage—love, joy, anxiety, infatuation, pride, security, happiness, optimism, fear

---

[13] Not everyone will experience all of these particular emotions. The extent to which an individual experiences embarrassment, anger, guilt disappointment, regret, shame or relief in abortion, for example, depends upon a multitude of social, psychological, spiritual and other forces.

- Serious illness—worry, anxiety, depression, discouragement, frustration, fear
- Starting a business—exhilaration, pride, worry, fear, anxiety
- Undesired childbirth—sadness, regret, confusion, shame, joy, embarrassment

Day-to-day, we bounce around among our emotions when we have time. If you don't recognize the following example, take a few minutes to observe your feelings next time you take a drive:

You get in the car to drive somewhere. Your mind starts to think about someone at work—perhaps someone who is incompetent, upon whom you depend. Your *frustration* level starts to rise as you wonder how much damage the person will do before he's fired. That leads you to think about your own career. You become genuinely *happy* for a few seconds as you recall a job accomplishment a couple of months ago. In your thoughts, you reexperience some of the *exhilaration, confidence* and *security* you felt when your accomplishment was recognized. Then the economy pops to mind. What would be the impact of an industrywide slowdown? Sales were off a little last month. You're *secure,* but *how* secure? Then you start to feel a little *insecure.* You remember what it felt like last time you were laid off or what happened to a friend who was laid off. You decide to switch on the music. Great song. A few minutes of *distraction* hit as the lyrics pop back from long-term memory. The song reminds you of something that was *enjoyable* in high school or college. Ahhh, those were the days. That goal you made, or award in class or social accomplishment. Some of the *exhilaration* comes back for a moment. A little *pride* and *joy* . . . until the song ends. The next song is *annoying.* You turn down the radio. Then you *worry* about whether you paid a certain bill. Not another late fee . . .

Such strings of thoughts and emotions can be experienced in a few minutes or less. The nature and intensity of your emotions may be influenced by caffeine or medication you are taking. The emotions may be weak or strong. How many times a day do you make the kind of rapid emotional transitions that are illustrated by the above example? Are you aware of it? The following section discusses why it is critical when you make a Big Decision to know what you're feeling and how you want to feel in the future when today's decision will have an impact.

How Emotions Affect Big Decisions, Sometimes Behind the Scenes

You're not just a cost-benefit analysis machine (even if you like to think you are!). You not only want to do what's best on paper, but you want to wake up in the morning and feel happy, motivated, optimistic and complete. The drive to find emotional comfort and satisfaction strongly influences the decisions you make, especially Big Decisions. Here's a simple illustration of how a business executive's emotions may influence a business decision at the office:

> Martin is the vice president of operations at a fairly small product manufacturer with $6.5 million in annual sales in the United States. A woman who is a friend of Martin's best friend approaches Martin to propose that she open and run a Latin American sales office for Martin's employer. Martin brings the proposal to the CEO, who flips it back to Martin and says, "I'll go with what you recommend." The strategy requires the company to risk three hundred thousand dollars over the next eighteen months (not chump change for this company!) and would mark an unplanned departure from the company's traditional markets. The proposed Latin American manager says she is confident she can generate sales of $1.5 million during the first year and grow quickly from there. That's certainly a respectable amount of business growth. She has an impressive track record with another company's Latin American sales operation in a related field. The CEO comments, "It looks a bit risky, Martin . . . but I don't want to miss an opportunity."

Traditional business analysis would launch into the size and growth characteristics of the Latin American market, demand for the product, competition, logistical issues, how long and costly the ramp-up would be, a financial analysis of the expected return on investment, a thorough review of the experience and qualifications of the manager, the company's other possible uses and costs of capital, and so on. All of this would become spreadsheets and memos attempting, as best as possible, to quantify the probable risks and returns of a Latin American expansion. That is all good, important work. At the end of all the analysis, though, one thing will be certain: Nothing is certain. A decision still must be made about taking the risk. The same numbers on the spreadsheet will look different to each manager. One manager will see great revenue potential and acceptable risk; another will see a decent idea that's not worth the risk; another will see only three hundred thousand dollars flying down the tubes. Depending on the company's culture, a contingent of backstabbers and vice-president wannabes might even refer to the initiative as "Martin's Folly."

Martin is responsible for making a major recommendation, which the CEO has told Martin probably will become the CEO's final decision. Who is Martin? Martin the Risk-Taker? Martin the Extreme Risk-Taker? Martin the Conservative, Stick-with-What-Is-Working Guy? Martin the One Who Always Comes Through for His Best Friend?

That's when emotion kicks in. Maybe Martin's oldest daughter is about to begin college, and fearful thoughts start running through Martin's head: *Heck, I don't want to lose this job over some folly.* Maybe Martin's investment portfolio is up and self-assurance kicks in, fed by boredom at this job: *Worst-case scenario is I get canned and start my own company. Boy, I'd love the personal freedom that would go with my own business. This Latin American project will be a training ground for me, if nothing else.*

Perhaps Martin is feeling unmotivated and doesn't want to do the work required to generate an analysis. Martin knows pride would prevent him from turning in an inadequate analysis, so he comes up with an excuse for the CEO and his friend's friend and lets the idea drop. Nobody will miss it, right? What Martin feels affects how he perceives his task and the consequences of being right or wrong. Although Martin is staring at a spreadsheet, his thoughts, conclusions and ultimately his recommendations are not all numbers.

Considering this scenario, your first reaction might be that it's irresponsible for Martin to allow his personal feelings to intrude so heavily on an important business decision (even if you do it all the time). From the company's perspective, an emotion-based approach is irresponsible—and wrong and lousy. It decreases the likelihood that Martin will make the optimal decision for the business. Some "Martins" will take less business risk than is warranted by the facts; others will take too much. Lousy or not, the impact of individual circumstances (including all the emotions wrapped around them) on business decisions is a fact of life. The company's best solution is not to hope that Martin and other decision-makers will ignore their personal emotions and career circumstances. That solution would be impossible, and an instruction to ignore emotions and self-interest would only lead to denial, concealment and misrepresented motives. The company's solution is to make sure major decisions are based on input that reflects a variety of emotional profiles, experiences, strengths, career goals, incentives and personal values—in other words, input diversification for the decision-maker.

If the decision is truly important, the CEO should regard Martin's initial recommendation merely as a way to work up an analysis, rather than a final decision. The CEO has ultimate responsibility for what happens at the company. In discharging that responsibility, the CEO must consider the impact of self-interest and personal influences on Martin and other players, then take steps to ensure that personal influences don't undermine the company. If this scenario had occurred at a different level in the business, the CEO might not have been involved. In that case, the responsible manager should have made sure that Martin's personal considerations didn't take over and dominate the decision process.

Investment banker Andy Hirschberg learned a valuable lesson about weighing individual propensities and self-interest from his father, who began as an accountant, then developed a niche transaction advisory practice that he passed to his son. Hirschberg keeps this lesson in mind when he deals with people in the business context:

> The best advice I ever got from my dad was, "When you start working with a person, you've got to find his or her 'morality line.' Once you know that, you'll know how to deal with them." What does this person's handshake mean? Do I have a sense of whether and when this person is likely to take advantage or become corrupt? If I know that, I can protect my clients and myself. It's important to determine the morality line of people on the other side of my deals as well. My clients need to think about how much they can trust the other side.

Whether you're making a decision for yourself or your business, you'll have to determine the sources from which to seek input and weigh the input from all of the sources. The credibility of your sources always is a question: How much can you trust the source? If the person who is providing you information or advice has a conflict of interest, where is that person's "morality line"? What standard of conduct makes *that person* feel good? In this process, you must go beyond merely understanding the biases of each source as you did in Step 4. In Step 6 you also need to consider the impact of people's emotions, personalities and morals on the information you receive from them. What are they saying and doing—and how do they *feel* about it?

What remains after you, the decision-maker, have considered the biases, emotions and other circumstances of third parties are your *own* emotions. The next two sections discuss when and how to bring your own emotions into a Big Decision and how to harness them.

When to Bring Your Own Emotions into a Big Decision

You may not have much choice about when to bring your emotions into a Big Decision. Emotions have a way of showing up on their own timetable. In Step 1, we asked you to think about your emotions early on to determine whether emotional barriers were causing you to focus on a decoy rather than the "real decision." Now at Step 6, you have identified the real decision, broken it down into manageable pieces, isolated the target questions, chosen your advisors, liberated yourself from misleading anecdotes and assessed the odds of success as well as possible. You've finished the set-up for your Big Decision and are about to enter the processing phase. If you haven't done it already, *now* is the time to confront how you feel about the issues. Your emotions not only will affect the decision-making process, but also will influence timing, your perception of risks and benefits, and what "success" and "failure" mean.

Bring your emotions into the Big Decision *now.*

How to Bring Your Own Emotions into a Big Decision

For some people, bringing emotional considerations into a Big Decision is second nature. These people are comfortable saying, "I'm too distracted today. Let's make this decision tomorrow," and "I like the opportunity, but I don't have the mind-set right now to see it to the end," or "I'm leaning toward this choice, because if I go the other way I won't be able to sleep at night. Too much risk for me." A business decision-maker in this category is comfortable saying, "Let's not get greedy. We'll take the good offer on the table and lock down the deal. Why worry about losing it over a few bucks?" or "I messed up once before on a similar deal. I'm a little gun-shy this time around." These people are adept at integrating their feelings into a decision. Even if the emotions expressed in these examples ultimately should be overcome, to permit different considerations to guide the decision, the decision-maker's ability to bring his own emotions to light is a valuable skill. It helps the decision-maker understand how and why he's making the decision.

If you're not accustomed to doing a personal emotion-check when you make major decisions, start now. You'll need to make a conscious effort until it becomes a habit. The following approach will help you bring your emotions into a Big Decision:

Move Past Denial. It's a Big Decision. You have a lot of feelings about it. Admit it. Is your first thought on reading this, *No, I don't have any feelings about this decision,* or *I have feelings, but they simply aren't playing any part in making this decision*? Be very careful if these thoughts sound like yours. Even indifference may be an important emotion. It is a child of frustration and apathy, as in, "I simply don't care about the entire issue anymore. I give up." Genuine indifference about a Big Decision is rare. It's far more likely that you're simply denying your feelings.

Explore Your Emotions and Their Source. Is pride driving you? Anxiety? Fear? Love? Anger? Frustration? Greed? Perhaps you're being stubborn because you don't want to let someone else "win." Maybe your choices look worse, riskier or less likely to work out because you're depressed or feeling pessimistic. On the other hand, maybe you're on a high, and the "sure shot" isn't so sure. Are you doing something just because you're concerned what other people will think if you don't do it? Are you motivated by a desire for revenge or because your feelings are hurt? Look beneath the surface. Answer basic emotional questions, even if they seem silly. *Am I happy? Am I mad? Am I afraid? Do I feel stupid or intimidated around this person?* What is your mood today? What is your mood lately? What has your mood been for the past few years? Some people are angry or depressed for decades without admitting that it has any impact on their decisions. One clue that you're riding an emotional train is if success seems inevitable or impossible. In most cases, life is not so definite—but your moods and other emotional phases can make it seem so.

Assess the Impact of Your Emotions. For each emotion you're feeling, ask how it influences your thoughts about a decision. Challenge yourself. Start with the assumption that your emotions influence your thoughts; your job is to figure out how. If you admit you're angry, ask, *How is the anger changing the way I see my decision?* Don't simply dismiss emotion as irrelevant. Look for misdirected emotions. If you had another terrible day at work, but ended up in a petty fight with your daughter, connect the dots: Anger may be affecting your decisions at home *and* work, even if there is little connection between the source of the anger and any particular dispute or outburst.

Talk to Someone You Trust. Your "bounce"—a person you can bounce ideas off without fear of being judged harshly—can give you a reality check on the emotional issues. Self-assessment has limits. Many people have trouble identifying their own feelings. If you have trouble identifying your own feelings, and you know it, don't be embarrassed to talk to others. If you can't identify your own feelings *and* you can't talk about them with others, you're going to have a real problem. Don't be worried that you'll look weak, stupid or unprofessional. Don't be afraid that you'll be exposing some vulnerability. If you do, you're back to the same defect we addressed in Step 3: the potentially disastrous consequences of a go-it-alone mentality.

Experienced decision-makers have a network of bounces. The bounce's role is to listen to your ideas, possibly offer advice and always give an honest opinion. The more important and diverse your decisions, the more bounces you need. A good bounce is frank, but nonthreatening—a person who can tell you without making you feel silly that you're getting carried away, are too negative or otherwise are off on a tangent. Amazingly, you'll often find that the mere process of talking about the decision with your bounce will move you toward a better understanding of the decision. Most of us have had the experience of describing a problem to someone else and making the decision while we described it.

In summary, you bring your emotions into a decision by recognizing them, accepting that they exist and working them into your thought process. Because you're intimately tied to your emotions, involving third parties who can help identify your feelings and put them in perspective is often helpful.

Hang-Ups: What to Do When Your Feelings Are a Bit Kooky

As you work your emotions into a decision, you may conclude that some of your feelings are misplaced, excessive or inappropriate. A variety of psychological conditions—phobias, anxieties, extreme moodiness, obsessions and compulsions—may influence your decisions. The fact that you recognize you have "an issue" doesn't mean that moving past the issue and making the right decision are easy. Millions (perhaps billions) of people wake up every day with such issues, of which they are well aware and about which they can't seem to do much.

How do you make a decision when you realize you're being driven in part by a neurotic condition or a hang-up? The key is to address the psychological issue and the decision separately, each on its own terms. Your initial reaction might be to say, "If I could separate my hang-ups from my decisions, I wouldn't really have a hang-up!" In fact, you often (but not always) can separate your hang-ups from your decisions. You probably do it every day. You want to go on a trip, but your fear of flying holds you back. You're well aware of the impact of your fear on this decision. You know exactly what you'd do if you had no fear. In such a case, your fear isn't destroying your ability to make a good choice; it's destroying your ability to act on it. Acutely aware of their neuroses and hang-ups, most people are reminded every day of how their decisions and behavior are affected (your friends' teasing may help you some in this area). When a psychological condition could affect your Big Decision, you must determine how to separate that condition from the decision.

For example, let's say you know that fear of public speaking is the main reason you haven't applied to law school. It's no mystery. You have thoughts like, *I am very interested in the law, and I'd love to go to law school, but I couldn't possibly answer hard questions in front of the whole class or speak in court!* You know that many people have overcome a fear of public speaking, but you don't have complete confidence that you can overcome the fear. If you're prepared to work toward overcoming the fear, you can "separate the fear from the decision" by applying to law school on the assumption that you'll overcome the fear before school starts. Come up with a game plan to overcome the fear, and execute the plan between the time you apply and your first day of school (or start when you're accepted). If you don't get into law school, you won't spend years thinking you didn't apply because of fear. You'll have some backtracking to do if you get into school and can't overcome the fear, but you gained by moving forward on the assumption that you could do it. Besides, just getting into law school may build confidence and help you conquer your fear of public speaking.

The law school example was too easy. After all, in a worst-case analysis you simply don't show up on the first day of school. Or perhaps you show up, find you can't handle it and leave school. The stakes are relatively modest. Let's say you're afraid to get married because the idea of a marital commitment terrifies you. The person you're dating seems to be "the right one" for marriage. There's nobody else in the picture (that is, another person with whom you want to have a relationship). On many levels, you do want to get married. Then fear kicks in. Is it too soon? Are you too young? Is this really the right person? Can you handle marriage? You've spoken with other people, and you're pretty sure that your fear of commitment goes far beyond normal apprehensions that most people have.

To become engaged and assume you'll overcome your fear of commitment by the wedding day would be very risky. When the stakes of going forward with a decision are so high, try to address the psychological issue before you make a decision. When a decision is truly important to you and others, your approach to the psychological issues should reflect that importance. Don't ask a significant other to wait around for years to see if you'll grow out of your fear of commitment. Address the issue aggressively by reading, counseling, psychological therapy and whatever else it takes so you both can move toward a timely resolution. It's unfair to say, in effect, "I can't make a decision yet because I have psychological issues and, by the way, I am not going to address my issues any time soon."

When your neuroses and hang-ups affect a decision, try to unwrap the psychological issues from the decision. If you're not comfortable with your decision because of the impact of a neurosis or hang-up, take steps to overcome that neurosis or hang-up. Meanwhile, move the decision forward to a comfortable degree while you resolve your issue.

How to Make Decisions When You're Extremely Angry, Depressed, Infatuated or Distraught

In the ideal world, you wouldn't make a Big Decision during truly extreme emotional episodes. Certainly, a person who is hysterical or otherwise so overcome by intense feelings that a deliberate thought process can't be achieved should make only those decisions that absolutely can't be deferred. Hysteria aside, Big Decisions often are accompanied by a slew of strong feelings and a timetable that requires faster action than you'd prefer.

Here's a simple strategy for making major decisions when you must act during an emotional crisis:

Get Some Physical Distance. Isolate yourself from the immediate emotional stimuli. You might want to leave the room if something in the room is upsetting. Take a walk down the hall or outside, or go to church or a chapel. Many people are calmed in emotional situations by spending time in places of prayer, worship, meditation or relative solitude.

Create Some Emotional Distance. If possible, sleep on it. Shelve the decision for at least twenty-four hours. A day to gain perspective can make a huge difference.

Acknowledge Your Emotional State. Overcoming denial comes up again and again in this book. It's all right to close your eyes, take a deep breath and say, "I'm a mess right now," or "I'm so angry I can barely think," or "Everything looks so bad. So hopeless. I'm so sad and afraid and lonely right now." Likewise, learn to admit that "I am riding an emotional high right now. The world might look different when I come down."

Seek Help—Both Support and Advice. Some of your most important resources are the people who help you cope and make your decision. Spiritual advisors, counselors, physicians and nurses, hospice workers and a host of other professionals are highly skilled at helping you. Take the help. They are doing what they do because they want to help. Assume they wouldn't have their jobs if they regarded helping you as an imposition. Even people who aren't usually religious find themselves turning to God for help with hard questions when the going gets tough. Look to friends and family members who are calming, supportive and wise. If your emotions are extreme on the positive side, talk to your most sober bounce, perhaps a skeptic who can throw a bucket of cold water on you. You don't need to follow that person's advice, but go ahead and hear it. Another person's perspective may be helpful, even if it's not reassuring.

Be Cautious. Is someone you rely on trying to take unfair advantage of your highly emotional condition? Don't be railroaded into anything. Be especially careful about signing any papers. Don't assume that you can get out of a commitment just because you believe you're under emotional duress. Don't assume that people will forgive what you say because you were distraught. Find out all the facts. If a medical issue is involved, use your time with the physicians to ask questions. If you don't understand, keep asking.

Take the Decision One Step at a Time. Decide what you must decide and put off issues that may be deferred until you're in a more normal mind-set.

If you don't have an advisor available to give you perspective, consider what professional advisors typically say to help emotional clients calm their minds during a decision:

A Physician Discussing Treatment with a Patient Who Has Just Learned That She Has a Chronic Illness

"You know, a lot of ground has been gained in caring for this illness in the past few years. There are now treatments available to you that were never available before. We have a great team at this office. We've cared for a lot of patients with this illness. Everyone in the office will know you. We're going to start right away. The first step is to make some basic decisions about your treatment plan. You'll be very involved in decisions about your treatment. Let me start by going over your options and a timetable. . . ."

A Family-Law Attorney Talking to a Woman Whose Husband Unexpectedly Left Her for Another Woman After a Twenty-Year Marriage

"You'll look back on this, in time, and realize that what happened to your marriage is more about your husband's behavior than anything you did. It's very normal to feel betrayed and to have all kinds of other feelings about what happened. Don't blame yourself for your husband's actions. I'm sure that after twenty years of marriage, this is the last place you expected to be. You're going to be happier down the line. If you're like most people who come into my office, your marriage hasn't been good for a while. And while there are exceptions, the spouse who's left behind usually comes out stronger and better than the other one. The length of your marriage will entitle you to more substantial financial benefits. If you're having a lot of trouble handling the emotional issues, let's talk about getting you to counseling. The legal case is a business proposition. The court is not concerned with who's at fault. It's an accounting of assets and liabilities. My job is to try to get you the best result under the law. We're ready to get started."

An Employment Attorney Talking to a Person Who Has Been Unexpectedly Fired from His Job

"I've seen a lot of people in your situation. It's a real shock, isn't it? You'll come through it. Five years from now, this will be a tiny blip in your job history. You'd be surprised at how many people actually benefit from a layoff in the long run. Some get better jobs; some start a career they like more. The bottom line is that the old job is gone, and the new job is coming. The first thing to do is to start getting your résumé and references in shape and develop a job-search plan. I'll take a thorough look at the legal issues with your former employer, of course. The most important step is to get a grip on the future and move forward."

A Bankruptcy Attorney Talking to the Owner of a Small Business Who May Have to Declare Bankruptcy

"Years ago, bankruptcy was considered a huge personal embarrassment. That's changed a lot. The tendency these days, even in big, well-known corporations, is to treat bankruptcy more as a strategy. Many, many people have come through personal and business bankruptcies and done great. The day after the bankruptcy filing, you will be doing much the same thing you were doing the day before, but now you have legal protection. It's going to affect your credit, of course, but you'll just start working on rebuilding that tomorrow. There will be other impacts and considerations, which we'll discuss in detail. The process is going to add structure to what feels like a mess at that moment. Today we need to start working on how that structure and process will unfold."

The common thread is clear: The professional advisor will put the emotional event in context and emphasize forward action. The client needs to know that she's not alone and that others have worked through the same problem. The advisor focuses on (1) action that will be taken to address the problem; (2) the importance of addressing the parts of the problem that can be managed today, rather than speculating and obsessing about the uncertainties; and (3) emphasizing that the client will benefit from the efforts of a very competent and responsive team.

The approach of professional advisors is advice that you should try to keep in mind.

When Emotions Will Mess
You Up: Buying and Selling Property

In one situation, emotions are almost categorically detrimental to your decision-making process: figuring out the market value of property that you want to buy or sell. Property valuation is not based upon what the property is worth to you. It's based on what the property is worth to other people. When you're trying to figure out what something is worth on the market to other people, your own values and emotions are irrelevant, even hostile, to the entire process. You can't figure out what property is worth to other people if you consider your personal likes, dislikes, preferences and other feelings. You must consider only what others in the market think, even if you feel differently or vigorously disagree with it. It's critical in valuing property not to confuse "what it's worth" with "how badly I want it" or "how great I think it is" (that is, "what the property's worth right now *to me*").

Most of us would agree that when we buy a home, we should

like it (or love it, depending on how much we value the "home experience"). It's pointless to analyze the decision whether to purchase a residence in an emotional vacuum. No residence is a great deal if you detest living in it. For most people, a home-purchase decision can, and should, have an emotional component. However, unless the home's resale value is irrelevant, part of the decision involves fair market value. Market value is critical if you're buying the home, in whole or part, because you plan to resell it for a gain—or at least to get out what you paid. Accordingly, there's a point in a home-buying transaction when you should remove your "Gotta live here!" hat and put on your "What is a fair price for this place?" hat. At this point, you must separate the attractiveness of the property to you from its attractiveness to other parties in the market and consider the condition of the market itself. Although you're the buyer today, someone else will be the buyer when it's time to sell.

Value also is critical for the non–real-estate investments you make. If you make an investment, you presumably want the investment to appreciate over time. Whether the investment will actually do so depends heavily on whether you bought it at a reasonable price. The fact that a company has a great business does not answer the question of whether that company's stock sells at a reasonable price. Early-stage investments in companies that are not publicly traded are among the hardest to value. A public company's stock price reflects a consensus of many buyers and sellers about value. Valuation is much more complex when a company's shares have no market. The same is true of cars and other assets—the larger, freer and more informed the market, the easier it is to investigate value. For these reasons, eBay and similar online markets have made two great contributions to commerce: (1) They've created extremely "liquid" (available) markets for items that used to be hard to locate, buy and sell, and (2) they provide a readily available source of information on the value of items that are hard to find and used items.

In some cases, paying more for an item than it is worth to others may be a sound decision. A lifetime spent getting the best deal on everything would be a boring and unproductive life. You'd spend all of your time investigating and negotiating your acquisitions. Perhaps you're the kind of person who plans to fall in love with your home, have a smooth, friendly purchase transaction (free from "nickel-and-diming"), move in and live an idyllic life in the home. If so, you value the aesthetics of the home purchase much more than the money you'll part with by not proceeding in a more value-conscious manner. Is it worth it? To you, perhaps it is. Every day, financially prudent and sophisticated people decide to buy vacation homes they'll use for a couple of weeks every year, at a price that would pay for three months at any hotel or rental unit. Is it worth it? To them, it is.

If we suggest that you never make an emotional purchase, we would be telling you what values to have—how to live your life, not how to make a decision. Our message is simply "Don't fool yourself!" When you throw caution to the wind or buy property for non-financial reasons (such as the prestige of owning a second house), admit it so you won't be regretful later. Make reality a part of your decision. Say "I might be paying twenty thousand dollars too much for this house, but it's worth it not to face the tension of negotiation or risk that someone else will take it while we are negotiating." Remember what you said when it's time to sell the house.

When you think about buying a house, making an investment or otherwise acquiring property that you may want to sell in the future, consider the factors that valuation experts consider when going through the valuation process as part of their profession:

- What is the *real* total cost to you of acquiring, holding and later disposing of the property? Here's an example. What will cost you more money in the long term: (A) a three-hundred-thousand-dollar house in a neighborhood where you won't feel comfortable unless your three children attend private school or (B) a four-hundred-thousand-dollar house in a neighborhood with great public schools? All things being equal, Home A (the three-hundred-thousand-dollar home) will cost more. A thorough analysis of the real cost to you goes far beyond the purchase price. The twenty thousand dollars-plus in annual private-school tuition you'll pay to live in Home A will far exceed the additional annual mortgage cost to buy Home B.

- What evidence do you have about the property's value to other people? A typical way to figure out how much property is worth is to consider the price at which comparable items have recently changed hands in arm's-length, voluntary transactions (that is, deals made between people who are not related to one another in some way or forced to make a deal). A good real-estate agent can provide information on "comps." For used items (other than real estate), a little research on eBay can give you ballpark information on what a particular item will fetch in a reasonably quick sale. Businesses are valued using a more complex set of techniques, but all of them in some way apply historical data to predict what price the market will accept today.

- What factors, especially emotion, influence the valuation placed on the property by other people? Large groups of people may be swayed by emotion and overvalue property. In its extreme version, this reaction is called a "mania." The media like to report on manias because they are fascinating. Over the past two decades, we've seen manias in the stock market (Internet stocks), toys (Cabbage Patch Kids, Beanie Babies, Tickle-Me Elmos) and in several real-estate markets.

During a mania, the credibility of what appear to be arm's-length, voluntary transactions is diminished. During a mania, consider the views of people who are not swept up in it. A mania presents the difficult task of separating the reality from the mania. Manias often start with a fundamentally real aspect—for example, Beanie Babies are cute toys and fun to collect; the Internet will change business productivity forever; beachfront property is desirable. When a mania occurs, an item's benefits are exaggerated. Buyers then expect and therefore pay for unrealistic benefits (such as permanent explosive value) and use other maniacs to validate their actions.

A Big Decision that involves buying property raises a red flag for emotion. Consider both: (1) What is the property worth to you? and (2) What is the property worth to other people who may have different values and objectives?

How to Identify When Emotion Is Driving a Property Decision

To identify when you're making an emotional decision in a property transaction, consider the following indicators of emotional conduct:

- You convince yourself that you must have a certain item or you won't be happy.
- You believe that you can never lose on a transaction, that the value will keep going up.
- You believe that an acquisition will solve an unrelated problem (for example, buying your dream house or a piece of jewelry will save your marriage).
- You make a mistake buying something, then make the mistake of not selling it because selling it would signify failure. When you pay eighty dollars for a share of stock that is worth

ten dollars, then refuse to sell it for twenty dollars because you're unhappy that it went down and don't want to admit you overpaid, you've made two mistakes!

- You find yourself making arguments for why problems with the property really aren't problems at all. Justifying value to yourself won't make the property any more valuable to others who don't hear or accept your arguments.
- You believe you can't walk away from a purchase. You *can* walk away.

Unless you like to overpay, manage your emotions if you want to make a decent deal.

We leave Step 6 with the following points to remember about the role of your emotions in decision-making:

- Your emotions are part of making a Big Decision. Make sure you understand how you feel about a decision and what impact emotion will have on your decision.
- If you'll be required to execute a decision, be sure you've considered the emotional resources you'll need to make it work. Be realistic with yourself. Many people are not meant to face the fear, uncertainty, anxiety and other stresses of starting a business. Are you ready to make a marriage work . . . for a lifetime? Do you have the emotional qualities and resources that each course of action would demand? An alternative that you can't execute is not a real option.
- Bring your emotions into the decision no later than Step 6.
- Take enough time to make your decision so the impact of temporary mood swings is minimized.
- If you have hang-ups or obstructive emotions, deal with them

on their own terms. Try not to confuse the psychological problem with the Big Decision.

• If your Big Decision requires you to value property, manage your emotions. Consider having an appraiser or other valuation expert give you an independent opinion on the value of the property under consideration.

Career: A Relationship-vs.-Career-Direction Decision Is a Lot Tougher When Mid-Thirties Love Is on the Line

People told Sharon Wayne not to leave her successful
West Coast music teaching career and move East
without an engagement ring on her finger. Did she listen?

Sharon Wayne picked up a guitar when she was eight and never put it down. She started with folk guitar, and at the age of fourteen began to study classical guitar. After four years in high school, Sharon was accepted into the University of Southern California (USC) undergraduate program in classical-guitar performance. In 1987, Sharon received her bachelor's degree in music. She completed her master's degree in 1989. When Sharon finished her formal education, she moved to the San Francisco Bay area to start her career as a classical-guitar performer and instructor.

For six years, Sharon slogged through a series of part-time retail and other nonmusic jobs as she steadily built a base of classical-guitar students and planted the seeds of a performing career. Finally, in 1995, Sharon taught enough students to support herself solely by teaching music. For an artist, the ability to support oneself through one's art is a major milestone. Sharon also had a budding performing career. She had recorded CDs for several classical labels and performed around the United States and Japan. Although Sharon loved performing, teaching paid the bills. And she was good at it. By 1999, Sharon had accomplished almost everything she wanted in music teaching. Yet there was one teaching goal that Sharon had not achieved: Sharon wanted to be on the teaching faculty at the San Francisco Conservatory of Music.

The San Francisco Conservatory of Music was founded in 1917. Housed in a classic building on Ortega Street, the conservatory nurtures the most promising Bay Area musicians. The conservatory's faculty is composed of master musicians who have a passion for instruction. To Sharon, the conservatory was "as good as it gets" for a classical-music teacher. Faculty positions at the conservatory rarely become available. Sharon kept her eyes open for spots at the conservatory almost from the day she moved to San Francisco.

In the fall of 1999, when Sharon was thirty-three years old, the conservatory announced that it was accepting applications to fill a classical-guitar teaching position. Sharon and dozens of other classical-guitar teachers applied for the position. The application process was rigorous, starting with résumés. Based on the résumés, a committee chose six finalists. Sharon was a finalist. Next came personal interviews, during which the applicants were required to teach a real student in front of the committee. Sharon also did a guitar performance for the committee. The application process took six months.

In July 2000, the conservatory offered Sharon a faculty position. Sharon was ecstatic. "I got it! I got it! I got it!"

Sharon screamed into the telephone when she called her family and friends. She couldn't sleep. At 5:00 A.M., Sharon called an East Coast friend just to tell someone else. *My career is exactly where it should be right now,* Sharon thought. It crossed Sharon's mind that being accepted onto the conservatory faculty might be the most important milestone in her life. Indeed, since she had graduated from USC, Sharon's life had centered around her music. She socialized and dated, of course, but Sharon's career grew and prospered, even when personal relationships did not. Sharon shelved dreams of expanding her performing career, at the possible expense of her teaching, when she got the conservatory's offer.

Sharon was scheduled to start at the conservatory in the 2000 fall semester. Sharon's faculty position did not require her to give up her pool of private students, so her teaching career was in full bloom. She spent August 2000 preparing to start teaching at the conservatory. That month, Sharon also fell in love:

Frank Welte was a student of mine. He was my student during the conservatory's application process. He was thirty-three, single and in medical school. I was then thirty-four and single. Taking classical-guitar lessons was something Frank had always wanted to do. After his first year of medical school on the East Coast, Frank took a couple of years to do some research in San Francisco. That gave him a freer schedule, so he started taking lessons. For six months we'd been working together professionally and getting to know each other. In August, we realized we were in love.

Frank's research stint in San Francisco was scheduled to end in mid-2001. In July 2001, Frank would go back to medical school in the Boston area. Over the next several months, during Sharon's first year teaching at the conservatory, the relationship between Sharon and Frank quickly grew serious. The more time Sharon spent with Frank, the more Sharon became convinced that Frank was "the one." By all appearances, Frank felt the same way about Sharon.

Sharon's realization that Frank might be "the one" created a three-thousand-mile dilemma. Sharon had no students, no conservatory, no career and no family on the East Coast. After medical school was over, Frank would have to complete his medical residency, which most likely would last four to six years at a yet-undetermined location. Suddenly, all that Sharon had built up in San Francisco for eleven years, which culminated in her acceptance onto the conservatory faculty, was at stake—weighed against love, marriage, parenthood and everything that might come if she went with Frank.

Neither the Silicon Valley nor Route 128 had a technological solution to Sharon's problem. She and Frank considered a long-distance relationship—talking on the telephone, taking trips across the country to visit each other and using e-mail. That approach might have been acceptable if they were younger, they agreed. At this stage, however, Sharon and Frank wanted to be together physically. E-mail isn't a hug in the morning or a candle-light dinner:

We were in love, and our relationship was very new. We wanted to be together. I had dated enough to know this relationship was really right. A long-distance relationship might not last for just a couple of years. Once Frank was done with med school in three years, he would do a residency. I didn't know where that would be. I could be in the same position in three years. I didn't want to bide my time like that. We talked about having kids. I didn't want to be apart for several years and jump into instant family life. Neither of us wanted a long-distance relationship.

They talked about Frank transferring to a Bay Area medical school, but didn't pursue it. The odds of a Bay Area medical school allowing Frank to transfer were minuscule. By the standards of an admissions committee, "I'm in love with a woman from San Francisco" seemed like a pretty tough sell. Putting aside the likely futility of a transfer, they barely had time to pull a transfer application together, and it was unclear when it would be decided.

In March 2001, Sharon was seven months into her relationship with Frank, six months into her teaching position at the conservatory and closing in on Frank's return to Boston. Zero hour on Sharon's decision was fast approaching, and Sharon started to feel the pressure:

There were two choices: break up, or I move to Boston. I had dated for a long time. I was in my mid-thirties. This relationship was not something to throw away lightly. We knew Frank wasn't going to transfer. I had to wrestle with the decision whether to go to Boston with him. It wasn't just the conservatory. It was all the private students I had built up for eleven years. It was everything I'd worked for in terms of teaching in the Bay Area. I was planning to buy a house in Berkeley. I discussed with Frank what I would be giving up. I cried. He felt terrible and guilty.

Word got around that Sharon was considering a move to Boston so she could continue her relationship with Frank. The advice, solicited and unsolicited, started to pile up. Despite talk of a future marriage, Frank had not proposed to Sharon and wasn't going to be put on any timetable for making a proposal. For her part, Sharon was incapable of giving Frank a marriage ultimatum:

We weren't engaged. I heard people say, "Don't go without a ring on your finger." I heard a lot of "That's the kiss of death. You'll never get engaged if you move." Two of the people who told me this had been in a similar situation. They made sure they were engaged before moving to San Francisco. They said I shouldn't mess around at my age. I almost gave Frank an ultimatum a couple of times, but I felt horrible after considering it.

Sharon wasn't just guessing about Frank's intentions, though. She believed in Frank and the relationship, and she felt she had enough indications that the relationship would end in marriage:

I thought Frank was just being traditional. I didn't want to interfere with that. I believed he would propose. He signaled to me that marriage and a family were his direction. This level of uncertainty was acceptable. Yeah, I wanted to be married, but I didn't want to get engaged on the basis of an ultimatum. If I were engaged based on an ultimatum, I wouldn't trust the motivation for the engagement. If someone proposes out of fear of losing me, rather than desire to spend their life with me, it would be hard to trust that proposal. That's my feeling. I trusted my judgment in the past, and my life has gone okay. I have been fortunate in my life. I have made good decisions. From the first moment, I knew Frank was a good person. I knew I trusted him. There was a connection instantly, a mutual respect. I hesitated to rush getting involved with him because I knew that this wasn't a person I could just mess around with. I had complete trust in the relationship.

All the trust in the world wouldn't restore Sharon's teaching career in San Francisco if things didn't work out with Frank. Sharon asked the conservatory if she could take a leave of absence, to keep a foot in the door. That didn't work. From the conservatory's perspective, once Sharon was unavailable to teach, she had to be replaced with another instructor. A leave of absence was a lot to ask of the conservatory. They had accepted her over many applicants, and now she wanted to leave for a guy. When Sharon talked to the director of the classical-guitar program, he intimated that the conservatory had Sharon on a fast track and had been very hopeful for her conservatory career. Sharon felt pangs of regret as she left his office.

Sharon's father in Los Angeles was another issue. He didn't want her to move so far away. Sharon recalls, "My father said he was concerned that I had achieved great things in San Francisco and sacrificed so much to get them. He was worried that I'd be throwing them away." Sharon had a very close relationship with her father, but didn't completely buy what he said: "My dad said he was concerned about my career, but I think it was more the geographical separation. I have a close relationship with my father, the closest in the family."

Sharon also talked a lot to her best friend in San Francisco, "Hashing through it, talking about all the details." In the end, Sharon relied on her best friend for support, but found little advice:

She supported whatever I said. She wanted me to be happy. She was a sounding board more than anything. She mostly just bounced back what I was saying. I chose to be around people who were accepting and not opinionated. I would dismiss the people who were very opinionated. I just felt they weren't seeing all sides of the issue.

Sharon also was concerned about going where she

didn't know anybody. She had visited Boston before, but hadn't been to the suburb where she and Frank would live. She was happy they would pay half as much rent and get twice the space. That was a pro. Among other cities, being close to Boston in particular was a pro. The classical-music scene in Boston is alive and thriving. *Much more,* Sharon thought, *than in California.* She had heard that Boston was a good place for a classical musician. Sharon did some online research, which confirmed what she had heard about the Boston scene. Leaving a place as naturally beautiful as the Bay Area concerned her, although she knew New England was pretty. She would have to leave her rent-controlled apartment. Her rent in San Francisco had gone up only 2 percent a year as Bay Area rent went wild in the 1990s.

The financial picture was not as simple as "marry a doctor and the future is set." Frank was only a second-year medical student. There would be a decade of school, residency and building a practice before Frank would see a doctor's paycheck. When he did, a chunk of that paycheck would go to pay back Frank's student loans. Sharon could expect to be the main breadwinner for the foreseeable future with Frank. The bad news, and the good news, was that by going back to student life on a shared basis, Sharon could expect lower living expenses.

Sharon decided to move. Instead of lamenting the loss of her San Francisco teaching career, Sharon focused on building a performing career based on the East Coast. Sharon had been trained as a performer and loved performing. Her position at the conservatory—gratifying as it was—had meant making sacrifices to her performing career for teaching:

I felt my professional career would just take a different direction when I moved—more of a performing career than a teaching career. Performing had the additional benefit of being something I could do from many locations. That fit well with Frank's future, which would involve a residency at an undetermined location. With a Web site, I can move my residence and have a stable performing career. The fear and excitement of starting a new performing career had appeal. In terms of the relationship, I was weighing having the security of a long-term relationship, having someone in my life and living together before I started a family.

In July 2001, Sharon Wayne said good-bye to her San Francisco students, resigned from her position at the San Francisco Conservatory of Music and moved out of her rent-controlled apartment. Still single, not engaged but in love, she moved to Massachusetts to be with Frank.

Postscript: In Sharon's Own Words

While the relationship was the catalyst for my move, I'd been feeling consumed with all the teaching I was doing. I had thought about reshaping my career for quite some time. I had put those thoughts on hold after I got the conservatory position. Although there definitely was a risk that my teaching career would suffer a setback when I relocated, I felt that the Boston area was a land of plenty for a performing classical musician. That has turned out to be quite true. Even though the move had some career disadvantages, I knew there were pluses, too.

Before I left San Francisco, I started looking for a teaching job on the East Coast. That was successful. I contacted an affiliate of an organization through which I had been teaching. I cold-called, received an interview and got the job. One friend was a serious inspiration. She had moved to San Francisco from Montreal. I met her at a guitar convention. She was a very outgoing person who became president of the guitar society in San Francisco shortly after she arrived. She was a guitar lover, not a pro guitarist, who wanted to manage musicians. She got involved with a radio station and did a guitar show and classical show. She took the city by storm. I thought, "Yeah! That's what I have to do." I didn't have a specific discussion with her. I just saw what she did in San Francisco. She wasn't waiting for people to come to her. She was assertive and outgoing. She didn't seem to fear being rejected. She was open to all different possibilities. I took on that attitude.

I had a clear vision of what I wanted in Massachusetts because I already had it in San Francisco. When I started in San Francisco, I only had a vague idea of what I wanted. When I moved East, I knew how many students I wanted and how to get students. It was easier. It wasn't like starting over. I know what I'm qualified for and what I'm not. I called the Boston Guitar Society and got on the board. People started calling for gigs. I hit the ground running in Boston, and it worked.

On a personal level, the first two months were very difficult. We got there during the summer. I had a lot of time on my hands. I didn't have friends to hang out with, or any real focus or direction. The social part of it was the hardest. Frank is not a very social person. I am an "introverted social person"; it's hard for me to meet people, but I like to call people and have coffee. There were times when I would be really, really frustrated and feel like I wasn't getting enough emotional support from Frank. Given my age and experience, though, I recognized the importance of this relationship and its strength. I knew I would get through the adjustment period.

January of the first year was a real turning point. The holidays were hard. September 11 was part of that, I am sure. In January,

I started working with a flute player who was a nice person and became a friend. Things started getting better.

Thinking back on my decision, leaving the conservatory and everything I'd built up was the biggest issue. I had private students at home. I was teaching at three schools. There were a lot of emotional pulls on me in terms of letting go of students and that position which meant so much. Letting go of students and saying good-bye was the hardest part. When I made the decision, I didn't realize how painful it would be. The pain of saying good-bye hadn't been a factor in the decision.

In the end, the lack of a marriage commitment wasn't a big part of the decision. The people who told me not to go without a ring didn't understand my relationship. It weighed on me a little, but in the end I didn't give it much credence. It was important to get my father's blessing. When I showed him what I would gain by going and enumerated everything, I got his blessing. It was one of the things I needed. I talked it out with him. I cried it out of him. My goal was for him to see why I was doing it. His perception up to that point was that I was throwing everything in my life out the window to be with some guy. I believe I convinced him.

A little bit of regret comes up once in a while, but there have been enough changes in my career in the direction I intended when I moved. I haven't burned too many bridges in the Bay Area. I make a point now to visit my family whenever I am out there. I probably spend more time with my family now. I never sold my car in San Francisco. It's more a talisman than anything else. I could rent a car when I come out for the insurance I am paying to keep a car sitting in San Francisco.

I've learned that I was overly optimistic about a few things. I might have stayed an extra year in California if I could do it all over again. It bothered me to get the conservatory position and stay only for nine months. I'd like to have stayed and built it more, even at the price of a year of a commuter relationship. The initial part of the move was really difficult. It was maybe a little sooner than it should have been. Frank wouldn't have ended the relationship if I had said that I wanted to do long distance for a year. But it would have been hard. Frank definitely expressed that he preferred to have us be together. I did, too. We were just beginning.

AUTHORS' NOTE: Frank surprised Sharon during a trip to Maine, two months after she moved East. On a cliff overlooking the Atlantic Ocean, Frank pulled out a ring and proposed. Frank and Sharon were married on September 1, 2002.

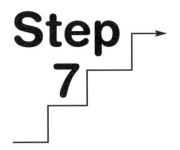

Step 7

Suffer the Hard Choices Now and Get Real Results Later

My basic principle is that you don't make decisions because they are easy; you don't make them because they are cheap; you don't make them because they're popular; you make them because they're right.

—Father Theodore Martin Hesburgh

The important thing is this: to be able at any moment to sacrifice what we are for what we could become.

—Charles DuBois

Two critical aspects of great decision-making are the ability to define a long-term plan and the mental fortitude to make choices that cause some short-term pain, but which advance the long-term plan. We're all told from the cradle, "Make a long-term plan and stick with it." Why is it so hard to do? The reason is simple: We gravitate toward what is most convenient, enjoyable, popular, fun, tangible and available at the moment. We try to avoid pain, disruption, deprivation, controversy, confrontation and benefits that seem speculative because they won't be realized *now.*

If you make the same decisions most others make today, placing instant gratification above all else, you'll end up about where most others do tomorrow: at an "average" place. That's fine if you want no better than an even chance of making your marriage work, you want to retire on Social Security payments, and you can accept plenty of regrets about the choices you made in life. You're probably reading this book because you think you can do better! Only if your day-to-day choices are consistent with a long-term plan can you achieve long-term benefits.

Step 7 talks about the long term—why and how you should pay some dues today.

Personal and Business Wants
That Require You to Make and
Carry Out Long-Term Decisions

The long term wouldn't be important if all of your wants, desires and objectives could be obtained in an instant. Despite our instant-gratification world, most of us have many personal and business goals that take much longer to achieve. Consider the following:

- Your personal and professional reputation, or a business's reputation, credibility and goodwill
- Your sense of self-esteem and accomplishment
- Close relationships with other people, including mates, friends, family, business associates and, for a business, a

loyal network of suppliers, customers, advisors and employees
- Financial resources (unless you're a lottery winner or you receive a large inheritance or windfall)
- Your business's track record and the value of its brands

Absent truly unusual events, no quick or easy way is available to build these assets or resources. Henry Ford was right when he said, "You can't build a reputation on what you're *going* to do." You may claim you're successful and pay for lots of good PR, but that doesn't add up to a reputation. A reputation develops over time and arises from consistent performance. You may form relationships and make deals with others, but the loyalty and trust of your partners arises over time from actually working together after you make your deals. You may have a good year and make a lot of money, but whether this translates into long-term personal or business security depends on how you manage your resources over an extended time.

The process of building personal financial resources almost always requires you to forgo some immediate gratification so that you'll have what you need when opportunity (or misfortune) knocks. This process requires you to take mental pleasure in executing a long-term plan, even if you must make some immediate sacrifice. Many successful savers seem to value the discipline of a financially prudent life. They like to pay a fair price, avoid waste and put together the best outfit for their kids from a store that sells at a discount, rather than paying the top dollar that others are paying. Their lifestyle doesn't have the panache of a loose pocketbook, but these people know that the real payoff for short-term financial restraint will come when they can make key midcareer decisions without fear, help their children buy a first home, choose when and where to retire, and leave a financial legacy to the next generation.

Long-term thinking also is critical in key domestic and work relationships. In the short run, the steps required to make a major change to a personal or job relationship often are difficult. For example, extricating yourself from a hopeless, damaging relationship may be more difficult *in the short term* than staying in it. The consequence is personal inertia; you stay in the relationship until you're shoved along. The "shoving" that gets you moving may be more than a metaphor. Some people stay in violent relationships beyond the point when they realize the relationship is dangerous. Sometimes the trigger to leave is that the relationship becomes virtually unsurvivable. Some people never leave. Likewise, personal inertia may keep you in a job that isn't working out until you're fired or demoted. While staying in a bad job may be the path of least resistance in the short term, in the long term you may dramatically reduce your employability if the job ends poorly.

Just as long-term thinking may require you to leave a bad relationship, it also may require you to stay and try to fix it. Long-term relationships have benefits that are difficult to replicate. Temporary issues arise in most long-term relationships. Even severe issues may be temporary. Maintaining a long-term relationship always takes work, and some issues that arise may appear quite substantial. Taking for granted the benefits of a long-term relationship is easy, until you no longer have them. When a long-term personal or job relationship develops flaws, decide whether the flaws destroy the relationship's viability, or whether the relationship merely needs repair. If you don't know, try repair first to preserve the long-term benefits.

Symptoms of Short-Term Decision-Making

Your own internal logic—the thought patterns and rationales you use to make a decision—provide valuable clues to whether short-term thinking dominates a decision. Consider whether you've made a decision using one or more of the following rationales of short-term thinking:

- "I'm young. What I do now won't matter in ten (or twenty or thirty) years."
- "Who knows what will happen? I may not be around to deal with the consequences."
- "I know what I am doing is worse in the long run. I just don't want to deal with the immediate repercussions if I do something different."
- "The problem will work itself out by itself."
- "I have so little that anything I save would be a drop in the bucket."
- "Nothing I do will make a difference."
- "Who cares what will happen down the line? Heck if I'm going to pass this up . . ."
- "There's always time to fix it."

The 1950s actor James Dean died at twenty-four in a fiery sports-car crash. He is quoted as having told America's youth to "dream as if you'll live forever. Live as if you'll die today." Dean's sadly prophetic statement embodies a common and unfortunate decision-making practice: Sit around dreaming about becoming a movie star, or a sports star, or a wealthy person, but use your time and money on today's overpriced impulse items. Dean's first piece of advice—"dream as if you'll live forever"—is strong and inspiring. If you only dream of goals that can be reached in a short time, you'll deprive yourself of the truly great successes that take more time to develop. If you follow Dean's second thought, you'll unfortunately lose your ability to see big dreams come true. If you want your dreams to come true, you must use time today to take a step toward making your dreams a reality. Don't become a *Run for Your Life*-style wanderer who's more likely to end up dissatisfied, disgruntled or broke tomorrow than a movie or sports star.[14]

Short-term logic doesn't necessarily indicate short-term decision-making. Some decisions truly won't matter in ten years, and sometimes you shouldn't tip the apple cart with a bold initiative. Nonetheless, short-term logic is a clue. How many young adults fail to save money for retirement, reasoning that "I'm so young, retirement planning is the last thing I need"? What this argument fails to consider, among other things, is that while it is a nest egg for retirement, a retirement account is also a component of what famed Chicago columnist Mike Royko quaintly referred to as "F**k you money."[15] While a twenty-eight-year-old certainly is not near retirement, a little FU money can make the difference between staying in a dead-end job and moving to a better situation *now*. While retirement money usually shouldn't be tapped for speculative career or investment leaps, when the other stars are lined up, having money stashed away makes a huge difference in your decision because you know that in the unlikely event that all else fails, you have an extra cushion.

The Difference Between Short Term and Long Term Is Time, and Time Is Valuable

What's the magical difference between short-term and long-term thinking? Why is there a difference between what is desirable now and what will be most helpful later? The difference returns to the fact that certain benefits necessarily are acquired over time. While a stellar act may give you sudden fame and

---

[14] *Run for Your Life* was a 1960s crime-drama TV series, the premise being that the leading character, attorney Paul Bryan (Ben Gazzara), believes he has a fatal, but not debilitating, illness and has only one or two years to live. Bryan resolves to "live life to the fullest," so he gives up everything stable (home, career), hits the road and does whatever's most thrilling and dangerous. It makes good television, but it's a poor way to achieve any long-term success.

[15] To be precise, Royko defined this level of financial resources as "enough money so that if you needed to, you could tell your boss, 'F**k you,' and you wouldn't be eating Alpo afterwards."

notoriety, the fame or notoriety won't last if your stellar act is followed by underperformance. Most personal achievements are in marathon events. The winners are the ones who last. Sprinting and pooping out after a couple of miles just doesn't cut it. You don't show up at work on the first day, challenge the boss to a duel, then take the leadership role or leave the battlefield defeated. You show up every day, learn the skills you need and progress up (and across) the rungs of the ladder until your progress at some point stops. If you become dissatisfied, you may move laterally to participate on another ladder. To rise to the top, you must go through preparatory steps. If you have extraordinary ability, talent or capacity for work, you may be able to jump a few rungs, but your ability to achieve any pinnacle of career success overnight is extremely unlikely. Don't bank on it.

The notion of overnight stardom—in the arts and entertainment, sports and business—is greatly exaggerated. While a significant accomplishment may take a few people from relative obscurity to fame "overnight," few individuals other than lottery winners and notorious criminals achieve fame (or infamy) or other "success" without years of groundwork, training, planning and practice. The fact is, becoming good at almost any endeavor takes time. Being great takes even longer. Becoming so great that you distinguish yourself among the other great people takes longer still. Once you've done that, having your skills recognized and rewarded takes more time. Greatness take years, decades or a lifetime to achieve.

Long-term thinking recognizes that your dreams require you to proceed over stepping stones. The early stones and the middle stones offer little or no gain or glory. They are successes nonethe-less. The short-term satisfaction offered by the early stepping stones is that once you've stepped over them, you're closer to your goal. If moving closer can satisfy you in and of itself, and it drives you forward despite current sacrifices, you're acting in the long term.

The Hidden Costs of Short-Term Decision-Making

Why suffer a painful or unpleasant decision today so that you *might* be in a better place five or ten years from now—*if* you're around? This question comes up again and again in intimate relationships and career decisions. In both situations, you may find yourself quite "moved in" (literally, figuratively or both). To change may require you to alter major elements of your life, some of which are enjoyable—a friend at work, a job location, a home—incur economic costs or risks, have possibly unpleasant confrontations and, in general, disrupt the current, familiar flow of your life. You may have to replace your job or your mate, and you may not know exactly how, where and with whom you'll land. While perhaps imperfect, the current flow of your life is a known quantity. A known quantity may be much more comfortable than an unknown quantity, even if what you know is difficult or even dangerous.

Many good reasons exist to act in the long term, even when it requires short-term sacrifice. Poor decisions and inertia have long-term costs, and many of them multiply as time passes. Here are examples of costs you incur when you put off doing what's best in the long term:

- *You lose better opportunities.* So long as you stick with what's not working, you lose the opportunity to identify, develop and situate yourself better. Whether it's a relationship, a job, a hiring mistake or something else, the time you spend going in the wrong direction is time you aren't moving in the right direction. Why continue on a path that's creating new problems rather than better opportunities?

- *You dig a deeper hole.* If you wait until a situation becomes intolerable, your options may become more limited because you're in too deep. Is it easier to find a new mate when you're in a battered women's shelter? Is it easier to land a job when you were fired from your last job for having a "poor attitude" because you hated work? Abusive relationships, debt and involvement in a crime or fraud are good examples. The deeper you are, the harder it is to extricate yourself. Take action while you can still see some sunlight at the top of the hole. Don't wait for the last shovel of dirt.

- *You get older.* You can't replace the years you lose when you defer a correct decision. This consideration is especially important for retirement planning decisions. Every year you don't save, the harder you will find it to meet your future needs. In contrast, if you implement a savings plan soon enough, you'll start feeling much more secure about your future after just a couple of years. If you are going to defer a Big Decision, make sure you know whether age will be on your side when you get to it.

- *Your habits become more ingrained.* Habits arise from doing something so often that it becomes natural. The longer you live with a bad situation, the more natural it seems as you become "habituated" (accustomed) to the situation. To some extent, this familiarity helps you cope. When you break out of a bad situation, you can start to break any bad habits you developed to cope.

If you suspect you're controlled by short-term thinking, go through the above list and ask if you're likely to suffer from any of those costs if you continue to sell out the long term.

Look at the positive side as well. Just as problems compound over time, so do solutions. If you start to save for retirement now, rather than waiting another five years, your retirement fund should be substantially larger when you retire. If you start your new career this year rather than in two years, you could be well-established in two years rather than fighting to get in the door. The same is true of education. It's a long road; get started. This is certain: You won't reach the end of the road before you reach the beginning. Likewise, the time you spend in a dead-end relationship is time that you could use to find a better relationship or at least enjoy the benefits (and incur any costs) of freedom from the current relationship.

Of course, the best long-term decision-making often does not involve leaving a bad situation or making any major change. If you constantly make small, but important, adjustments to your relationships and situations with an eye to the long term, you may not need to make a big change. The best long-term strategy often is to identify and repair a flawed situation. Don't be the one who moves from a divorce into a new relationship with the same problems as the old relationship. Don't leave a good job that has a few problems for a job that has lots of problems. The idea is to *improve!* Most personal relationships and jobs deliver a mixture of positives and negatives. Long-term decision-making makes full use of counseling, intervention and other techniques to separate permanent problems from temporary problems.

No-Win and No-Lose Decisions: Choosing the "Lesser of Evils" and the "Greater of Goods"

Some life decisions don't offer a "good" alternative. From time to time, you must choose among several options, all of which involve physical or emotional pain, financial burden or other detriment. These decisions are inherently difficult because any choice will cause some harm. If you're like most people, every instinct in your body wants to avoid harm, not choose it. What propels such decisions usually is that more harm will flow from the absence of a decision. The classic illustration is a choice between two painful medical treatments; both will cause pain, but the absence of treatment may be worse. The term "mercy killing" seeks to find the good (mercy) in a euthanasia decision. Few people who've participated in such decisions feel that much good is involved. Many end-of-life decisions are, at best, rocky compromises with fate. The decision to fight a war inevitably brings pain, hardship and loss—even to the victor. Brazen wars of conquest have been disfavored in the postcolonial world. Accordingly, contemporary wars typically are rationalized as the lesser of evils to defend against an enemy's threat.

If you're confronted with a lesser-of-evils decision, don't let fear of a rough choice freeze you. When consequences flow from doing nothing, indecision may be the worst of all evils. The choice is between managing the situation as best you can, or being devoured by whatever fate or chance deals you. Consider all of the alternatives, including the ones that cause pain. In many cases, the best decision will cause the most short-term pain, cost and inconvenience. Keep a very open mind as you go through the alternatives. Steps that you wouldn't take under normal circumstances may become viable, and even necessary, at this point in your life—such as changing your residence, pleading guilty to a crime, surgery, arming yourself, resigning from a position or declaring bankruptcy.

Consider a serious situation that repeats itself all too often:

Tara is in a bad domestic relationship with Paul. The relationship deteriorates, and Paul begins to threaten (or commit) violence against Tara. Tara is afraid, and a friend or family member advises her to seek a court order against Paul's harassment. Tara tells Paul that she's thinking about going to court. Paul threatens that if Tara gets a court order, Paul will kill or seriously hurt Tara and, to make the example more extreme, Tara's child. Adding credibility to the threat, Paul is stalking Tara and "acting crazy." Tara is reluctant to obtain a court order out of fear that Paul will carry out his threat. Tara believes a court order will only make things worse and will not protect Tara because she feels, "How can a court order stop a madman?"

The choice between evils is clear: If Tara goes without a court order, convincing law enforcement to intervene may be harder, and Tara loses a deterrent to Paul that could result from bringing in the law. If Tara obtains the court order, this action may indeed provoke Paul. Most people can't afford to move out of town and disappear for a time period. The situation is especially difficult when children are involved because an abused person may be prohibited from simply disappearing with a child. Tara must make a decision.

In the short term, Tara's reluctance to seek a court order has plenty of logic. Tara's reasoning is: "Without the order, Paul might try to hurt or kill me, but with the order Paul *most likely will* try to hurt or kill me." Tara leans toward choosing the apparent lesser evil of possible harm over what she perceives as probable harm. In the long term, however, if Tara is going to improve her life and get past Paul, she needs an approach that has a chance of making him stop. Doing nothing won't make Paul stop in most cases. In many cases, this decision requires a multifaceted strategy in which the following occur: (1) Tara demonstrates to Paul that Tara has legal remedies against Paul so Paul will not face Tara alone in any future confrontation. (2) Tara increases her personal protection to as high a level as possible. Depending on Tara's resources and capabilities, this protection may include new steps (arming herself, buying a guard dog, moving to a secure environment). (3) Tara demonstrates that she will not be defeated by Paul, starting with enforcement of a court order and full cooperation with law enforcement. Many people have been through what Tara is going through. Private and public resources are available in nearly every city to help people in Tara's position, which is among the most terrifying lesser-of-evils situations that a person can experience. One of the best pieces of advice to a person in an abusive relationship is to put away some money if at all possible. Some financial resources can make a huge difference.

Now let's look at a greater-of-goods decision:

> Connie has a high-paying job at an international investment bank. She receives regular promotions, challenging work, worldwide travel and a collegial work environment. Everyone agrees that it's a great job. Connie loves her job, but she also loves spending time with her young children and would like to have more family time. There is no reconciling Connie's job and her family; to continue getting the work Connie loves, she needs to be available every day and night, ready to travel at a moment's notice. Connie is becoming uncomfortable with the trade-off. Something has to give.

Connie needs to find the greater of two goods in the long term. Personal inertia probably will keep Connie going at the status quo for quite a while, but resentment (or frustration that she "can't do everything well") may start to build unless she reconciles the conflicting demands on her time. If unchecked, this resentment may lead to marital, work or even parenting problems. Connie probably needs to reassess the long-term picture, that is, the impact of time on all of the moving parts in her life. She also needs to do some soul-searching on what is *most* important to her in a situation that demands a choice.

How should Connie approach her career-plus-family decision? Surely more facts are needed. How old are Connie's children, and does she want to have more? What is Connie's living situation and financial condition (flexibility)? Is Connie close to a key career point, which might affect the timing of any change? What is the genuine attitude of Connie's employer toward work adjustments by employees who need increased family time? What are Connie's reentry options if she tilts her priorities toward family and sacrifices some advancement in the short term until her children are older? What other work options could Connie pursue in the short term that will offer much (or more!) of what Connie enjoys about her job?

When Connie completes her decision process, she may be surprised to find that very little on either the job or family front must be sacrificed forever. For the most part, Connie's career adjustments will merely rearrange when Connie experiences particular satisfactions in the long term. It will be helpful for Connie to get past a harsh career-vs.-family mentality and think of the choice as "tilt toward career right now vs. tilt toward family right now." Having it all is possible, but rarely all at the same time. Make time work in your favor.

The message of Step 7 is that you shouldn't let short-term pain derail your long-term plan. Just as what you are today is the consequence of the steps you took in the past, your future is built from today's decisions. Stop treating the future as "a big if" that might never arrive. Build your future piece by piece with long-term decisions. Learn to live on a budget that allows you to build for freedom in the future. Form lifelong bonds with other people who deserve a part in your life. Separate yourself from relationships, personal or business, that are destructive instead of constructive and productive. Risk adventuring into the unknown, especially if the known is not working for you.

Every good decision-maker has said on more than one occasion, "This isn't going to be fun. And it isn't going to be pretty. But it is the best step for the long term, so I am going to do it." The sense of self that you feel when you take control of your future is better than any shopping spree. Good decisions may require big sacrifices, tough conversations and deferred gratification. If you come to appreciate the long-term benefits of doing what's best, even with sacrifices today, those decisions will empower you to move your life a big step forward.

We leave Step 7 with the following points to remember about making decisions for the long term:

- Make decisions that advance your long-term plan, even if some short-term pain is involved.
- Determine the necessary stepping stones to meet your long-term objectives.
- Make decisions that advance you from stone to stone. Don't just hang around one stone and dream about jumping over all the rest in a single, glorious, improbable leap.
- Learn to derive satisfaction from your progress along the path.
- Be patient about reaching your objectives, but not about the steps you take along the path. Move from step to step with energy and a sense of personal immediacy.

Education: A Troubled Young Mother Makes a Choice to Come Back from the Edge of Society

*Terri Harris didn't want her children to grow up
on the same painful streets where she got her education.*

When Terri Harris[16] was young, her mother told Terri that she was special because she was adopted. After all, Terri's mother liked to tell her, Terri had been "selected." Terri's mother undoubtedly believed that Terri was special. In contrast, Terri's father wasn't interested in children, didn't want to bring Terri into the

---

[16]A pseudonym.

family and didn't have any interest in her. Terri's father was, as Terri puts it, "emotionally absent" from her childhood. Don't jump to conclusions about the Harris family's financial condition: Terri's father was an executive at a well-known corporation. Money was not a problem at the Harris home.

Terri might have come through her youth intact if she'd merely had a loving, caring mother and a father who didn't pay much attention. When Terri was eight, however, fate dealt her a cruel blow. Terri's mother became ill and was hospitalized. The original illness became complicated, and Terri's mother had additional lengthy hospitalizations. For the next eight years, Terri's mother was almost constantly hospitalized. Terri's father spent most of his nonwork hours at the hospital. Terri rarely saw her father when he left for work in the morning or at night when he returned from the hospital. The family crisis didn't cause Terri's father to reevaluate his feelings about parenthood. Indeed, Terri's father let Terri know she'd become even more of a burden. Terri became accustomed to his grumble, "I never wanted a goddamn child."

Terri felt twice abandoned: first by her biological parents, later by her adoptive parents. She was a bright, inquisitive little girl who lacked the most important ingredients of a stable, successful life. Terri had no love, no support, no companionship, no guidance and nobody to tell her who she was or could be. Terri recalls:

I was driven by unanswered questions that pertained to my existence. The fact that I was adopted only increased these feelings. My adolescence was in full swing by the age of thirteen. I experienced early puberty and became fascinated by the gawking response I'd get from male passersby as I waited for the school bus. I was initially uncertain why the men expressed such interest.

Over the next year, Terri discovered what gawking men were looking at. By the time Terri was fourteen, she was sexually active. Drugs also became a part of Terri's life and, for the first time, she found an advantage in her empty home: Terri could come and go as she pleased without the questions a concerned parent would ask. By the end of eighth grade, Terri had stopped going to school. In a short time, she was in and out of detention facilities:

I became very resentful and angry. My anger fueled a deliberate defiance. This led to a series of incarcerations. Although I didn't like being detained and labeled, for the first time I felt protected . . . protected by the incarceration. I had what I'd longed for: a structured routine. I had time to think and get to know myself. I felt relieved to be removed from my family. I learned that my anger was a source of power that could keep people at whatever distance I wanted. It gave me a sense of grandiosity. By the age of sixteen, I was the living definition of "hell on wheels"—angry, alone, defiant, uncaring about what others thought. I didn't think I was worthy of anything good. It seemed that nothing good had come to me so far.

When she was sixteen, one of Terri's consorts convinced her that she should profit from her sexual conduct. The "logic" led Terri to make the worst decision of her life: to sell her body for money. At seventeen, Terri gave birth to her first child. She wanted to have the baby. She had a burning desire to have a genetic relative, and now she'd made one:

Three months before my eighteenth birthday, I gave birth to my first child. Finally, I thought, here is another human being with whom I share a bloodline. I didn't concern myself with the role of the father, as I saw this as a small detail not worthy of consideration. I had two more children by the time I was twenty-four.

In her early twenties, while Terri lived in a phony world of luxury cars, furs, expensive meals and lavish trips, she had no self-respect, no stability, no freedom and little to look forward to. At twenty-four, Terri wanted to make a long-term change, but it took a message from her child to commit to do it:

I had been in a turbulent relationship. My first child, who was then six, saw me bruised from head to toe and drenched in tears. She looked at me so innocently and said, "Why do you let him hurt you? Please don't cry." I was ashamed and humiliated at what I allowed my child to witness. "Look at the environment I have created for this child," I thought. She didn't feel secure. I was doing to my little girl what my father had done to me. It made me think about the direct correlation between the choices I'd made and the consequences I endured. I became empowered by the reality that I had something to do with how things turned out. My first child was now a little person. This required me to act both responsibly and as a role model. From that moment, I wanted to change the entire direction of my life. I realized I still had a choice.

Once Terri vowed to change her life's direction, Terri's commitment to her long-term plan was total:

I took the defiance and the steam that were within me, which made me so angry, and I turned them into a passion to build a life that would be regarded with respect, of which I could be proud. I didn't want to live a less-than-respectable life anymore. I knew it would take a long time, a lot of effort and a lot of sacrifice. But I had to start. I knew I had to be fearless. That's where not being driven by what other people thought was a benefit to me. It became critical later on. Much of what I did, other people told me I could never do after the life I'd led.

Terri had no skills to form the basis for a new life. She'd left school in eighth grade. She'd had run-ins with the law. She had three children, from six months to six years old. She wasn't married and had no source of financial support. What appeared before Terri was a very, very long road with guaranteed frustration. Yet, Terri didn't doubt she'd succeed. Terri's first step was to accept responsibility—for getting into her position and for getting out:

I struggled to accept the position I was in. I came to understand that as a result of poor choices, impulsive behavior, a lack of self-regard and the thrill of living in the face of danger, I'd created a terrible destiny for myself. I could use my childhood to explain what had happened, but that wouldn't help me out of where I was in life. I made a promise to myself, and indirectly to my children, that by the age of forty I would no longer be struggling to survive. I accepted that the next fifteen years would be a period of self-sacrifice and a type of absolution.

Terri gave up a life of easy money and high living on the fringes. She enrolled in community college to finish her education. For two years she received state financial support for her children. That was humiliating, but it was necessary. Terri's children needed medical coverage. Terri struggled through low-paying part-time jobs, lived in tiny apartments and barely made enough to pay basic living expenses. It was far from how Terri had been living, but she began to regain her self-respect. She cried sometimes, but never forgot her vow and never sacrificed her progress.

It took Terri two years to receive her A.A. degree. Four years later, Terri earned her B.A. degree in humanities, while holding multiple jobs and raising three children. Six years later, Terri received a second B.A. in business administration.

Terri chose a career in the criminal-justice system, counseling and assessing serious law-breakers. Terri's style is no-nonsense. Each day, men and women come into Terri's office (or she visits them in jail) and talk about criminal life. They like to tell Terri that she simply doesn't understand them, that she's just part of "the system." They tell Terri how abused, neglected and misunderstood they are. She hears how their parents failed them and caused it all.

Terri listens patiently. She knows there's truth to it. Neglectful parents cause kids to go in the wrong direction. Terri knows it's the parents' fault when kids are allowed to go off track, and nobody is around to guide them back. But when the person on the other side of her desk finishes his speech by telling Terri that he doesn't have a choice anymore about which direction to go in life, Terri looks straight into his eyes. "Bullshit," Terri Harris says. "That's where you're wrong."

Postscript: In Terri's Own Words

I reached my original goal—to become educated and mainstream—by forty. In fact, I was pretty much there at thirty-two when I got my first B.A. degree. I feel good about how far I've come.

One of my goals as a woman approaching middle age is to further develop my tolerance and understanding of humans and why they are so imperfect. In my youth, I assumed that all the people in the mainstream community were ethical and law-abiding. I can understand broken laws on the street much better than I understand the kinds of crimes that CEOs and other college grads commit. It fascinates me.

As I get older, my big desire is to leave something of myself in the world. I see my children as a kind of contribution to the world. I believe strongly in their abilities and fortitude. My relationship with my own kids is far from perfect. My oldest daughter went to a major university. She's goal-oriented and analytical. We grew up together. In a way, she represents my past, present and future all put together. Because of it, there's friction between us sometimes. My two grown children always assert their independence by challenging my opinions. When they were younger, they claimed I was the strictest parent in the universe. It was definitely true.

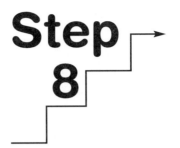

Step 8

Time, Time, Time—Be a Brilliant Procrastinator

Never do today what you can put off till tomorrow if tomorrow might improve the odds.

—Robert A. Heinlein

My evil genius Procrastination has whispered me to tarry 'til a more convenient season.

—Mary Todd Lincoln

One of the biggest misconceptions about decision-making is that a decisive person makes rapid-fire, on-the-spot decisions. The word "decisive" means firm or resolute. A decisive person is one who does not lightly waver once he or she has made a choice. Neither a decisive person nor a great decision-maker must work with lightning speed. The amount of time you spend to make a decision affects the quality of the decision. Some decisions should be made quickly; others *must* be made quickly. Many decisions, however, can and should be delayed for a period

193

of time. In fact, some decisions must be delayed, or you'll invite a disastrous result. In many situations, your most important decision is whether to make a decision at all—or when to make it.

In Step 1, we showed how a Big Decision initially may present itself as a decoy. In the same way, the time for you to make a Big Decision may not be presented accurately. You need to figure it out. Two factors drive the timing of a decision: (1) the situation and (2) you. "The situation" includes all aspects of the decision that are affected by when a decision is made, including offers and opportunities that may disappear, deadlines, costs connected with a delay (for example, interest, a financial penalty) and other time-sensitive factors. "You" includes all of the personal factors—personality, emotion, convenience and preference—that impel you to decide now or later.

Step 8 shows you that you can actively manage the timing of a Big Decision to improve the likelihood that you'll make a great decision. Step 8 explores the difference between "tactical procrastination" and "procrastination because you can't make a decision." Tactical procrastination is an intentional delay that you impose to help make a better decision. Procrastination because of obsessiveness, insecurity, fear or other incapacity is a decision-making barrier.

Tactical Procrastination: Deciding to Put Off the Big Decision

Experienced decision-makers are able to make sound judgments in a rapid time frame—if necessary. The same decision-makers know how to avoid, delay, stall, prolong and defer a decision beyond when other people think the decision "should" be made. Robert's Rules of Order, which govern formal parliamentary procedure in vast parts of the world, provide abundant tools for legislators to table (defer) an issue. Often, more matters are tabled than voted upon. If you've ever watched *The West Wing* or another semirealistic treatment of leadership, you've seen a leader presented with loads of items that seem to require action. Yet the leader says "pass," "next," "not now" and "later" after many items that seem to be pretty important. At other times, the leader hears out his trusted advisors, then dismisses them without a decision. Why?

Skilled decision-makers know that a premature decision may be much worse than no decision. A decision is premature if it's made with poor information when better information could be obtained without an unreasonable cost or harmful delay. A premature decision is one that is made before resolution of a separate situation that may affect the decision, if waiting for the separate situation to be resolved will not cause major harm. A premature decision is one that is forced on the spot, when the decision-maker really needs more time to think about it, to obtain input or perhaps just to get some sleep. A premature decision is one that takes precious time away from a more important decision, when this one "can wait."

Premature decisions have many drawbacks. Decisions that are made with sketchy information are less likely to be correct. Pride-driven decision-makers may be slow to change course, even after a basic assumption behind a decision clearly turns out to be flawed. This can create a situation in which a bad decision is made too soon, then is corrected too late. A premature decision also may consume unnecessary time and energy. You'd be surprised at how many so-called "pressing decisions" simply go away if they're deferred. In some cases, a little benign neglect can work much better than action. "Let's just wait and see what happens" can be very powerful words. In the wrong situation, of course, a failure to take immediate action may turn a minor problem into a major problem. The decision-maker's true skill is tested when she decides which approach is correct. Finally, decisions that are made quickly, impulsively or in a highly emotional context may over-emphasize short-term factors, such as temporary feelings and out-side pressure.

Every important decision has its time. The time may be today, tomorrow or yesterday. It may be a month or a year from now. It may be a decade from now or never. Learn when to decide not to decide.

Examples of Tactical Procrastination

Over the past quarter-century, U.S. policy with respect to the defense of Taiwan has been a fascinating example of tactical delay in making a decision. While the United States clearly supports Taiwan's independence, the United States has left ambiguous where the edges of its support lie. Would the United States send troops to defend Taiwan? Shoot missiles at China? Use nuclear weapons? U.S. policy often is called "strategic ambiguity." The United States undoubtedly has a variety of military contingency plans. The United States knows its options if circumstances warrant action. The precise response would depend on a huge number of factors, including the nature of the challenge to Taiwan, the U.S. relationship with the parties, the issue in dispute, and the opinions and assistance of the rest of the world community. Publicly, the United States has decided not to decide right now—not because U.S. leaders are especially indecisive, but because not deciding may serve U.S. objectives better than a firm decision. Part of the theory of strategic ambiguity is that the ambiguity causes China to make conservative assumptions about the U.S. response (in other words, to assume that *all* options are on the table). This tactical-delay policy has been in effect for more than twenty-five years.

Personal decision-making may require you to take time that cannot be measured in days or even months. Putting a decision off until later may be the best decision you make. Some of the smartest words ever uttered are "I am not ready for _____." You fill in the blank: (1) marriage, (2) marriage to you, (3) a child, (4) an intimate relationship, (5) you to move in, (6) alcohol or drugs, (7) "anything else you want me to do that isn't right for me now."

Sharon Thom, an experienced spiritual practitioner and grief counselor whose views on intuition in decision-making are considered in the final chapter of this book, incorporates timing into the analysis when she helps a client face a major decision. Thom asks clients these questions:

- Do you believe what you want to do is possible?
- Do you want it for yourself?
- Are you ready?

Saying that you're not ready to make a Big Decision usually is a sign of great strength, maturity and self-confidence, rather than a sign of "weakness." A weak person may not have the courage or self-esteem to resist another person's entreaties—even those that will quickly and predictably lead to all kinds of harms and disadvantages. Of course, if you know you will *never* marry a certain person or do something else that someone wants you to do, procrastination and excuse-making can be cruel, selfish and pointless. While you may think you're saving the other person from hurt feelings or other pain, you're simply denying the other person the right to move forward with his or her life. For this reason, you should use deferral honestly in your personal life. You may be deferring other lives as well.[17]

Shifting from personal to business illustrations, let's look at

---

[17] If you tend to "just go along" with what other people want in situations when you should say "no," you need to learn refusal skills. Refusals skills are how to say "no." Many schools now teach refusal skills as a way to combat child abuse, date rape, drug use and other social problems.

how venture capitalists commonly harness the value of putting it off. Consider a start-up company that goes to a venture capitalist with a two-year budget that requires $6 million to develop, design and launch a product. Will the business get $6 million? There's a very good chance it will not, even if the business receives funding from the venture investor. A common strategy is for the venture investor to make an initial funding (perhaps $1 million) and reserve the right to decide on later fundings as events progress and milestones are reached. This approach allows the venture investor to make a smaller decision today and defer the rest. What the investor hopes to gain in the interim is more information about the company's chances of succeeding before the investor puts more funds at risk.

Business offers many chances to act too quickly or too slowly. Others with strong vested financial interests will push and pull your business mercilessly, often with a tenacious team of executives and salespeople. Businesses need to control, as much as possible, the timing of their decisions. In today's competitive environment, a business that defers decisions that should be made today is clearly at a disadvantage. Businesses that make decisions too hastily, driven by fads, waste a lot of time and money. A business must have processes in place to ensure that managers who have a handle on the importance of timing address important decisions. A basic technique is for a company to have "escalate" policies—guidelines in each department for when employees should take a decision or a situation to a more experienced manager.

Remember that the timing of each decision is unique. The best time for you to make your own Big Decision may be different from someone else's time to make the same decision. Putting a decision off is a totally legitimate tactic. When procrastination can help you make a better decision, use it. When it won't, don't abuse it . . . move forward.

How Do You Know When to Make a Decision?

Challenge the timing of major decisions that are presented to you. Learn who and what are driving the timing of the decision. Decisions to administer emergency medical treatment, to use deadly force in self-defense and to respond to other classic emergencies obviously don't allow the luxury of significant delay. The situation drives the timing of these decisions. You can't do much to change it. On many occasions, however, the decision is not as urgent as you initially think. Other people may tell you a decision is urgent (or unimportant) because they have an interest in an especially fast or slow decision from you. Don't blindly buy into the timetables that other people set. Figure out what works for you and try to establish that as the timing.

Here are three areas in which the parties to a decision frequently have conflicting timetables:

Marriage and Children. Couples often are at odds about the timing of a marriage decision. The discussion typically centers around age, health, values, and attitudes toward marriage, family and children, career status, career objectives, current financial resources and financial goals—not necessarily in this order! Many times, the Big Decision is actually the culmination of a series of decisions. *Am I ready to think about marriage? Are we ready to talk openly about marriage? Is it time to get engaged? If my partner wants to get married, when should I decide? If we get engaged, how long should we allow before the wedding?* What is too soon, too fast and too pressured for one person may be too late, too slow and too slack for the other.

The same is true of parenthood. Couples may go for years without seriously discussing children, beyond early screening questions along the lines of, "Sure, I want children someday. How about you?" In early years, a couple may focus on their relationship and perhaps education or careers. As time passes, discussions start to occur about when to have children. Both parties want to reach a consensus, in theory, but the road is often long. The transition from a couple-centered life to a family-centered life may require years of development and adjustment. The parties often don't reach the same point at the same time.

If a marriage or parenthood decision is pressuring you, think about whether the pressure exists mostly because you and your partner have different timetables. Once you identify timing as the issue, try to understand and communicate honestly about the timing. Quite often, the difference is completely well-intentioned. Matthew wants to start having children now. Denise wants to put it off because she does not feel confident about the family's financial status. Both want the best for the family. Once both parties understand that their differences are well-intentioned, they can get down to nuts and bolts: creating a plan to get Denise comfortable with the family finances and begin having kids.

Career. Many career decisions seem to present a tension between the Forces of Patience and the Forces of Boldness. The Forces of Patience tell you to stay the course and that good things come to those who wait. The Forces of Patience, often represented by your current employer, set the timetable for your progress based on what the employer needs and when. The Forces of Patience exhort you to "Stay on track!" The employer defines what is on track. Even if you're on the fast track, the employer defines the fast track, too. You typically must adapt your schedule to the institution's. It won't adapt much to you.

The Forces of Boldness are impatient, perhaps frustrated, with whatever track exists. The Forces of Boldness want to risk the benefits offered by the track for the possible greater benefits of rapid, self-determined progress. More often than not, the Forces of Boldness start inside you. Harvard accepted Bill Gates and would have kept him there "on track" for four years. Gates made the decision to leave. Cal State Long Beach didn't tell Steven Spielberg to quit before he earned his degree (the USC film school wouldn't take him in the first place). Spielberg decided it was time to go make real movies.[18] When a successful employee leaves one position to make a lateral move, it's usually not because the current employer thinks it's time. Such a move is designed to speed up the employee's career by moving over and up to a level that is several steps ahead on the career track. Improving your compensation dramatically without making a few well-timed lateral career moves is often difficult. While having a successful career at one company is possible, lateral moves often create opportunities where compensation is concerned.

That being said, boldness does not always triumph over patience. For every Gates, Spielberg, Faulkner, Jobs and Fitzgerald (F. Scott) who dropped out and made it, a few million people who you've never heard of—and never will—boldly jettisoned the slow and steady track only to find that life off the track can be tougher and slower.

Whether Patience or Boldness should prevail in your career decision depends on where the other 10-Plus-1 Steps lead. Step 8 simply asks you to recognize that the timetable set by the Forces of Patience may be protecting institutional interests. Your own interests may lie in a more accelerated approach to a decision, on a timetable set by the Forces of Boldness.

Company Takeovers. A difference in opinion on timing often arises for employees when one company buys another company. Employees of the acquired company are very interested in moving employee issues to the top of the buyer's agenda. After all, the acquisition could have a huge impact on the employees' lives, including where they work and live and how much they're paid.

---

[18] Spielberg returned to Cal State Long Beach thirty years later to complete his bachelor's degree.

The career track suddenly is redefined, which is a matter of great concern to all who are on it. For the buyer company, though, matters related to employees end up lower on the list, with financial matters, legal matters, public relations and other issues taking the front seat. This situation becomes awkward for employees of the sold company, who may feel like ships without rudders until they can force the issue. This difference in perception often causes a tug-of-war for the buyer's attention. Lacking legal leverage, employees often rightfully pursue a squeaky-wheel strategy to get noticed.

Certainly in the above situations, your antennae should be up for timing-related conflicts. In all situations, consider the possibility that your decision schedule may differ from that of someone else in the picture. Before you become frustrated that someone else "just won't focus," take a moment to figure out his timing concerns.

How to Put Off a Decision and Why Sleeping on It Works

You may be concerned that delaying a Big Decision, even for all the right reasons, will earn you a negative reputation as a procrastinator. It won't, and it shouldn't. Don't tell people, "I just can't make up my mind on this," or "I'm stumped. Gosh this is a toughie, way beyond what my brain can handle." You don't have to be embarrassed about taking time to make a Big Decision. Tell people, "I need to explore a few matters before I decide this. Let's come back to it in a few days." Or, if you can make only part of the decision, say, "I can go with part one of what you want. As for part two, I don't see any reason to decide that right now. We're going to know a lot more next week when we talk to Helen from XYZ about what she's doing. Let's just get part one rolling right now." A well-executed delay demonstrates that you appreciate the subtleties in each decision.

We've all told people that we want to "sleep on it" or "take the weekend" before making a decision. The connection between sleep and decisions is partly physiological. Sleep has a proven impact on judgment. Sleep deprivation impairs judgment. You clearly should try not to make a Big Decision in a sleep-deprived state. Sometimes, however, you should sleep on a decision even when you're not sleep-deprived. Sleep and dreaming reduce stress. The passage of time, even if it's just overnight, may make issues clearer by giving you some distance from the pressures of the moment. You've looked at the situation in today's mood, but how about tomorrow's? What was unbearable today is something you may endure and see with more clarity tomorrow. Practice asking yourself in the morning, *How do I feel about the decision now? Has anything changed overnight in my thinking?* Although sleep may not resolve the big issue, a partial decision may be ready: "Yes, I will take the time to talk to a counselor before I go any further," or "I will not spend more than $225,000 on the house, no matter how the rest of the negotiations go. I can walk away from it."

The benefit of sleeping on it is universally recognized. The English, Irish, French, Danish, Spanish, Italians, Swiss, Germans, Russians, Chinese and other cultures have expressions that mean, in essence, "If you sleep on it, you'll make a better decision." American novelist John Steinbeck observed, "It is a common experience that a problem difficult at night is resolved in the morning after the committee of sleep has worked on it." A Danish proverb puts it more simply: "The best advice is found on the pillow." Eighteenth-century British author Horace Walpole was correct (if not concise) when he observed a connection between sleep and sound judgment:

The sure way of judging whether our first thoughts are judicious is to sleep on them. If they appear of the same force the next morning as they did overnight, and if good nature ratifies what good sense approves, we may be pretty sure we are in the right.

Four centuries earlier, Leonardo da Vinci commented on the relationship between relaxation and judgment:

Every now and then, go away, have a little relaxation, for when you come back to your work your judgment will be surer, since to remain constantly at work, you lose power of judgment. Go some distance away because then the work appears smaller and more of it can be taken in at a glance and a lack of harmony or proportion is more readily seen.

Unless disaster will happen today, it won't hurt to ask the waiting world for the courtesy of a night's sleep before you make a Big Decision. If a true emergency is not involved, and someone else denies your request for a day, be suspicious of that person's motives.

Skills for Emergency Decision-Making

You'll inevitably face situations in which you must make a Big Decision quickly. Even so, there is *quick,* and there is quick. A job offer that expires in forty-eight hours must be analyzed quickly compared to a decision about which of several colleges to attend. A decision whether to loan bail money to a friend or employee must be made more quickly. A decision whether to try to save someone from a burning building must be made almost instantaneously.

In a true emergency, such as when your life is in danger or other extreme factors exist, you may experience instinctual physical and emotional responses. Your fight-or-flight responses may cause your heart and mind to work much faster than usual as your body generates a surge of adrenaline. In earlier evolution, the fight-or-flight response gave humans the resources necessary to protect themselves from physical threats or attacks. In developed society, where physical danger is less constant, fight-or-flight responses often come into play during psychological threats or attacks.

Studies have shown that the fight-or-flight mechanism affects the way the mind processes information. For evolutionary reasons, when a human perceives a fight-or-flight-level threat, the mind becomes increasingly efficient at responding to danger. The body shuts down unnecessary bodily functions and devotes itself to assessing the danger and responding to it with a "fight" or a "flight." This response allows rapid evaluation of a large number of stimuli as your mind sizes up the threat, considers response options and takes responsive action. The human factor manifests itself in the details. Just as everyone has a different ability to manage in calm circumstances, people vary widely in how well they manage a physical or psychological attack.

A lengthy laundry list of considerations would not be helpful for dire emergencies. Advice to emergency workers, who must respond to unexpected, immediate threats of serious personal harm more often than most people, typically incorporates the following principles of quick-response decision-making:

1. Protect yourself as much as possible by moving to a place of comparatively less danger.
2. Request assistance as soon as you can do so.
3. Follow procedures that were established before the emergency unless inappropriate. (This creates a presumption that pre-planned procedures are sound, although circumstances that make the procedures inappropriate may exist and warrant an alternate response. In other words, if your standard fire procedure is to go out the side door, you may go out the front door if the side door is on fire.)

If you can influence the pace of events, consider whether you are able to freeze or slow down an emergency situation. A classic example is the Federal Aviation Administration's decision to ground airplanes and close airspace over the United States almost instantly after the September 11 attacks. Clearly there was an emergency, but the precise nature and scope were uncertain at the outset. The attacks involved multiple airplanes that appeared to have been commandeered and intentionally crashed into landmark buildings. The immediate response was to ground all planes: Planes that are on the ground can't be used to crash into landmarks. Next, move the key decision-makers to safety: Put the president on Air Force One and protect Air Force One, a place of comparatively less danger. Protect other key leaders as well. Finally, activate systems and procedures that were set up to respond to emergencies, especially communication channels and an emergency decision-making command chain.

A more common example occurs when you're driving along the freeway at sixty miles per hour, and you suddenly see something strange going on just ahead. Cars are swerving or skidding, and you see red taillights and maybe smoke from skidding tires. What is the first thing you do? You slow down to create more response time and reduce your personal exposure to the risk. You focus on the situation, scanning the road, looking for the source of the problem. Having given yourself more time to address the situation, you focus all of your attention on it until you understand it. Then you "do what you're supposed to do" given the type of situation. Because your mind becomes more alert during emergencies, you are able to use the few additional seconds you created when you slowed down more efficiently than in normal conditions.

Of course, you should not respond slowly to a dire emergency. You should respond quickly to a dire emergency, but you often will benefit if you can buy even a small amount of time to structure your response.

Many situations do not involve a dire emergency, but still require a fast decision. If you're fully equipped to make the decision, an accelerated schedule may present no problem. The problem arises when you feel both pressured and out of your league. In such circumstances, you need to evaluate the following factors before acting:

1. Is there so much immediacy to the problem that it would be harmful to defer action? In other words, is this a real emergency or something that can be put off for some time?
2. If you don't do anything right now, is there a serious danger that something will happen that can't be fixed later?
3. Will you risk more harm by not acting at all than by taking some amount of possibly incorrect action now?

If the answer to each of these questions is "yes," you probably need to take some action. When you do, take action that will solve the urgent part of the problem; buy time and seek guidance as soon as possible. If your decision is wrong, chances are the sooner it is corrected, the less damage there will be. If you lack knowledge in an area, you may know little about your options. Therefore, keep your options open as much as possible. Here's an example of how to manage a rapidly developing workplace issue for which you are largely unprepared:

> You've just been promoted to supervisor of a corporate department. You have never been a supervisor before. It's your first day on the new job, and a female employee comes into your office and reports that a male coworker is sexually harassing her. She asks that he be fired because she "can't take it anymore." You call in the male employee privately and inform him of the allegation. He tells you that he was dating the female employee, but broke it off. She became enraged and promised that she would "get even." You don't know whom to believe. You call in the female employee and advise her that the allegation was denied. The female employee says that unless the male worker is terminated "today," she will quit and pursue "a multimillion-dollar sexual-harassment suit." She says she is

"shocked that the company is tolerating sexual harassment." The male employee tells you that if he's terminated, he'll sue for slander and discrimination.

Congrats on the job promotion. The female employee has set a timetable that you can't meet. You don't want to take action against the male employee until an investigation reaches at least a preliminary conclusion he's at fault. The female employee's ultimatum seems firm. The situation clearly passes the three-question test; you must do *something*. What can you do to bring the situation to a much more comfortable place?

Certainly, a potential harassment/discrimination claim should send you to your superiors, your company's legal counsel or both. Most businesses would require a legal threat to be escalated. Your first decision is not to handle this situation on your own. It's very delicate, and you don't know all the rules and approaches that might apply. If your company's standing policy is to speak immediately with the company's attorney, you should adhere to that policy. Let's say, however, that the harassment issue reaches your desk at 6:30 P.M. and counsel is unavailable. You try to call two of your superiors but cannot reach them. What do you do?

You Defuse the Dynamite, Freeze the Facts and Defer the Decision until you reach higher ground:

Defuse the Dynamite. Remind both employees that you just became aware of the situation, and company policy requires you to bring it to the attention of the company's attorney. The attorney cannot be reached. Given that it's the end of the day, you suggest that both employees go home. Make sure you have the home numbers of the employees with you and leave your number with the company's counsel so you can hear some advice as soon as possible. Assure both employees that you'll do everything possible to respond promptly.

Tell the employees that if one or both feel uncomfortable coming to work tomorrow until a more definitive conclusion is reached, he or she should stay at home on standby tomorrow morning. If one of the employees must be at work for the business to function, arrange for the other employee to be on paid standby until further notice, to work very temporarily at a different location or perhaps to take a paid morning off to give you time to consult counsel. If both employees must work together and can't be replaced on short notice, you might want to come up with a way to supervise their work together.

You'll have much more advice, support and clarity tomorrow morning. If someone overrides your decision to allow employees to stay home, that decision can be undone at little cost. You rarely will be chastised for overcautiousness in matters of legal liability. Compare the cost of a lawsuit with the cost of an employee coming late to work one morning.

Freeze the Facts. Tell the employees that you've been presented with conflicting facts, and you must proceed in a way that's fair to everyone. You expect both of them to cooperate. Consistent with your company's policy, you may want to advise the employees to preserve any evidence, such as e-mail, that is relevant to the dispute.

Defer the Decision. You've already made a number of interim decisions. None of these decisions, however, resolves the original situation presented to you. You preserved the status quo as much as possible while you waited to hear from superiors or legal counsel, while protecting all parties' rights and the company. You made the decisions you needed to make to buy critical time. Once the immediate crisis has passed, keep up your efforts to bring in other people to manage the situation. If you compare these steps to the response steps above that apply to dire emergencies, you'll see that the tactics are identical. Get safe; call for help; follow procedure. It's only a matter of degree.

Move Forward, Even If You Wait to Make Your Big Decision

Don't use the fact that you're deferring a Big Decision to justify a state of total paralysis. Move forward! In many cases, *all* your options will require you to take the identical next step. So take it. C. E. James, the entrepreneur-turned-technology executive, would rather have a team risk a little waste than sit idle, waiting for a final decision to materialize:

> Someone sitting at a desk, waiting for something, is a total waste. And so I think that when you look at your alternatives, you can in many cases start down a path—what seems like the more reasonable path—even if you have not made the final decision. Now you're ahead of everyone else, ahead of the game, ahead of the market, because you started the process. You can call it a "step" decision, or say you've set your general direction and you're willing to change it and adjust as you go along. I find those to be the most rewarding situations: the situations when I have not had full information and made a decision knowing it might be changed as I went along. A week later, I may have wasted a day's worth of work, but gained four.

Reflecting his entrepreneurial heritage, James's approach might strike some corporate decision-makers as chaotic. An entrepreneur knows that you sometimes must act without full information. Each exhaustive analysis of a decision is costly in time and money. An entrepreneur must pull the most out of the resources for which she's already paid (such as employees). This approach requires a culture of action, in which most analysis is done in real time. If James's protocol seems chaotic, it's chaos borne of reality in certain stages of a venture, which is not just true in business. You likely have similar constraints in your personal life: uncertain prospects, limited resources and a need to advance your cause.

The life lesson from the entrepreneur's world is to keep moving forward. Don't put your whole life on hold while you sort out one piece of the puzzle. If you have a decision that can be made today, make it today. If you can take a step to advance your cause today, no matter which direction the Big Decision will take, go ahead and take that step.

We leave Step 8 with the following points to remember about timing your decision:

- Timing is a part of most, if not all, decisions and should specifically be considered.
- Don't assume that now is the best time to make a decision. The better approach may be to make a decision when more facts are available or a related situation has worked out.
- Emergency decisions are undesirable and, if possible, you should slow down the situation while protecting yourself and marshaling as much assistance as you can.
- Nobody makes a decision with *all* of the facts. Don't use a lack of information as an excuse to avoid an unpleasant or painful decision.
- If you decide to defer a decision, perhaps until you have more facts or a related situation works out, keep moving forward. Don't wait to do things that should be done now. Be willing to accept some wasted effort for the sake of making progress during the time you'll lose if you defer the Big Decision until a later date.

Sexual Orientation: Timing a Decision to Come Out as Gay or Lesbian Is Complex with Friends, Family and Career Involved

Jen Dennis comes out in steps over twenty years as she and society become more comfortable with Jen's personal choices.

Jen Dennis[19] was born in Michigan and raised in a Catholic family. She is now in her early forties. In mid-1981, Jen finished her freshman year at Michigan State and was looking for a summer job. Like most college freshmen, Jen had an active social life. She dated several men in her freshman year and never questioned her sexual preference. Brought up conservatively, Jen had never, to her knowledge, socialized with a gay or lesbian person.

During her freshman summer, Jen applied for a job as an intramural softball league umpire. Jen got the job, and she began to meet and work with a group of women who were sports referees and umpires. Jen hit it off with this group. Although she didn't drink, as did these women who were mostly juniors and seniors, Jen felt comfortable in the group and liked the way they interacted. They played sports together, had parties together and socialized together. Jen felt a certain genuineness about these women. Jen found herself thinking, *I've been looking all my life for a group like this.* Jen had no idea they were lesbians.

One night, Jen's new friends threw a small party. During the party, one of Jen's friends showed her a trophy that she and some of the others recently had won at

---

[19] The names in this story are pseudonyms.

a softball tournament. The trophy was engraved, "Winner, Women's First Place, Gay Softball League." The shock must have shown on Jen's face. "Did you know we were gay?" Jen's friend asked, laughing. "Oh, of course!" Jen lied poorly. Jen recalls vividly what happened next:

I went on as if nothing was different until I could get back to my dorm room. I went into shock. I was immobilized for twenty-four hours. I literally laid on the floor of my dorm room. I had so much in common with these women. I felt that this must say something about me—something I had been completely unaware of. It had never occurred to me in my life that I might be gay.

Jen spent the rest of the summer with her new friends. For Jen, it was a time of experimentation and, ultimately, crisis. Jen kissed a woman for the first time. Yet when Jen's friends took her to her first gay bar, Jen met a guy and kissed him. Jen started a romantic relationship with another woman, Tracy. The relationship ended when Tracy moved out of state.

Jen went home at the end of the summer and told her parents what had happened in her personal life—and that she was in an emotional crisis. Jen recalls that first visit home:

I was close to my mom. I was not a particularly rebellious teenager. I told my mother that I had met a group of gay women at school, and I had kissed a woman. I cried. I told her I was unable to handle it. I was emotionally stuck. My mother was not supportive. She seemed angry. I don't know if she was angry at me or at the people I was hanging out with at school. My parents sent me to a counselor who would provide therapy from a Catholic perspective. I felt that if I was gay, my options were to deny it and

fake my life—which meant get married and have kids—or alco-
holism or suicide. I was raised a Roman Catholic. I was very into
church when I grew up. I listened carefully to the sermons. I was
not aware of anybody who lived his or her adult life as a gay per-
son. I believed I needed counseling. I knew I had these feelings,
and I didn't want them. I thought therapy would help me over-
come them.

The therapist didn't try to convince Jen that she
wasn't gay or even talk about religion. "The therapy was
about coping, dealing with the fact that I was freaked
out and talking about suicide," Jen says. After a year of
therapy, Jen considered herself not gay anymore. Jen
told the therapist that she had moved past her feelings.
Jen almost believed it. She didn't socialize with her gay
friends during her sophomore year. She avoided them.
During one of her last therapy sessions, Jen commented,
"I am sure I will run into these issues again." "Yeah, I
think you will," was the therapist's response. Both comments were foretelling.

For three years of college, Jen felt as if she was "in an
emotional fog and a struggle." She painted her fingernails,
which she had rarely done before, to be "very heterosexual." There was no hanging out with lesbians. No gay
bars. No gay parties. She dated men. "At the time, I
believed that if I could avoid those people, I would be a heterosexual. If I hung out with them, I felt I would not be
able to separate myself from their lifestyle. They had a
lifestyle I wanted, and they had emotional relationships
that I wanted." Jen now believes she tried so desperately to
be heterosexual in college at least in part for her parents:

There was a part of me that felt that, while I was in college, I
shouldn't be gay. My parents were putting me through college.

Because I was accepting support from them, I shouldn't disappoint them. I shouldn't betray their trust. They didn't impose that on me, but that's the way I thought about it. I thought I owed it to them not to be a lesbian while they were putting me through college. During that summer when I was hanging out with the lesbian women, I lied to my parents. I had let them down. I also was afraid about possibly being cut off, as others I knew had been. They hadn't done anything like that before, but I did have some economic fear along those lines.

Things changed the day college was over. At the end of Jen's senior year, the intramural referee squad threw a senior party and invited several past members of the squad. Now Jen was finished with school. At the party, Jen saw Tracy for the first time since their breakup:

That party was a turning point. When I saw Tracy, I thought to myself, "I have wasted three years. I am a fool if I think this is not who I am. I am done pretending." The last three years hadn't been terrible, but they were fake. I dated men I didn't care about. They cared more about going out with me than I cared about them. This was very unfair to them. Where other people did things naturally, I had to think hard about how to act on a date. I wasn't looking to get married. I spent a lot of energy trying to be like other people. I watched what other people did, and I tried to dress like them and act like them. I tried really hard to be the same as they were. The only time I didn't feel like that was that first summer.

Jen describes feelings of relief, freedom and fear when she "came out to herself" at the party. Jen says the relief came from not having to pretend she was someone else anymore. The sense of freedom, according to Jen, came from being able to live life as she believed she was meant to live it. Nonetheless, Jen feared rejection by her family and friends, and she feared that she would not be accepted by the gay and lesbian community. After all, she'd rejected her lesbian friends—even shunned them. Jen also felt guilt that her family would have to deal with people who might look down on her parents because they had a lesbian daughter. When Jen came out, she lost her guilt about being a lesbian and acquired guilt about what her family might go through.

Jen came out to Tracy at the year-end party. Jen didn't tell her straight friends at that point. It was too soon. Jen needed time to adjust before she was ready to risk others' rejection. During the summer, Jen decided she would leave Michigan to live with Tracy on the West Coast. Jen told her parents she was going to live with some friends from college. Jen's parents probably knew Jen was going to live with Tracy, but they didn't ask. Jen didn't tell.

The week before Jen left Michigan, she told two of her closest, straight college friends she was gay:

I told them, "I'm moving to California, and I'm moving in with Tracy. I'm gay. I thought you should know." I knew that if I left Michigan and didn't tell them, I would never communicate with them again, because that was going to be my life. My decision was, "Do I tell you and include you in my life, and give you the opportunity to live in my new life, or not?" I wanted them in my life. One of them said, "I totally don't get it, and I don't care. I'm glad that you're happy." The other one said, "I don't understand it, and I think you're making a big mistake. But you're my friend, and I love you." She'd experimented with it in high school and thought it was something you outgrow. She didn't think there was such things as gay and lesbian people. She saw me date men. My friends were pretty good about it. They were supportive.

Other than these two close friends and a few lesbian friends, Jen was still straight to the world. She moved in with Tracy and landed her first post-college job at Hewlett-Packard Company:

I was living with a woman, but I couldn't talk about it at work. People at HP tried to set me up with men. I got good at deflecting. If I showed up at a work function without a date, people wanted to set me up. They worried that I was alone. When they asked about setting me up, I made excuses. I'm a poor liar, so I was very uncomfortable. I had a male mentor who took a strong interest in the progress of women at HP. I always wondered whether he would stick with me if he knew I was a lesbian. There were three or four other lesbians at HP, but they were all pretty quiet. I heard people make disparaging comments about gays in the office. Tracy and I got each other rings, but I wore mine on my right hand to avoid any questions. When I broke up with Tracy, it was easier at work. I was simply single.

That was Jen's experience at HP in the mid-1980s. The world changed, she recalls, when the AIDS crisis caused people to start talking about gay and lesbian relationships, and when Bill Clinton was elected and talked about gays in the military. For most Americans, President Clinton's public position on gays in the military was little more than a policy sideshow. To Jen and many other gays and lesbians, Jen recalls, it was a watershed. The president of the United States acknowledged that the gay community existed. "Before that, people didn't talk about it. Now the discussion was in the open."

In the early 1990s, Jen took a so-called "early retirement" incentive from HP and enrolled in law school. She wasn't sure she wanted to be a lawyer, but HP made Jen an offer that gave her a free year. The United States was in recession. Jen thought it was a good time to acquire some professional training. Jen met Theresa a few months before starting law school and began a new relationship. Unlike Tracy's family, which never acknowledged Tracy was gay, Theresa's family embraced it:

Theresa's mother used to "out" me to everybody. She was a travel agent. I would go to her office, and she'd tell her coworkers excitedly, "This is Theresa's girlfriend, Jen." I really liked it that Theresa's family was so open. They didn't just tolerate our relationship, they embraced it and were proud of it.

Before Jen started law school, she decided that she was done pretending she was straight. She didn't want to live the double life she had lived at HP. She felt that society had changed as well. That summer, Jen and Theresa joined a country and western dance ("clogging") team. They were very involved in performing, and they went to the gay rodeos that were held half a dozen times a year. At these events, there were hundreds of gays and lesbians. Jen no longer felt isolated. Through this experience, Jen decided she wasn't going to lead one life during the work or school week and another on the weekend. At that point in her life, Jen felt that "if you are a closeted person, you make a choice not to tell people who you really are. You shut them out. I decided I'd rather be open from the beginning and let people choose from the beginning. I had consciously closed people off at HP."

Jen also had become part of the gay political community and now believed that "it mattered to come out":

The theory is that the more people who come out, the more straight people in society will say, "Those are my neighbors, those are my family members." People should see that I am not a radical or a truck-driving, cigarettes-rolled-in-my-sleeve kind of gal. There is a connection between coming out and tolerance, and moving past tolerance to acceptance.

National Coming Out Day is in October, close to the start of the law-school year. It was a landmark day for Jen. The school's Gay and Lesbian Student Association (GALA) planned to staff a table in a very public location. Senior GALA members asked Jen to staff the table. Jen had never done anything so public before a nongay audience. Table staffers would stand before the entire student body, in a central location, at a table that had a huge banner that said "Gay and Lesbian Student Association." Jen did it, and in so doing came out to her colleagues at school. Jen described her experience coming out at school:

I was nervous the whole time I was sitting there. When you sit at the table or when you tell people that you're gay for the first time, you're telling them something they don't know about you. People have to absorb it for a minute. Most people are okay with it, but they have to say, "Oh! I didn't know that." They have to figure out how they feel about it. That's how it was at the table. As people from my law-school class walked by, I kept hearing "Oh!" as they put it all together.

Three years later, Jen was offered her first job at a law firm. Before Jen started at the firm, she decided she'd come out at work. She didn't know when or how the opportunity would arise. It didn't take long:

I arrived at the office and was put in a room with another woman. She was typing and chattering the whole time. She wanted more and more information about my personal life. So I told her right away, and that was it. I'd come out at work. My face got hot when I told her. It still gets hot. You never know whether you'll get rejected. There is a fear of the unknown—how other people will react. She accepted it.

Jen's law career progressed, and the question of when and how to come out professionally became more complex. There were colleagues at her firm, lawyers on the same side of a case, lawyers on the opposing side of a case, clients, judges, law firm staff and others. Each category brought its own considerations. "When I meet with new clients, I go with nondisclosure. If they ask, I tell them. For other lawyers, I have to make a conscious decision whether I want each one to know this about me. For some people, I decide not to tell." Jen's current law partner, who is not gay, is a sounding board for Jen when professional issues and Jen's sexual orientation cross paths. "Sometimes I just don't get it," Jen laughs. "Somebody will do or say something odd. My law partner will say, 'Don't you think maybe it's because you're gay?' She's a no-nonsense person who will give me an honest take. She won't gloss over something just to make me feel better."

Jen's professional stature increased when she became the chair of the local Bar Committee on Diversity. When the committee secured a seat on the Bar Association's Board of Trustees, Jen became the first openly gay trustee. "Now I am sitting before twenty-five people wearing the 'Big L' on my forehead." When the Bar Association decided to take a public position against an antigay measure on the state ballot, Jen had to take her show on the road. She went from place to place as the representative of lesbian lawyers. "At this point, I was not just a lesbian," Jen said. "I had become 'The Lesbian.' It was strange, sitting in front of groups of people, basically saying, 'I want to validate my relationship with my lover.'"

At one point, Jen considered asking her nongay law partner to present the ballot issue to the group of family lawyers with which their firm dealt every day. Jen decided she had to do it herself. Jen's rationale was simple and consistent with how her decisions on coming out had evolved over twenty years: "If I can't say gay rights are important, why should anyone else?"

Postscript: In Jen's Own Words

This is what I would tell gay people who have career and family concerns about coming out: You have to do everything in your own time. There are reasons to make decisions at various times. With respect to telling people who are close to you, such as friends and family, when you come out you'll learn who is going to be part of your life by how people react. If you choose to lie to them, you will have made the decision for them. You won't have a relationship with them in which they understand your life. If you tell them, and they choose not to be a part of your life because you are gay, you gave them a chance.

After you come out, the people who stay in your life accept you and want to be there. There is no barrier of deception. Even so, there are some people you simply may not want to tell. I never told my seventy-five-year-old grandmother, not because I was afraid she would reject me, but because she was from such a different time that I thought it would make her sad. There was no point. There are situations where I still choose not to bring it up. There are some times when it just wouldn't be kind. What would be the point? If my grandmother had asked me directly, I'd have told her. I made a decision not to lie.

I regret going back in the closet when I was in college. I wasted three years of my life pretending to be somebody I wasn't. Most of my college life was directed to doing what I thought I was supposed to do, as opposed to naturally being who I was. Yet I'm not sure I had a choice. I'm not sure I was ready to handle the repercussions. It's harder when you're younger. High-school kids are pretty bold these days, but a lot of gay kids take abuse. It depends on the kid, whether he or she can handle it. There is so much pressure in high school, not just sexuality. I would never pressure a kid to do something she couldn't handle at the time.

On the work question, the big issue is whether you're working at the right place. If you're at a place where you can't be openly gay or lesbian, do you really want to be there? If you really think people aren't going to make you a partner or promote you if they learn you're gay or lesbian, how important is it to you to work there? If you're good at what you do, get a job someplace that will let you be who you are. Otherwise, you're not living a whole life. I feel it is emotionally, personally and physically detrimental to deny who you are.

When I lied at HP, I was denying my relationship with Tracy. I won't do that with Theresa. It's no longer acceptable to me. Theresa is an important part of my life. It is important for me to acknowledge her to other people. I have a picture of her on my desk, but it is tucked back a little. There is still a certain amount of double life. In my area of law, people tell me very intimate things about their lives. I think some of them want to know something about my life, sort of as an exchange. I have to make a conscious decision how much to tell each person.

There are other reasons to come out at work. If you hide it, people can use it. The fact that you hid it will be an issue. They think that you are less than forthcoming. Dishonest. In many states, there are legal reasons now to be out at work. You can't discriminate in employment in some states. Although discrimination still happens, it is easier to protect your rights when it is known that you're gay. The work choice is still hard, especially for people who work at a place where it will cause a problem. If you're there, think about getting a different job.

The main change in the past twenty years is that there is a lot more information available to people who make these decisions. Most parents are better educated. The American Psychiatric Association and American Academy of Pediatrics have declared that homosexuality isn't a disease, and children of gay or lesbian parents are as well as or better adjusted than kids of straight parents. That really matters. When I was in college, I wanted to know if I was sick. There was a doctor in New York who gave shock treatment to "cure" homosexuality.

Religions have come a long way. Most religions allow commitment ceremonies, and some have ordained gay ministers. When I first came out, I tried to find anything I could to read up on homosexuality. I went to the library. I read Ann Landers. Anything I could find. Now if you go to the library there are even books written for kids. There is less "I am a sick human being. They better fix me or I have to kill myself. And I will go to hell." There are still many people who have a hard time with it, but there are many more resources.

AUTHORS' NOTE: Although Ms. Dennis is openly a lesbian, as described in this piece, she chose to have her story published under a pseudonym to preserve the privacy of others in her story, both gay and straight, who may not wish to have their stories so freely told.

Step 9

Keep the Risks of Failure (and Benefits of Success) in Perspective

The greatest mistake you can make in life is to be continually fearing you will make one.

—Elbert Hubbard

We're not going to tout the so-called "benefits of failure." Failure is not a wonderful thing. Nonetheless, failure is poorly understood, and the fear of failure often irrationally influences Big Decisions. If the risk of falling on your face makes you fear an important step, you need to evaluate your view of failure and how it affects your decisions.

The "fear of failure" and the "fear of being a failure" are two different concepts. Concern about the physical, social, emotional or financial costs and risks of a decision is a normal part of the decision-making process. Fear of failure (or, more accurately, fear of the consequences of failure) is a problem only if it's excessive and causes you to avoid risks that you should take. In that case, as suggested in Step 6, you need to address your excess fear as a psychological issue, separate as much as possible from your Big Decision.

The fear of being a failure is a different matter. The fear of being a failure is a thought pattern that says, "If I fail, then not only will I suffer the regular risks of my decision, I will suffer an additional consequence because I invested myself personally, perhaps publicly, in trying to do something, and I fell short." The "additional consequence" is the self-assessment that you lack the qualities required for success, often combined with fear that others will hold you in less esteem. Bluntly, the difference between fear of failure and fear of being a failure is the difference between the fear of what it will cost if you don't succeed and the fear that if you don't succeed you'll be "a loser."

Your ability to keep the fear of being a failure in check is a huge factor in whether you'll make good decisions. Not getting what you seek, and suffering physical, emotional, financial or other pain, are possible outcomes of almost all Big Decisions. Disappointment is a risk of proposing marriage, auditioning for a part in a show, playing a competitive game, pursuing an ambitious career path, asking for a raise or taking a case to trial. Financial loss is a risk of leaving a steady job for a less steady position or investing in the stock market. The disapproval of certain people is a risk of controversial marriage or taking an unpopular political stand. If you can't bear these risks and can't change them, you probably shouldn't take them right now. If you can accept the risks and want to accept them—and should accept them—you need to overcome fear that you'll be a loser if the decision doesn't work out.

Step 9 shows you why and how to overcome the fear of being a failure when you make a Big Decision. At the end we also address the opposite problem: delusions about the benefits that success will deliver.

You Have Nothing to Fear
but Fear of Being a Failure

Not every lawyer who tries a case and loses feels like a failure, although all of them feel lousy. A person whose marriage proposal is rejected may generally feel successful, self-confident and respectable, although the rejection is a discouraging event. Others would be devastated by the rejection and feel that it reflects a larger failure. Some actors can audition week after week, with little or no success, and not become incapacitated by feeling like a loser. Other actors find after a couple of unsuccessful auditions that the repeat ego blows are too painful to continue. A person who asks for a raise will be unhappy if it's not given, but might just as easily conclude that the employer is deficient. Others would see the rejection as a highly personal attack full of implied—even justified—criticism. The extent to which a person translates a loss or a failure to achieve a goal into feelings of larger inadequacy is highly individualized.

The fear of being a failure rears its head in many ways. Here are some examples of how the fear of being a failure may influence a decision:

- Your child increasingly has problems at school. Competent professionals have said it is in your child's best interest to be held back a grade. You tell the school that is out of the question because you fear that other parents and children in your community will look down on you or your child as "not cutting it." Your fear of being a failure as a parent in the eyes of others may keep your child in a situation that doesn't work.
- You have a job at a large, prestigious company. You don't like your job. In fact, you're miserable. You're extremely well-qualified and could land other jobs. You refuse to leave your company because you believe that a successful person should

be at a prestigious company, and others might think you weren't good enough. Your fear of being a failure keeps you unhappy.

- You made a decision at work, and you learn that it was a bad decision. You won't admit the decision was wrong or change courses. It would humiliate you, you believe, to acknowledge that you made a mistake. You try to justify the decision, twist the data to show a better outcome, claim it just hasn't had time to work and blame factors other than your decision. Your fear of being a failure drives the decisions you make while you're trying to recover from the initial error. Your fear makes things worse.

The fear of being a failure feeds stubbornness and inertia. By protecting your self-esteem against bogeymen who might call you names like "loser" or "failure," you escalate the perceived cost of taking action so high that no benefit is worth it. The key to moving past fear of being a failure is to realize that much of the fear is self-created, and it is more a reflection of your ego and pride than a real risk of the decision.

How to Take the Fear of Being a Failure Out of the Equation

The fear of being a failure is an emotional thought process that must be identified and kept in check. The biggest clue is an exaggerated view of what other people will think if you fail. If your Big Decision is influenced excessively by fear of being a failure, try these steps:

- Eliminate that part of your fear which is essentially just fear of the unknown. Everybody experiences *some* fear of change or the unknown. Nobody wants to fall on his face. But are you really going to fall on your face? Faced with a mortal fear of standing in front of a jury and presenting a court case, many future trial lawyers take mock trial courses, where they try a hypothetical case using a real courtroom. When it's over, everyone has the same comment: It's not as hard as it looks. Life offers lots of opportunities to float trial balloons, do dry runs, research the facts and talk to other people who've been through a challenge. Before you let fear of the unknown dominate you, reduce what's unknown. Knowledge is the antidote to fear of the unknown.

- Be realistic about the harshest consequences. Feel free to play out the Parade of Horribles in your mind. Wallow in it for a while and taste the paralysis it causes. Get it out of your system. Once you've laid out each disaster scenario, go back and assess the real likelihood of each consequence. Then consider the likely costs and risks of standing still and doing nothing.

- Determine whose standards you're trying to meet. Are you concerned about failing to meet your own standards? Those of your parents? Your colleagues at work? Your teammates on the playing field? Your friends? Your neighbors? Your spouse? This analysis is critical because the more audiences you have to please, the easier it is to fail. Everyone defines success and failure differently. If you must meet all definitions of success and avoid all definitions of failure, success will be awfully hard! If you try to please everyone 100 percent, you'll find yourself stuck. Acknowledge that you can't please everyone, then go forward with a plan to meet those standards that are truly important to you.

- Remember that "losing" and "failing," on the one hand, and "being a loser" and "being a failure," on the other hand, are very different concepts. You "lose" and "fail," in some senses, whenever you don't reach a goal. You only become "a loser" or "a failure" when you *choose* to measure your self-worth by that goal.

Skillful stage performers have fear management down to a science (although they may tell you otherwise). The audience expects perfection. It's not all right to remember 90 percent of your lines or play a whole lot of the notes right. A stage performer is presented with a choice: do what you love doing, totally exposed, and risk a screw-up every time you perform, or choose another career. Those who make it are those who master their craft and manage the fear sufficiently to perform night after night. Even among this group, many fear playing the lead or doing a solo, and plenty of up-and-coming actors fear being famous. Every entertainment agent has heard, "Wow, I got the part. . . . Oh, @#*! I got the part!" Don't make ego protection your religion while opportunities pass you by. Worse things can happen than falling on your face once in a while. Others don't care nearly as much as you think about your failures, mishaps and, yes, your successes.

Let's look at a divorce decision:

> Just two years ago, Elizabeth stood in front of all her friends at a no-holds-barred expensive wedding, declared that she'd found her eternal soul mate in Brian and committed herself to Brian forever in marriage. All of their friends and family members gave sentimental toasts and predicted everlasting happiness and gorgeous children. Elizabeth believed in the relationship. Unfortunately, the relationship began to deteriorate just a few months after the wedding. After two years, Brian pays no attention to Elizabeth, insults her, is unfaithful and lies. He refuses to participate in marital counseling. There's never been a divorce in Elizabeth's family, which her parents always mention with great pride. To make things worse, Elizabeth's sister told Elizabeth not to marry Brian in the first place. Elizabeth is distraught, but not by the idea of divorcing Brian (she wants to end it). Elizabeth agonizes over the public aspect of divorce, a humiliating announcement to everyone she knows,

including all the wedding guests and her parents, that her marriage failed.

If nobody else existed, Elizabeth would file for divorce tomorrow. The emotional relationship is over. Thankfully, no children were born of the marriage. Elizabeth is ready to move on. Yet Elizabeth is hesitant to take the final step. Elizabeth is concerned that she'll be a failure in other people's eyes and, to some extent, her own. She second-guesses her decision to marry Brian. ("Why couldn't I see this coming? All the signs were there!") Elizabeth imagines other people talking about her mistake getting into the marriage or managing her marital problems with Brian. Elizabeth is convinced that her marriage decision will be ridiculed, her judgment about men will be questioned, and she'll be the subject of gossip. She's concerned that she will be seen by men as "second-hand goods" or someone with "baggage." Fear of being a failure is driving Elizabeth's divorce decision.

The most important characteristic of fear of being a failure is that it's usually overblown. In many cases, a little investigation dramatically reduces the fear of being a failure. The key for Elizabeth is to acknowledge the fear of being a failure and confront it as an issue that is separate from the decision whether to divorce Brian. If Elizabeth confronts her fear of being a failure and investigates her concerns, she'll probably reach conclusions that help her move forward. Her concerns include:

What will my parents think? Even though Elizabeth's parents don't like divorce, they may be strong supporters of a divorce when they learn about the marriage. Has Elizabeth been sparing her parents the details? It's time to talk. The problems probably aren't news. Family lawyer Andrew Ross tells clients, "Trying to hide a bad marriage is like trying to hide a fire truck in your driveway. You can't do it." Even if Elizabeth's parents are categorically or religiously opposed to divorce, more information may help them understand Elizabeth's position.

What will my friends think? Elizabeth's friends may be more in favor of the divorce than she is, and they will help her get through it. Elizabeth's probably been unloading her marital problems on certain friends. Discussing her fears of failure with friends may help Elizabeth. Good friends will give Elizabeth reassurance that they understand what she is doing and will not think she is a failure.

Will I be "secondhand goods"? Elizabeth's fears of being treated as "secondhand goods," or someone with "baggage," almost certainly are overblown. Divorce is not a cure-all by any means, but it's not a show-stopping stigma in large parts of contemporary society. Plenty of men will marry a divorced woman. There are clubs, support groups and matchmaking services specifically for divorced singles. Moreover, the fact that Elizabeth doesn't know who her future mate will be is no reason to stay with Brian. If Elizabeth thinks it will be challenging to find another mate, and the relationship with Brian can't be fixed, that's a good reason to put Brian in the past sooner. She needs to get started with her future.

Will I be the subject of gossip and ridicule? Like most bad news, today's shock and surprise are old news tomorrow. Sure, a period of adjustment will take place, but Elizabeth's genuine friends before the divorce will be genuine friends afterward. Is Elizabeth going to stay in a terrible marriage just to avoid gossip from people on the street? Do they really matter? Do they respect her for staying *in* the marriage?

Will people think I'm a loser? Humans are more compassionate and understanding than Elizabeth thinks. People know that everyone makes some decisions that don't turn out well. When others learn that Elizabeth was in a bad marriage, they won't judge her on her marriage decision nearly as much as they'll judge her on how she handled the difficulties that surfaced. We've seen time and again what a short memory people have for scandal and how popular "redemption" is.[20]

The same process applies to fear of being a failure in careers, parenthood, school, business and elsewhere. We all make mistakes. We all know that others make mistakes. We all sometimes fail to succeed when we didn't make any mistake or bad decision. Don't let a fear of being a failure make it impossible for you to take steps that will help you move forward. Is it better to suffer the temporary embarrassment of rehab, or to suffer from a drug or alcohol problem that may kill you? It's far better to play in the World Series and lose than never reach the World Series. The risk you'll lose is virtually always the price of the chance to win. If your fear of being a loser prevents you from taking steps to move your life ahead, you must overcome that fear. Your fear of being a failure isn't the same as the risks that normally go with your Big Decision. It's a separate issue that concerns how you feel about yourself. Work on it. Don't let it hold you back.

The Parade of Horribles Trap

A major effect of the fear of being a failure is that it causes you to exaggerate the *likelihood* of failure. If you're terrified you may become "a loser," you'll start to believe that failure is certain, even when it's not. You'll also tend to exaggerate the consequences of failure, so both the odds of failure and its effect on you are overblown. If you wade too deep into this mire, your pride and desire to protect your self-esteem take over, and you can't make a decision that involves any risk. Mostly imagined risks are paralyzing you.

---

[20] We intentionally do not address any religion-based concerns that Elizabeth may have about divorce. If Elizabeth believes divorce is a sin, and this belief causes her to hesitate, she should consider appropriate spiritual consultations. Working through the conflict between Elizabeth's religious values and the values that are violated by Brian's conduct may be a target question: "Can I address my problems with Brian and not commit a sin in my religion's eyes?"

Many people experience the fear of being a failure as a "Parade of Horribles" or failure spiral. The Parade of Horribles is a series of failures and worst-case scenarios played out in your mind that bring about crushing financial, emotional or other disaster.

Perhaps your mind has gone through the Parade of Horribles shown in these examples:

- "My teenage daughter wants to spend the night at the home of a new girl at school. I don't know this girl or her parents, but I hear she has a seventeen-year-old brother. Two years ago, in the next county over, a couple of girls got in a car with the brother of one girl. He'd been drinking or taking drugs or something. They got into a head-on collision. The brother survived, but both of the girls were killed instantly. There is no way I'm going to let that happen to my daughter. She can just forget it!"

- "I have some money to invest for retirement. I need this money when I retire. Nothing can happen to it. I'll never put any of it into the stock market. Look what happened in the 1929 stock-market crash and the Great Depression. People lost it all. They committed suicide. Then there was Black Monday in 1987. That trimmed out a few retirements. Then there was the dot-com debacle. I am going to put it all in a CD. That way it will always be there, no matter what happens. I guess there's the possibility of the bank going under. It's insured by the government, though, whatever that means. Am I going to trust the government? These are the same people who were supposed to be watching Enron and WorldCom. Gold always has value, especially in a disaster. I could buy gold—but what if it tanks? Look what happened to silver. . . ."

- "I have a great idea for my company's next product line. It's aggressive, though. Perhaps too aggressive. Maybe it's New Coke all over again. That guy who thought up New Coke probably thought he'd hit on a brilliant idea, too. Coke spent zillions on it. In a year, New Coke was gone. Everyone had egg on their faces. If this doesn't work, I'll get canned, and everyone will point to me and say, 'He came up with the stuff that blew us up.' We're not The Coca-Cola Company. A disaster could bankrupt us. I'd never get another job in this industry. And I have no other skills. I'll be on the street. Jack Taylor lost his job and worked down to his last dime before he got another job—in Podunk. I'll just keep my big mouth shut."

A Parade of Horribles thinker can come up with lots of arguments and anecdotes to back her up. "All those businesses that declare bankruptcy every year thought they had a great idea, too, right?" "Did you hear about the guy who became homeless after he lost his job?" "What about all of those celebrity drug-addiction stories on television? Forget about an acting career, son. Get in with a big corporation." These thumbnail anecdotes efficiently feed disaster psychology, but bear no relation to the risks and benefits of a decision. So many people die, are maimed, are bankrupted, become homeless and otherwise meet tragedy each year that you can find a story to support any point you want to make.

You can try to justify Parade of Horribles decision-making on the ground that you're "just being cautious," "looking down the road" or "considering all the angles." There's a hint of merit to this argument. It makes sense, when making a Big Decision, to consider as many possible outcomes as you can bring to mind, no matter how improbable the outcome. The disaster scenarios are worth pondering if there's any real possibility they will arise. The Parade of Horribles becomes a defect in your decision process when your fears and anxieties elevate mere possibilities—often very remote possibilities—into probabilities that inevitably will crush you.

How to Manage the Parade of Horribles

Parade of Horribles thinking typically surfaces when a very bad possible outcome of a decision is combined with incomplete information about the real odds of the bad outcome. Imagine that a physician hands you a prescription form and says, "I just have to warn you in advance that this medication has been shown to cause seizures and death." Your immediate reaction, based on that limited information about a severe outcome, is to assume the worst. You won't respond, "I'm not too concerned about that." You'll say, "What??? How often does that happen?" If the physician says, "One in four hundred thousand cases and never in your age group," you'll feel better. If the physician were to say, "I really don't know," you'd stay in the Parade of Horribles. Because of the high stakes (your life) and inadequate information about the threat, your self-preservation instinct hears a mortal warning.

When you find yourself in the Parade, you need to fill the information gap that causes you to assume that you'll wind up in a failure spiral. Investigate! Get good advice from a more experienced person, someone who's seen similar situations play out. If your concerns are medical, see a doctor. If your concerns are legal, see a lawyer. If your concerns are financial, depending on the issue, see an accountant, financial planner or investment advisor. If you've got career concerns, find someone who's been there. Stop imagining all of the awful possibilities in areas you don't know about. Do what it takes to assess the real likelihood of a horrible outcome and act accordingly. In many cases, you'll find that the awful outcomes that you thought were likely are totally unlikely or impossible.

Don't march in the Parade of Horribles!

How to Deal with Bankruptcy, Flunking Out and Other Universal Symbols of Failure

It's worth saying a few words about the fear of bankruptcy, flunking out of school, failing an important test, divorce (to some people) and other events that sometimes are treated as symbols of failure. These events rarely have an impact that is anywhere close to what you think. The world's full of people who went through a bankruptcy, many now wealthy and creditworthy. Major law firms employ plenty of high-powered attorneys who once failed the bar exam. Skyscrapers are designed by architects who sat for their qualifying exams more times than they wished. Juilliard graduates mess up recitals, pro tennis players double fault on match point, and diplomats say undiplomatic things when the microphone is open.

Embarrassing setbacks and mishaps make for a bad day, a bad week or even a bad year. They rarely affect your long-term progress, unless *you* can't get over it. If you pick yourself up, regroup and move forward, you'll have every chance to get past the problem. If your "failure" was a fluke, you'll build success on your adjustments and future performance. If you failed because you weren't yet ready for the challenge, go back and practice, train and do what it takes to get ready. If you failed because you don't have what it takes to achieve this goal, failure is a message that you'll have to find success somewhere else. Change your target.

Many stigmas have disappeared or are destigmatized: divorce, addiction-recovery programs, alternative schools and special education, psychotherapy and psychiatric care, non-Western medical treatments, antidepressive drug therapy, "fat farms," illnesses and counseling (marital, academic, financial/credit). As more people are willing to talk about common problems and solutions, public acceptance and understanding of those matters have grown.

If fear of a stigma weighs on your Big Decision, find out more about that stigma. Don't be shackled by stigmas you picked up in bygone days. When many of us were raised, cancer was regarded as a terminal illness, ulcers were thought to be caused by the personalities of nervous people, and sex therapy was a perversion. Years ago, the children of divorced parents were from "broken homes." Now we talk about "single moms" and "single dads." This change is more than just a shift to politically correct terminology; it reflects a general view in society that divorce does not inevitably "break" a home, and that in some cases it's the best solution to very serious family problems. Before you base your decision on yesterday's stigma, do enough research to learn, for example, that many cancers now are regarded as chronic (or curable) illnesses, the majority of ulcers are caused by treatable bacteria, and sex therapy may be recommended by a medical doctor. You'd be surprised to find that what used to be stigmatized is now regarded much differently.

How to Avoid Walking into Failure

Failure can be real, of course. In relationships and new businesses, more dreams ultimately die than come true. Investments may go sour overnight and affect your financial plans. There are disappointed people everywhere who set out to do something and did not achieve the success for which they had hoped. Miscarriages of justice and tragedies occur every day. You may win when you should lose, lose when you should win, and tie when you should either win or lose. Sometimes you fail because you were wrong or didn't make a decision properly. At other times, outside forces intervene and ruin your plan. Virtually every life endeavor carries with it a chance of failure. Indeed, more is expected of you when you succeed—sending you to a harder tier and ensuring that if your forward progress stops, more people will know about it.

When you make a Big Decision, get a grip on what "success" and "failure" mean for you. Your concept of success and failure may change—what would have been failure ten years ago may now be acceptable (perhaps even success). Don't allow past decisions made when you had different values, different experience or different priorities to overly burden you. Just as your definition of success changes over time, how you define failure will change.

Make decisions that allow you to sleep at night by honestly confronting your ability to accept the risks that go with your choices. If you can't take a risk without being petrified by fear of future failure, ask whether you should be taking that risk at this particular point. A few people seem able to "bet it all" day after day without blinking an eye. If you aren't one of these people, don't try to convince yourself that you are. Take risks that will not trigger unmanageable failure visualizations and Parade of Horribles thinking. The best failures are the ones that permit you to say, "At least I tried." The worst cause you to say, "I never should have done it." If you're at a point in life when you think you want to take more risk, experiment with it before you quit your job, leave a marriage or otherwise burn a bridge that took a long time to build. If you're at a point where you need stability and you can't sustain risk, do what's stable right now. If you can't sleep at night, how effective will you be during the day? Think about how much of your plan depends on your own committed and confident execution, and you'll see that if you take more risk than you can handle you'll set up a failure.

The Delusion of Becoming a Success

The flip side of the fear of being a failure could be called "delusions about the benefits of success." While the fear of being a failure stops you from doing what you should do, delusions about success may cause you to pursue a goal in the belief that if you achieve the goal you'll realize a variety of false benefits. Two significant problems flow from delusions about the benefits of success. First, the delusions impel you to pursue objectives that, without the false benefits, wouldn't be worthwhile. Second, you'll be disappointed if you achieve your goal and find that you receive much less than you expected.

Here are some examples of how success delusions may become part of a Big Decision:

- You believe problems that emerge when you're dating someone will go away if you get married. While it's possible that marriage will take your relationship to a new level of respect, fidelity, communication or whatever isn't there while you are dating (or living together), it's extremely unlikely. You should address the relationship problems before you decide to get married.

- You believe problems that emerge during your marriage will be solved if you have a child. Introducing the joys and challenges of a child might conceivably help you and your spouse overcome your problems, but more often it will complicate your problems and subject a new person to them. You should address the problems before you decide to have children.

- You believe that obtaining money and possessions will fulfill you. Money can reduce financial stress, provide financial security, allow you to make new choices and provide material comforts. Money can be used to do good in society and help the ones you love. If you believe that money will fulfill all your psychological needs, make you spiritually complete or make you happy forever, you have delusions about money. Be realistic about what money can buy before you make trade-offs that generate more money, but cost you elsewhere.

- You have an unrealistic view of the benefits of career success. To distinguish yourself at work, you may have to spend less time with your family and friends or on relaxation and personal-growth activities.

If your Big Decision relies upon a vision of success, make sure that vision is realistic. The Parade of Wonderfuls can hurt you as much as the Parade of Horribles.

We leave Step 9 with the following points to remember about failure, fear of being a failure and success:

- Distinguish fear of not achieving what you want from the fear of being a failure, then determine whether you really will be a failure if your decision doesn't work out.
- Understand and investigate the stigmas that are driving you. Are they real or remnants from your childhood when stigmas may have been different? Do you care about the stigma?
- Don't get sucked into a Parade of Horribles. Great decision-makers consider all of the awful things that might happen and work to reduce the chances they will happen. (This is an important strategy, which we discuss in Step 10.) Great decision-makers do not assume that everything will go awry in each Big Decision.
- Don't take on so much risk that you can't sleep at night. Everyone has a different risk tolerance. As a day-to-day condition, fear is unpleasant and will affect your ability to live happily. Don't be afraid to admit that you have a different risk tolerance than another person. It's not macho, cool or smart to take on risk that makes you a bundle of nerves all the time.
- Be realistic about the benefits that success will bring. There is no perfect life. Success in one part of your life may breed challenges, and even failures, in another. Miscalculating the benefits of a decision can be as dangerous as misapprehending the risks.

Relationships: The Emotional Risks Are High When an Adopted Man Seeks His Biological Mother After September 11

Dave Cook knew his birth mom's name was Susan Auerbach. He didn't know how she'd react when he sent her an e-mail thirty-one years after she gave him up.

Dave Cook learned Susan Auerbach's name as he was growing up. Susan was Dave's biological mother; she lived in the Bethesda, Maryland, area when Dave's adoptive parents took him home in 1970. Until January 2002, that's about all Dave knew about his mother. Dave was raised by his adoptive parents in upper-middle-class Northern California homes. Although Dave's adoptive parents divorced when he was five, their relationship was cordial, and Dave and his two siblings (who were not adopted) were raised in a stable, loving environment.

Dave harbored no anger about his adoption. Yet ever since Dave was a child, he wondered about his mother, Susan Auerbach, and thought about meeting her in person one day:

I always thought about finding her. I would see someone in a public place and wonder if it was Susan. It wasn't an everyday thing, but it happened through my whole life. My adoptive mom was very open about Susan. She told me as much as she knew, but she didn't know a lot. It was a private adoption. There were no public records. I knew that Susan was a teenager when my mom and dad adopted me. I never took steps to find Susan. I was busy with my life and my career.

Things changed in 2001 when Dave hit some severe speed bumps. In August 2001, Dave's wife had a miscarriage as they were trying to have their first child. The miscarriage hit Dave and his wife hard. Just when Dave was beginning to recover from the loss of a baby, September 11 occurred:

September 11 drove home that you don't know what's going to happen in the future. Who would have believed that we could be attacked like that? I felt a timetable. Finding my mother surfaced as something I had to do now. It became urgent. I was thinking that life is really short, and you don't know what's going to happen. I was thirty-one years old. I felt like time was speeding up. I had to find her. I had a real need to tell her I was okay, that I grew up and I was so thankful for everything I had in my life. I just wanted to let her know all those things. I wanted her to know it turned out okay. I thought it was something she might be thinking about. But if that's not what my mother was thinking, that was fine, too. What really mattered was what I would tell her—that I was safe and doing fine. After September 11, I knew I wanted to meet Susan before I died. Before then, I thought I wanted to do it—but it wasn't tangible. I didn't know if I had what it would take.

In November 2001, before Dave had a chance to do more than poke around the Internet for information about Susan Auerbach, he lost his job. Dave took that as another sign that he needed to do what he had put off for so long—try to find his mother. He started telling family and friends, but he only told people he knew would encourage him. Dave's adoptive mother's open attitude was important. In addition, although Dave did not know anyone who'd found an adoptive parent, Dave knew someone who'd given a child up for adoption. Dave knew the fear, guilt and other strong emotions that his birth mother might have experienced, and which she still might be going through.

Dave worked full-time through the end of October 2001 doing freelance work for the company that laid him off. At the beginning of December, Dave regarded finding his mother as his main mission. The Internet was Dave's research tool, but Susan Auerbach's contact information didn't jump off any Web pages. To find Susan, Dave pushed deeper into cyberspace:

I knew I was born in Bethesda. I started looking in the largest county next to Bethesda—Montgomery County. I looked at different schools and at local high-school alumni databases. I found one Auerbach and e-mailed him. He didn't know her. Several times it seemed I was close, then it didn't work out. Then I went to Classmates.com, which is a huge database organized by high-school class. I typed in "Auerbach," and the name showed up in New York, Ohio and Maryland. The Maryland entry was class of 1971. I thought Susan had graduated in 1972, and the school was in Prince George County. Because of the graduation date and county, I dismissed it at first. I went to Mapquest.com and started to look at the different counties around Bethesda. I figured out that Prince George County was only a dozen miles from the hospital in Bethesda. I still had doubts, but I told other people about it. They were convinced, even though I was skeptical. My mom and my wife said, "It's her." That's when I began to believe I might have found Susan.

Anyone can be listed on Classmates.com. You just sign up. To contact another person through Classmates.com, however, you have to pay a fee. For the fee, you don't see your classmate's e-mail address—just a name. If you want to contact a classmate, your initial contact e-mail is routed through Classmates.com. This allows a recipient to preserve his or her privacy. The recipient is free to answer the e-mail or ignore it. If the recipient ignores it, the sender doesn't get the recipient's e-mail address or other identifying information. In late December 2001, Dave paid for Classmates.com. Then Dave did nothing. Finding Susan Auerbach was one thing. Setting into motion a process that could lead Dave and Susan to a joyful reunion—or emotional disaster—was within Dave's power:

It took me a month to get up the courage to hit Send on the e-mail. I needed the time. The idea of totally disrupting her life is not what I wanted to do. Now it was a realistic possibility. It was the first time I seriously thought about the possibility of it not going well. The time between when I got the name and when I pushed the Send button was a month. I didn't think about it every day that month. I looked for new business. I spent time with myself. I hiked in the woods. I challenged myself working out. I had just come off the corporate grind. I am a physical person. I kept the issue on the cupboard shelf during that month. I talked to the people who would give support about the whole process and the things that could happen. What would the first e-mails be like? What would phone conversations with Susan be like? What would a face-to-face be like? That was the big thing.

In mid-February, Dave was ready. He sat down to compose an e-mail to send through Classmates.com. Dave wanted to keep it short and to the point. He got some coaching from his adoptive mom. She had done some adoption-related work and had read about first contacts. Dave crafted an e-mail that he hoped would communicate to Susan that he didn't want to interfere with her life. Dave definitely didn't want to create feelings of guilt on Susan's part. He just wanted to let her know he was fine.

Dave showed the draft e-mail to the people who had given him support all along. "Perfect," they all said. On February 18, 2002, Dave cut and pasted his draft e-mail into Classmates.com and pushed Send. "I woke up and was determined to send it that day. That evening, when I hit Send, I wanted to grab it back and maybe think about it more," Dave recalls. That was, of course, impossible. After thirty-one years of separation, Dave's message traveled at Internet speed through Classmates.com to Susan Auerbach:

From: D COOK
Sent: Monday, February 18, 2002 4:11 PM
To: Susan Auerbach
Subject: D COOK has sent you a Hi Note
Hi Susan, My name is David Cook and I have reason to believe I might be your birth son. I was born April 3, 1970 in Bethesda Maryland and was adopted shortly after my birth. I'm not sure how you feel about my reaching out to you. But I feel a deep need to thank you. I've been blessed with so much. I've grown up with a wonderful and loving family and have a great life. There is so much about me that I would like to tell you about and I'm obviously curious about you. Any contact would be in confidence if you prefer but I would love to learn and tell you more if you are open to writing me back. I eagerly hope to hear from you.
—David Cook

All Dave could do was wait. He had no idea where Susan Auerbach was or how often she checked her e-mail. For all Dave knew, Susan's Classmates.com entry was registered under an out-of-date e-mail address, and she would never get the note. If Dave didn't hear from Susan, he didn't know what it would mean. Would it mean she didn't get the e-mail? That she got it but didn't want to have contact with him? That she wanted to have contact with him, but didn't know what to say? That she wasn't alive?

Susan did check her e-mail:

From: Susan Auerbach
Sent: Tuesday, February 19, 2002 8:53 AM
To: David Cook
Subject: Oh my
Hello David,

I can only imagine that you are in great suspense as to whether or not I would respond so I am. I am filled with all kinds of emotions at the moment—joy, fear, anxiety, guilt. I have thought of you often your whole life but interestingly, in the past year, several people have asked me whether or not I would look for you. I always felt that it should be your move.

I would love to hear from you and to tell you about me and my life. Right now I'm a bit stunned so I doubt I could be coherent. Let me just tell you that I live in New Hampshire, I'm married, I was never able to have any other children, and I am a very happy person.

Yours,
Sue

The exchange of e-mails continued:

From: David Cook
Sent: Tuesday, February 19, 2002 6:43 PM
To: Susan Auerbach
Subject: Oh my
Hi Sue,

Thank you so much for writing back! I'm not sure this has really sunk in yet. I'm also feeling some anxiety but definitely joy. I'm so happy to hear from you. I want to tell you so much about me and learn about you, but I also don't want to overwhelm you. Let me know if any of this, at any time, is too much or too soon for you.

I can start by telling you that I've lived most of my life in different areas of Northern California. We moved out here when I was about 2 years old. I've been married for 3 years now to my college sweetheart and we live in Silicon Valley. We don't have any children yet. I work in Advertising as an Art Director.

I am so thankful for everything I have. I grew up with a younger sister and a brother and always knew that I was adopted. My mom has always encouraged me to reach out to you. I'm so glad I did. She told me your name when I was really young. After the crazy year this has been I decided it was time to get the courage up to try and contact you. I found your name through the Classmates site and hoped it was you and that you would be open to hear from me.

For the longest time I've wanted to let you know that I've lived a very happy healthy life.

There is obviously so much more to me. When, and if, you are comfortable, I can tell you more and if you want, send you pictures of me. And I'm curious and would love to hear more about you and your life.

I hope to hear from you soon.

—Dave

From: Susan Auerbach
Sent: Wednesday, February 20, 2002 10:44 AM
To: David Cook
Subject: Well hello then
Good morning Dave,

I must tell you that I have experienced all kinds of emotions in the last 24 hours. I put off checking email until 10:30 this morning in case this was all a hoax or a dream or something. I guess I always knew or hoped that you would contact me and thought about what I would do when you did. But what I didn't count on was the reality of the emotions it brings on. The predominant one is joy though. I'm so happy that you have had a good life. I think I met your parents very briefly at the hospital but I didn't really get any impression of them. I'm so glad you had siblings to grow up with. I have a sister and a brother and they become more important to me as I get older.

As I said, I live in New Hampshire. Have been here for about 20 years. My dad passed away ten years ago and my Mom moved up here about 9 years ago. We live in an old duplex in the middle of town and she lives on one side and my husband and I live on the other. I got my Ph.D. a year ago and have had my own consulting company for about 18 months. I love working for myself and have made quite a nice life for myself. Most of my work is with schools and non-profits. I do facilitation and organizational development work. Actually, I got my Ph.D. from the Fielding Institute which is in Santa Barbara so I was coming out there for a week every year for about three years. One of my friends who was in the program with me has a sister-in-law who lives in San Jose so we used to visit her too.

It is funny what 9/11 has caused us to do isn't it? Seems like a wake up call to humanity. My brother in law (my sister's husband) works at the Pentagon and was not far from the impact point. I think we all take life a little less for granted now.

I would love to hear more about you. And yes, this is a bit overwhelming but wonderful as well. Everyone in my life knows about you so I have no need of keeping your appearance in my life a secret. So, please do tell me about yourself. And ask me whatever you want to know. If I were you I'd have lots of questions.

Thanks so much for taking the risk of getting in touch with me. I can only imagine how scary that must have been.

Yours,

Sue

From: David Cook
Sent: Thursday, February 21, 2002 6:06 PM
To: Susan Auerbach
Subject: More about everything
Dear Sue,

I have to admit, I checked my email twice last night and I was so happy to read your beautiful note this morning. Thanks for writing back. At times this all just doesn't seem real. It's hard to describe.

I want to tell you more about me. I was the oldest of three growing up. After adopting me, my mom was able to give birth to my younger sister, who is 11 months (to the day) younger. Four years later my mom gave birth to my younger brother. We had a comfortable childhood, growing up in a Victorian House two blocks from the California Berkeley Campus. We have cute childhood pictures of me sandwiched between a brother and sister with blond hair blue eyes (I have brown hair hazel eyes.) Being adopted, I never felt different, if anything I felt special. My parents didn't treat me differently and were always open to telling me everything they knew about you. When I was younger I remember being in public places looking at women wondering if you were there.

My parents got divorced when I was about five. It was a friendly separation and from the age of 5 to 13 my brother and sister and I all lived with my mom. My dad started a very successful company that produced arts & crafts shows all over the western states.

As a kid I always had a lot of energy. As a toddler they had to put a leash on me. I was always jumping off of furniture throwing myself at things. When I was about 9 I started getting involved in sports which I seemed to do well at. Up through High School I played football, baseball, and ran track.

In 1984 I moved to Marin County (just North of San Francisco) to live with my Dad and start high school. I loved high school. I had a lot of friends (many I still talk to). My parents always encouraged me to pursue my passion. I was always drawn to Math, Science, Architecture, and Art. I got decent grades (B average) but I don't feel like I tried very hard.

In my high school years we were able to travel a lot. My dad loves adventure traveling and he would take turns taking each of the kids to exotic places. My dad and I did a lot of hiking and ice climbing in places like Peru, Argentina, and Pakistan.

After high school I went to San Diego State University for three years but ended up graduating with a degree in design from San Jose State. I was in a fraternity and that's where I met my wife Tiffany (she lived in a sorority across the street).

I would describe myself as a pretty social person. Tiffany and I almost never have a free weekend where we aren't doing something with our friends or our dog Harley.

I'm not very religious although I was raised Episcopalian. I believe in God and love being kind to people.

I'm leaving so much out. Like the time I almost cut my finger off when I was 4 years old. Or the time when I crashed my parents' new car when I was 16. But I can save these stories for later.

I do have so many questions for you. How old were you when you had me? What was your life like after you had me? When you said you weren't able to have any other children was it for physical reasons?

What's my nationality? I was told that it was German. Are your parents from Germany? Why do I tan so easily? :)

What can you tell me about my birthfather?

Are there any medical things I should know?

Are there any specific questions you want to ask me?

Ok. I'll stop here. As you can see, I have so many questions and things I want to tell you. Thank you for being so open to all of this. I hope to hear back from you soon (when you get a chance). I'm taking Tiffany away for her birthday for a couple of days starting tomorrow night and may or may not have email access.

Yours,

Dave

PS. I've posted a web site that I did of pictures from my wedding if you'd like to see what I look like. The guy on the microphone with the gray beard is my dad, the other guy on the microphone in the tux with glasses is my brother (he was the best man), and my mom is the one with curly hair kissing me on the cheek.

In April 2002, after several more e-mails back and forth and some trip planning, Susan Auerbach boarded a plane. At the other end of the trip, for the first time in Susan's life, she was picked up at the airport by her son—now a man—at San Francisco International Airport. Dave Cook and Susan Auerbach spent an emotional week together in the Bay Area. By design, they left the schedule very open. Susan met Dave's parents and saw the place where Dave and his wife had married. The weather smiled on the reunion, and they spent some beautiful days around the Bay Area.

Dave and Susan realize how lucky they are. They both were in the right place when Dave decided to find her. They count their blessings each day as the relationship grows.

Postscript: In Dave's Own Words

Looking back on what I did, it was extremely important that my adoptive mom wanted it to happen. She also wanted to let Sue know that I was okay and what a gift I was to her. It's hard to say what would have happened if my mom had been unsupportive. Knowing myself, there might have been a level of defiance. I might have done it sooner. That would not have been as good, because it would have been fueled by something other than my being ready to do it. Knowing that it was about when I was ready actually made me put it off until I was ready.

The main people I looked to for advice and support were my mom, my wife and a coworker who was especially interested and excited about what I wanted to do. They were able to listen and sort of reflect. If I would say something, they'd ask, "Why are you feeling like this?" and we would talk about it. I felt I could trust them with what I was feeling. I didn't tell my father for a week after I contacted Sue. I was nervous about how he'd react. I sought out the people who'd definitely support what I wanted to do.

I've spent a lot of time looking at Sue's pictures, especially shots of her as a young girl. She looked like me. I hadn't even thought of that when I decided to contact her. My whole life, I've never looked like anyone else around me. That was really amazing. I had no idea how I'd feel about meeting her, watching videos of her growing up. Being able to fill in the years of her life has been an incredible experience.

People who want to find a biological parent should be careful. Play all the scenarios out in your mind, even the bad ones. Make sure you're comfortable and are doing it for reasons you're sure of. Make sure the timing is right. I guess it's sort of like when the knock at the door gets really loud. When I approached Sue, I had the time to do it. Also try to play out what level of communication you'll have.

I've told some adopted people about my search, and they've had different reactions. Some have a lot of anger about their own adoption. I think that is a sign of a different kind; maybe it's not telling them to find their parent now, but to explore why they're angry. Some people are afraid of what will happen, that they won't like what they find. I dealt with that by saying that I just wanted to let my mother know I was okay. No matter how she reacted, I would achieve what I wanted. For anything after that, I sort of said, "We'll see what happens." I don't know how I would have reacted if things had not worked out well.

This will change my life. I feel like there's calmness. I feel at ease about a lot of things. I feel a sense of confidence—that anything's possible. There are amazing possibilities out there.

What would I say if I spoke with a sixteen-year-old who was in the position Sue was in when she gave me up? I would say that you have the chance to give a gift to someone else. You can give the gift of life to someone who can do good things and affect a lot of people. This mistake is an opportunity if you want to take advantage of it, but it's also a sacrifice. Sue definitely made a sacrifice to give me life, and I am so thankful for that.

Postscript: In Susan's Own Words

I am also from an upper-middle-class family. I grew up in suburban Washington, D.C. I got pregnant and had a baby two weeks shy of my seventeenth birthday. I was five months pregnant before I admitted I was pregnant. It was a very different world in 1969. It was pretty clear from the beginning that the best decision I could make would be to give the baby up for adoption—that it would be in the baby's best interest not to be raised by a seventeen-year-old girl, and in my own best interest. I was too far along for abortion. It wasn't an option. I was referred to a physician in Bethesda who was known for working with young women who were pregnant. He had a connection with an attorney, and they arranged the adoption.

I didn't know the Cooks' name. There were medical complications when Dave was born, and that was pretty traumatic. I needed to have a cesarean section. A couple days after Dave was born, they walked me down to the nursery. I looked at him. Then I had to carry him out of the hospital and hand him to someone else, not the Cooks. I never allowed myself to have regrets about the decision. I never allowed myself to think it wasn't the right decision. I now feel that decision has been confirmed.

Every year on Dave's birthday, I thought about him. Because of the cesarean, I have a physical scar that I see every day when I'm in the shower. I was never able to have children after Dave. I sometimes wondered if I was being punished for giving up Dave. I feel at times that I need to apologize to Dave, even though I gave birth to him and made the right decision. Maybe there's part of me that thinks I should have kept him, and I took the easy way out. When I think about this, I dismiss it. There's no basis for me to feel guilty. But guilt has been with me since 1970, and sometimes it's been severe.

I didn't know whether Dave knew he was adopted. I have known a lot of adopted people who have issues with their birth parents. I didn't want to mess up his life. I was very, very, very afraid of him being angry at me. That is why I never tried to look for him. I never knew what his name was. I walked around for seven years with a clipping from Dear Abby about the National Adoption Registry. I never acted on it. I was afraid he would contact me and be angry. It might have been different if I'd known someone who had a good experience. I might have posted my name somewhere to make it easier for him to find me if he wanted. For example, I might have put my name in the National Adoption Registry.

I put my name in Classmates.com because of my thirtieth high-school reunion. Dave's e-mail was beautiful. I got the e-mail from Classmates.com and I'm thinking "D Cook, D Cook, D Cook, I don't remember D Cook." I went to a fairly large high school. I opened it up. . . . My jaw dropped. I was in shock. I was hyperventilating. My palms were sweating. I was freaking out. I knew it was real. It was his birth date. It is a magical, special date in my life. I was really excited, but also quite anxious. I wasn't afraid, just really excited. For thirty-one years I had a fantasy this was going to happen. I always thought he'd come to the door. I was grateful it was an e-mail. My predominant emotion since then has been excitement.

What's amazing is that we like each other so much. This has worked out unbelievably well. When we were together in San Francisco, we worked on creating a relationship that we hope we will have forever. I am changed in so many ways. I will never be the same. It happened at the right time. Ten years ago it would have been harder because of things in my life—my father's death, infertility issues. Dave's timing was great. I was open for something. Earlier, I would have coped. I would have been okay with Dave coming into my life. But I am now at a place where I can really understand and appreciate what a gift this is to me personally.

Step
10

Make a Preliminary Decision
and Fine-Tune It with a Great Plan B

It is change, continuing change, inevitable change, that is the dominant factor in society today. No sensible decision can be made any longer without taking into account not only the world as it is, but the world as it will be. . . . This, in turn, means that our statesmen, our businessmen, our everyman must take on a science fictional way of thinking.

—Isaac Asimov

At any point on the path from Step 1 to Step 10, you might have made a preliminary decision: the decision you're "leaning strongly toward." If you haven't done it yet, now is the time to review your wants, concerns and practical factors; your investigation notes and advice from friends, family, mentors, experts and others; emotional considerations; timing considerations; and your reflections on values, priorities and objectives—and see where they direct you. Unless there's "only one choice," you should treat your thoughts as preliminary because there are two things you haven't done yet. You haven't done contingency planning, and you haven't considered your intuitions—the "Plus One."

Here are simple examples of contingency planning:

- You apply to a school that you know will accept you, along with more competitive schools. When you have a backup school, the decision is not whether you'll attend school next year, but which school you'll attend.
- You investigate residential options for elder care while you're trying home care for an ill parent. If home care doesn't work out, you know right where to go. The decision is not whether your parent will have sufficient, timely care, but merely where care will be provided.
- You consult a bankruptcy attorney before you embark on a business strategy that you hope will save your company. You'll keep what you learn in your pocket and avoid a mistake that will hurt you later in the bankruptcy process. The question is not whether your company can respond to the crisis, but which strategy the company will use to respond to the crisis.
- You earn a certificate by attending school at night while you start your own business, so that if the business does not work out, you're more employable in the job market. You won't fail if you don't succeed in your new business; you'll start another career based on the additional qualification you obtained at night. If the qualification also helps you in your new business, so much the better.
- You check out the job market before you learn whether you'll receive an important promotion. If you don't receive the promotion, you're prepared to move. The other opportunities you've identified are your metaphorical "parachute."

Step 10 is dynamic and creative. Contingency planning is the most fluid part of the decision process. A contingency plan (Plan B) may take more effort than your main plan (Plan A). As you work through Step 10 and project the impact of your decision on uncertain future events, you'll constantly adjust and refine your preliminary decision. This process will create a new preliminary decision for you to evaluate all over again. Step 10 creates a better Plan A and a solid Plan B. Contingency planning is a crucial step.

Your Preliminary Decision

Any decision that may be changed is, in a sense, preliminary. Many "final" decisions can be changed down the road. You see how a decision works, and you make more decisions and adjustments as you go along. Yet Big Decisions often involve a major change in direction—what's sometimes called a "watershed," a dividing point between before and after. While many Big Decisions can be adjusted to some degree, the costs often are high: bankruptcy, divorce, relocation, finding new employment, embarrassment and so on. Some Big Decisions—for example, life support and decisions related to civil or criminal liability—are difficult or impossible to undo. The extremely high cost of changing course is part of what makes a Big Decision difficult. The stakes of a Big Decision are high.

When we refer to a "preliminary decision," we're talking about a decision that you are leaning toward after you've put in a lot of thought and legwork, but before you're committed irrevocably. You can still reconsider it, adjust it or change your mind. You might be thinking that a preliminary decision doesn't sound like a decision. You're right. It's a hypothetical scenario, cast in the form of a decision. It helps you play out future events in your mind by projecting effects that will flow from the decision. The preliminary decision is a tool to help you think about how the future will play out.

You must be able to hypothesize how the future will unfold to do contingency planning.

The Contingency-Planning Process

Contingency planning is a process that is based upon five steps that form a simple loop:

1. Make your preliminary decision on Plan A.
2. Evaluate how the preliminary decision is likely to play out, starting with your list of wants, concerns and practical factors, and your assessment of how the unknowns most likely will be resolved.
3. Adjust your preliminary decision to reduce the risks that can be reduced by making acceptable changes to your preliminary decision (or how it will be carried out).
4. Go back to step 2 and reevaluate how your adjusted preliminary decision is likely to play out, then repeat steps 3 and 4. Move to step 5 only when you've made all the possible adjustments.
5. Develop approaches to deal with risks that can't be reduced any further.

Contingency planning leads directly to better decisions for several reasons. Contingency planning helps you identify and avoid problems that may arise as you execute Plan A, which results in a refinement of Plan A. By preparing for certain risks in advance, contingency planning reduces the magnitude of those anticipated risks. A reduced risk level will permit you to make a more aggressive decision and, with greater possible benefits, still take a risk that you consider reasonable. If your decision fails, contingency planning will reduce the cost and may even create benefits. Many Plan Bs end up delivering more benefits than Plan A ever could have delivered.

Let's revisit Robert's decision whether to report fraud committed by his supervisor, Dan. We introduced Robert's decision in Step 2 when Robert created a list of wants, concerns and practical factors. We identified and ordered Robert's target questions in Step 3. Let's assume that Robert's target questions were answered as follows:

Target Question #1: What would it cost Robert to talk to a lawyer about his supervisor's (Dan's) fraud?

Answer #1: $175 an hour, so Robert scheduled a one-hour consultation to get some basic advice from a lawyer who had background in employment law and white-collar crime.

Target Question #2: Is Robert committing a crime if he doesn't report Dan?

Answer #2: The lawyer said, "In theory, no, since you're not assisting the fraud—but you're in a dangerous spot because you know about it. Someone might claim you were involved. There's a real danger that you'll become embroiled in criminal proceedings if Dan's activities come to light. It's best to get on the right side before it's too late."

Target Question #3: Will Robert lose his job if he reports Dan's fraud?

Answer #3: The lawyer couldn't give much assurance, except to emphasize how important it would be to report Dan to the right person and to make sure Robert has good evidence. "If you're going to go after big game, you'd better kill it," the lawyer said. In the event Robert is terminated in retaliation for his report (perhaps by a manager who is friendly to Dan), the lawyer assures Robert that the lawyer is available to challenge the termination.

Target Question #4: Will Robert become unemployable if he reports Dan's fraud?

Answer #4: Also no assurance. The lawyer pointed out that it would be difficult for Robert even to know why a prospective employer rejected him. If Dan has friends, there's risk that Robert will be blackballed in his industry.

Target Question #5: How should Robert go about reporting Dan, if Robert decides to do it?

Answer #5: The lawyer had some ideas about how to make a confidential report, but says Robert should proceed on the assumption Dan will eventually find out about the report. The lawyer agreed with Robert's concern that Dan's direct supervisor might be too friendly with Dan. The lawyer advised Robert to approach a particular non-sales manager several levels above Dan.

Robert's preliminary decision after the legal consultation is that he should report Dan's fraud. The possibility of becoming embroiled in criminal proceedings is way too serious for Robert's comfort. Items 3 and 4 remain uncertain, however. These items are fertile ground for contingency planning. Robert starts by going back to his wants, concerns and practical factors, running through the "what-ifs" and jotting down some possible strategies:

Wants: If I can't keep my job, I want to maximize the chances I'll land on my feet.

Possible Steps to Reduce the Impact If I Lose My Job:

✓ Lawyer already lined up. Will try to force a rehire or, even better, negotiate a cash settlement of termination claims, an outplacement period and a mutually agreed-upon reference letter.
✓ Investigate job market now. Know what's out there. Create job-search plan.

✓ Review how safe savings assets are and put away more.

✓ File for unemployment benefits if terminated.

✓ Talk to my wife about short-term employment options for both of us.

✓ Update résumé.

Steps to Protect Employability:

✓ Let dependable references know I might be making a change.

✓ List potential employers (note places where Dan might have influence).

✓ Get lawyer's input on how to prevent Dan from "poisoning the well."

✓ Investigate opportunities in other geographic areas and industries.

✓ Read about the experiences of others who "blew the whistle" to see what issues came up and how the issues were handled.

Robert hasn't eliminated the risk in his Big Decision, but he's reduced it. He has a good plan and is a step ahead of Dan and everyone else in the picture. His comfort level is higher because he has a good plan that will help him make and execute a very tough choice.

Your contingency plan must be real, you must be willing to do it, and it must be feasible. A contingency plan that won't work, is too expensive or risky, or which you lack the commitment to carry out is no plan. If you know that you don't have a real backup plan, you won't make better decisions. You'll make the same decisions that you would make without a backup plan, because you *are* without a backup plan.

Managing Contingencies with a "First Strike"

Aggressive contingency planning goes beyond figuring out how to control future damage. In many cases, especially where emotional and public-relations issues are involved, contingencies often are best addressed if you take the initiative and make the first move.

Here's an example:

> You want to stop an immediate family member's substance abuse, and you decide preliminarily to go forward with a substance-abuse intervention. You wonder what distant family members will think when they hear about the intervention. Because you live with the abuser, you know more about the abuse than distant family members. In fact, you and your immediate family have covered for the abuser at family gatherings. You're worried that distant family members will misunderstand the intervention and see it as an over-reaction to a minor problem.

The concerns identified in the above example could be addressed with a first-strike strategy. What if you let the less-involved family members know what is happening before they hear rumors? The conversation might go something like this:

> Hi, it's Jean. I just wanted to let you know that we have taken some steps to get my dad into rehab for an alcohol (or drug) abuse problem. We hope it will be very brief. Over the past few months, my mother and I became worried that Dad had a problem. I'd rather not go into the details on the phone but, believe me, it's gotten very rough for all of us. And him. We were concerned he might hurt himself on the road or get sick. We spoke with a counselor, who suggested that we discuss the problem with Dad and get him into rehab. So we're doing that. I wanted to let you know what's going on. I didn't want this to catch you by surprise. I know you'll understand, and I'll keep you posted. If Dad calls you, please support our efforts. We really need everyone's love and support (or prayers) to get through this.

In this scenario, the person who initiated the intervention didn't wait until rumors brought family fallout. She took the initiative, preparing and educating family members. By bringing the other family members into the process, the intervener showed her respect for the distant relatives and probably gained quite a bit of reciprocal respect for an open approach. Like everything that involves people, the strategy has its own risks. Some distant family members might think nothing of trying to interfere with an intervention. Moreover, it is critical to respect and protect the dignity and privacy of the person who has the problem (Dad). At the end of the day, your judgment is very important on these "political" issues. If the distant family members would never know about the problem or the intervention, it may not be necessary to say anything at all.

If a problem is virtually inevitable down the line, consider bringing it to a head on your schedule with a first strike. The anticipated emotional response of a third party, for example, often can be managed better with a first strike. Even if avoiding anger, frustration, disappointment, sadness, hysteria or rage is impossible, almost all of these responses come in degrees and flavors. By anticipating a response and managing it actively, you'll be at a significant advantage.

The main risk of a first strike is that you may be doing something unnecessary or even harmful. The less you know about what actually will happen, the riskier it is to launch a first strike based on your *assumptions* about what will develop. Accordingly, it is important in contingency planning to investigate the facts, test your assumptions and, if necessary, get advice from someone who's "been there."

We leave Step 10 with the following points to remember about preliminary decisions and contingency planning:

- Remember that your preliminary decision is only a starting point. It should be followed by a dynamic and creative contingency-planning process through which you'll adjust the decision.
- Your contingency plans will enable you to make more aggressive decisions, which may lead to higher rewards.
- A contingency plan must be real, something you can actually go to if Plan A stalls.
- The more active, creative and thorough you are in developing a contingency plan (or plans), the better the contingency plan will be and the more it will help your decision.

Intervention: When Nothing Else Worked, an Alcoholic's Daughter Did the Unthinkable to Stop Her Mother's Drinking

Samantha Littlejohn was desperate when she decided to "drop a dime" on her mother, but Samantha may have saved her mother's life.

Samantha Littlejohn[21] remembers what afternoons were like when she was a teenager:

I came home from school, and I did what's called a "mood check." I searched the house to determine where my mother was: what room she was in and what mood she was in. There are so many moods that go with alcoholism. I'd have to figure out what to say to her about my day to appease her. Was my mom angry? Was she sleeping? The consequences of not knowing her mood could be severe.

Samantha's mother, Marjorie, was a vodka drinker for as long as Samantha could remember. Marjorie's drinking

---

[21]The names in this story are pseudonyms.

dominated Samantha's childhood and her adolescence. "In a lot of ways," Samantha recalls, "I was a girl who didn't have a mother." It created a strange alliance between Samantha and her father, who shared their despair:

My dad and I went skiing and rafting together. Mom was never there. She always stayed home. I always looked more mature than my age, and my dad looked young. We spent so much time together that strangers thought we were married. My dad and I kept each other company. He was the only person I could talk to about my mom and her drinking. I often felt like I was my mom's mother.

Samantha, Samantha's father and her brother Ted were always trying strategies to help Marjorie to stop drinking. Nothing worked. Marjorie was in classic denial. She did not believe she had a drinking problem—and if she did, Marjorie believed it was nobody's business. Samantha, Ted and their father went to Al-Anon, Alateen and back to Al-Anon. They visited family counselors. Marjorie and her husband tried couples counseling. In the end, Marjorie said, "My drinking has nothing to do with you. It has no effect on you or your father. So quit talking to me about it."

At the age of seventeen, Samantha graduated high school and moved out of her home, going to a different city to attend college. She met Craig when she was twenty and fell in love. Samantha and Craig were engaged when Samantha was twenty-one, and they planned to be married in the late summer of 1992.

Although she lived more than a hundred miles away, Samantha kept in constant communication with her father. He gave Samantha frequent reports about Marjorie, and the reports were not good. Marjorie's drinking problem wasn't getting better. Without Samantha around, Samantha's father became lonely, frustrated and despondent. At the beginning of the summer of 1992, Samantha's father told her that he had met a woman and planned to leave Samantha's mother. Samantha didn't blame her father, but both Samantha and her father worried about what would happen to Marjorie's health and safety when she was alone.

As Samantha put it:

When my father left my mom, I became really scared. My father lived pretty close, but he couldn't check on her all the time. Now there was nobody around. I didn't blame my father for leaving. He tried his best. But I now started to see my mom as being on a road that would end in death.

The summer of 1992 was a watershed for Samantha. Samantha's relationship with Craig was going extremely well, as Samantha and Craig planned their wedding. Samantha thought a lot about family that summer. Her mother couldn't help her with the wedding plans. That was completely out of the question. Samantha wanted her mother to attend the wedding, to play something of the role that a mother is supposed to play at a wedding. Samantha knew both extended families would be at the wedding. Samantha was terrified about what would happen at the wedding. During the same time, Samantha was becoming obsessed with visions of her mother's death, future car accidents and injuries caused to her mother and others, and embarrassment:

My brother and I would imagine the car accident she was going to get in. We knew all the people she did business with. We knew her doctors, the veterinarian, the pharmacy people. We even knew the storekeepers at the grocery stores where she bought her alcohol. We feared that one of them would call the police. It made so much sense to me that one of these people she saw on a regular basis would call the police and turn her in. Do we wait until she wraps her car around a tree? Or do we wait until, God forbid, she hits a child or a car? Wait until she hurts or kills somebody? I pictured all of these scenarios. Those were all things that I could picture. It was horrible. I imagined how things would look if they got better, and I imagined what would happen if they got worse. I wanted them to get better so badly. That summer it became my mission.

On a visit to her hometown two months before the wedding, Samantha picked up the phone book and started thumbing through listings for "Alcoholism Rehabilitation." She'd heard about interventions and wanted to find out more about them. Samantha and Ted made a secret visit to one of the places in the telephone book, a hospital with a rehabilitation unit, and met with an intervention specialist for the first time. The intervention specialist was a man who specialized in alcoholism interventions. He'd been through hundreds of them. After Samantha and Ted told the specialist about Marjorie, the specialist told them that he might not be able to help Samantha's mother. An intervention might not work.

This will work, is all Samantha could think. They begged the specialist to take the case. Samantha assured the intervention specialist that she, Ted and other people who were close to her mother would cooperate fully. They would do whatever it took, for however long, to get Marjorie well.

Several schools of thought exist on how an intervention should be conducted. The approach used at the hospital Samantha visited was a common one. The goal is to force the substance abuser to make a choice—a Big Decision—between addiction and the other things that the abuser values. The intervention often starts with a surprise confrontation, where loved ones are brought into the room. There's role-playing. One family member cries. Another reasons. A friend gets angry. The intervention specialist guides the process to a destination: a decision to stop the abuse and a plan of action.

The participants in this kind of intervention tell the abuser how the abuser has harmed relationships. They try to move past the denials. They assure the abuser that they love her (or him), and that the abuser is important to them. Ultimately, the group discusses the fact that the abuser has to make a choice: give up alcohol or risk losing what's truly important. Through the process, the abuser hits rock bottom and sees the need to make a major change. The group promises to support the abuser. The abuser's desire to change has to come from within. The intervention crystallizes the abuser's choice and forces the abuser to come to terms with everything that's at stake. Instead of allowing the abuser to destroy all of his or her relationships over a decade, the abuser is told the relationships already have been harmed. What would be said should have plenty of credibility to Marjorie, Samantha reasoned. After all, Marjorie had just lost her husband.

The first intervention involved tricking Marjorie to go to a hospital, where emotional meetings occurred with Samantha, Ted, Samantha's grandmother (Marjorie's mother) and the intervention specialist. The intervention seemed to work. Marjorie checked herself into a rehabilitation program. For a brief moment when Marjorie completed the program, the Littlejohns' nightmare seemed to be over. Within hours of coming home, however, Marjorie fell off the wagon.

Samantha, Ted and their grandmother did a second intervention. This time, they emphasized to Marjorie that relationships were at stake. If Marjorie didn't stop drinking, Samantha and Ted said they'd terminate all contact with Marjorie. Marjorie's response hurt Samantha more than anything she'd ever heard: "I'll still have my dogs." Nonetheless, after the second intervention, Marjorie swore she was finished with drinking, and she checked herself into a second rehabilitation program. When Marjorie was released the second time, the Littlejohns believed that their mother had finally beaten alcoholism.

On a subsequent visit to her mom's house, Samantha smelled the unmistakably familiar scent of vodka on her mother's breath. Samantha searched the house and found an opened bottle hidden in a cupboard. Samantha confronted Marjorie. Samantha's mother stood in front of her in the kitchen and said, "No, I haven't had a drink." Now Samantha hit rock bottom. *We really did fail,* Samantha thought. *Now we have to take the next step and terminate contact with her. We had threatened to do that, but now we needed to follow through.*

Samantha knew that if she and Ted didn't terminate contact with their mother, they would never again have credibility with her. If they did, they'd lose their mother. The intervention specialist was pessimistic. After the second intervention, the specialist asked Samantha if she wanted to quit trying. For Samantha it wasn't an option. The intervention specialist and the rehabilitation doctors started to talk about failure. Samantha had to continue.

As Samantha started to walk out of her mother's house, she looked at her mother's wall calendar. Her mother had an appointment to take her dogs to the veterinarian at 1:30 P.M. the following day. Samantha knew the route her mother would take, and she had some friends with a house close to her mother's destination. Samantha and Ted were desperate. They started to think about a different kind of intervention—having Marjorie arrested:

We'd put all this stock in the interventions. We attended them, and she drank anyway. I remember saying, "What if she gets in a car accident? What if the police came? They'd find out that she was drunk. It wouldn't be us; it would be the police." We would keep our side of the deal. We wouldn't contact her. But Mom would have to admit to being an alcoholic to someone else—the police. It was our only course of action. My objective was to create a real bottom for her. Nothing so far had stopped her drinking. Not me, not Ted, not her mother, not the interventions, not the rehabilitation. Maybe this would be a reason to stop drinking. I thought about the jail. I started to hope she'd have to spend at least one night in jail. I thought, "It would be okay if my mom had to spend one night in jail. It would be okay if she had to appear in front of a judge and admit to being drunk. She has a lot to lose, and she doesn't recognize that." I had to give her a reason to fix herself.

The next morning around 8:00, Samantha Littlejohn called the police station. She gave the dispatcher a simple report: "My mother's name is Marjorie Littlejohn. She lives at 377 Talmidge Street. She'll be at the corner of Veteran Street and Highway 136 at around

12:25 P.M. She will be intoxicated, very likely above the legal limit." Samantha provided her mother's license-plate number and a physical description of Marjorie. The dispatcher asked Samantha who was calling. "Samantha Littlejohn," she said, "Marjorie Littlejohn's daughter. She doesn't know I'm doing this."

"Oh," the dispatcher said, "I understand. Thank you for the information, Samantha." The dispatcher took the telephone number at the house of Samantha's friend.

Samantha and Ted waited. Five hours later, the telephone rang.

"Is this Samantha Littlejohn?" the man on the telephone asked.

"Yes," Samantha answered.

"You may want to come down here. We're in an alley just past Veteran and Highway 136. We've got your mother in our squad car. She's in custody with what appears to be a high blood-alcohol level."

"How is she?" Samantha asked.

"Shaky," the officer responded. "She's being cooperative. I think she's in emotional shock. We'll be taking her down to the station."

Samantha and Ted jumped into Samantha's car. Samantha recalls:

I was pretty shaky, too. When we got there, I saw my mother's empty car in the distance. There were two police cars. There was my fifty-year-old mother in the back of the police car. She hid her face. I introduced myself to the policeman in charge. One of the policemen was Ted's former gym coach at our high school. We hugged him. The coach was crying. I got in my mother's car and drove away. My mother later complained bitterly about how the police treated her. She claimed it was "the worst treatment." It was cold in the police car. They refused to roll the windows up. . . .

Marjorie didn't like being arrested. She also was concerned about how she'd appear in front of the judge. It was a shock like none other. The judge gave her a huge fine. Samantha was glad. "I didn't trust that the message would stay. The more the penalty, the better." Marjorie stopped drinking and entered a rehabilitation program for the third time after the arrest in an effort to show the judge that she was on the right track.

This time it worked.

Postscript: In Samantha's Own Words

It's been ten years, and my mother has not had a drink.

The whole intervention process gave me focus, a mission, something to do. For so long, I'd been helpless. The things we'd tried before didn't work. I had to be completely committed, so I became committed. Ironically, I used survival skills that my mother's alcoholism taught me. While I feel I was very brave and that I accomplished what I set out to do by the decisions I made back then, I still believe that I have a long way to go myself. I am still recovering from my mom's alcoholism. If our efforts hadn't worked out, I don't think I would have had any regrets about it. If my mom died as a result of her alcoholism, my mom would have chosen death, and I would have done everything I could to get her off that course.

I really believed my mother was going to die. Calling the police was the most difficult decision. It was not as safe as a hospital intervention. I didn't know what the police and the courts were going to say and do with her. It was my own strategy.

My husband Craig and I have faced some really big decisions in the past ten years. How I handled my mother's drinking had a big effect on how I make decisions. I know the lasting impact a hard decision can have. I got my mother back. Before this, my big decisions were, "Which apartment am I going to rent?" "Which

*car am I going to buy?" When big issues come up now, I say,
"What about five years from now? What about ten years from
now?" I can look ahead. I really look into the future. We talk
about this once or twice a year, which is pretty often. It comes up
when we talk about relationships. We talk about the longevity of
relationships and what can be done to maintain them. Every little
thing you do in a family you have to be sure you have no regrets
about it.*

*I also learned that I have the power to leave. I have the right to
take care of myself by getting out. Before this, I never would have
thought I had the right to leave my mother. I learned that I do. If
it had come down to that, I'd have done it. You have to do what
you can to save yourself. Put your own oxygen mask on first, as
they tell you on an airplane. Then use your strength to help others.*

*I would tell others who are in my position to speak to somebody,
go seek help. Keep trying until you find that right person to work
with you. You can't make the other person stop. It's got to be up
to them. They won't stop until they want to stop. They must have
a reason to stop. You can attempt to give them that reason, but you
can't make them stop. We couldn't take away the things that were
important to my mother—her house, her dogs. It hurt me a lot to
realize that I didn't make a difference to her. The threat that I
would leave wasn't enough for her. She needed more. The arrest
was it.*

*I hadn't planned to have kids. Home life wasn't a high point
for me when I grew up. I have two kids now. I am so passionate
about working with kids—for raising them right. I think a lot
about the relationships kids have with their parents, their relationships with each other, and how to teach them, what to read to
them, what will challenge them. I'm always careful to compli-
ment my kids more than I criticize them each day. I do the jobs at
school that people hate. I'll be there for my kids. I've learned that
passion can lead us down the path to make a difference.*

I'm so offended when I go to a neighborhood party and the other parents get drunk in front of their kids, even to the point that the parents aren't able to walk. I don't tell people what my childhood was like with my mother. It's very private to me.

My mother learned later that I had called the police. One of the Twelve Steps in the Alcoholics Anonymous program is to make amends to the people you've hurt, those who've been affected. When my mother was making amends, I wanted to make amends, too. She didn't say much when I told her. She just got real quiet.

What's important is that my mother hasn't had a drink for ten years. I love my mother.

Plus 1

Respect Your Heart, Your Gut, Your Instincts and Your Intuition—Then Go for It!

When making a decision of minor importance, I have always found it advantageous to consider all the pros and cons. In vital matters, however, such as the choice of a mate or a profession, the decision should come from the unconscious, from somewhere within ourselves. In the important decisions of personal life, we should be governed, I think, by the deep inner needs of our nature.

—Sigmund Freud

A hunch is creativity trying to tell you something.

—Frank Capra

I learned always to trust my own deep sense of what I should do and not just obediently trust the judgment of others—even others better than I am.

—Barbara Deming

T he 10 Steps will not make your Big Decision for you. *You will make the decision.* The risk of presenting 10 Steps is that our method will be misinterpreted as a mechanical process. A wide variety of factors affect how humans make major decisions, including:

- The unique combination of values, abilities, needs, perceptions and emotions of each decision-maker, the decision-maker's personality and even genetics
- The process applied by the decision-maker to make the decision (this is where the 10 Steps come in)
- The extent to which the decision-maker is ready, willing and able to execute the alternatives presented

The 10 Steps help you crystallize a Big Decision—to face the difficult issues that you must face, sort through the variables and travel the path with greater confidence. The 10 Steps bring structure to a fluid situation. The 10 Steps force you to analyze, and remind you that indecision, fear and paralysis have costs. *The 10 Steps help you move forward.*

Once you apply the 10 Steps, you have a better grasp of what the real issues and choices are, what factors influence your judgment, and what steps are most likely to lead you to the right (or wrong) choice. Even after you apply the 10 Steps, however, powerful internal voices and intuitions still may tell you what to do. If the voices are consistent with the conclusions you reached after applying the 10 Steps, the choice is easy. Yet what do you do with gut feelings or intuitions that say the opposite? What do you do with nagging doubts? What do you do with hunches and what your heart tells you to do? What do you do with dreams? Premonitions? What do you do when the answer comes to you in prayer?

Dismissing intuition as a silly basis on which to make an important decision would be easy. Yet we are swayed by anecdotes of intuition succeeding where logic failed.

The following story is true:

Early in World War II, sirens sounded air raid safety drills once or twice a week in Tokyo. As the war intensified, drills were replaced with warnings of real air raids. When the fatherless Kashiro family of Tokyo heard real warnings, the widowed mother and her two daughters were supposed to go to a subterranean bomb shelter at the local Shinto temple, as instructed by public officials. On March 9, 1945, real warning sirens sounded and firebombs started to rain from the Tokyo sky. The Kashiro family did not go to the bomb shelter. This time, after obediently participating in all of the drills and earlier warnings, mother Kashiro said, "No, we are not going to go to the shelter. We have to save ourselves. We don't have to listen to anybody." As Tokyo filled with smoke and fire from the firebombs, mother Kashiro pulled her daughters out of the house and into the streets. The family stumbled around Tokyo, trying to avoid the smoke and fire. There were bodies and pieces of charred flesh everywhere. Whenever the Kashiros saw a fire, they turned and went in another direction. They did this without sleep for three days. When the bombing was over, the Kashiros returned to their home. It had been burned to the ground. Neighbors who had never spoken hugged each other and cried together (which, in itself, was unusual in Japanese culture). The people who had gone to the bomb shelter were dead. The heat had been so intense that people in the shelters were baked. The Kashiro daughters are alive today, as are their children and grandchildren, thanks to Mother Kashiro.

What should we do with stories like this? Rationality, deference to authorities and wisdom didn't save the Kashiros. The Kashiros were saved by some kind of mother's intuition. Maybe even that's a stretch. Perhaps the Kashiros were saved by dumb luck or panic. Writing off this story as a fluky anecdote should be easy for a rational person. But it's not easy. The story stays with us. Stories like the Kashiros' remind us that, like intuition, pure logic also has its limits.

So often we find that purveyors of rational thinking are charla-tans and poor logicians. What is rational and logical—like what is commonsensical—is far more subjective than most of us admit. We rely on information that is biased by its source, then view the information through our own biased lenses. Our values often are conflicting, unformed or ambiguous. Our understanding of the risks, rewards and basic cause-and-effect is limited by our imper-fect knowledge and often is just plain wrong. Is logic what we use to make our decisions, or is "logic" a word we slap on decisions that are made with much less rigorous methods? Is intuition the opposite of rational thinking, or is it rational thought operating at a deeper level?

The risk you take if you disregard your intuition is that your intuition may serve you better than your conscious thoughts. You don't process all information at the conscious level, even when you're awake. You observe events that never become thoughts. Incidents that you've repressed or thoughts that you want to avoid are percolating under the surface. Your mind may refuse to call up certain thoughts, but they're not gone. You capture events in your peripheral vision and study them, even while your attention is directed straight ahead. You analyze life while you're sleeping, but you only get a glimpse of what you've figured out. More than any "bounce," mentor, expert advisor, friend or family member, your intuitive faculties study your situation, all day and all night, look-ing out for you.

Your intuition asserts itself in many different ways. You may have a nagging doubt. A solution may come to you during prayer, during the night or in a dream. You may believe that your intuition has a divine source. Intuition may be a hunch. A situation may not feel right, or it might feel very right. Regardless of how your intuition asserts itself, remember the following when a Big Decision is involved: *Intuition is how you tell yourself to consider and weigh a piece of information that you didn't find in other ways.*

The final step in making your Big Decision is determining what to do with your intuition.

Your Intuition Is Your Angel:
Respect Your Angel

Whether or not you believe in angels, treat your intuition as your personal angel (or "guide," if you're not comfortable with angels). Intuition is telling you something, trying to help you, for reasons that are real but not always obvious. The ultimate source of intuition is for psychologists, theologians and spiritualists to ponder. Whether intuition is from God or from mental operations that occur below the conscious level, for the purpose of a Big Decision, the message is the same: Never ignore your intuition, even if you choose to override it.

Sharon Thom has been a spiritual practitioner for twenty-five years, and for four years she was CEO of Esalen Institute. Thom's primary vocation for several years has been grief counselor of last resort. Thom's clients include parents who have very ill children, teenagers who self-mutilate or starve themselves, people who are involved in binge drinking and attempted suicides. By the time a client finds Thom, the client typically has been through psychiatrists, failed to improve with powerful medication and done everything else that the "traditional" mental-health-care system recommended. Nothing's worked. Thom's methodology uses trust-building exercises, conversation, music, poetry and a variety of very nonmedical spiritual practices and procedures. Thom claims her own decisions are "all intuition." She lives, studies and practices intuition.

Thom argues that intuition operates at a deeper level than

emotion. Thom doesn't know exactly where intuition starts, but she describes intuition as emanating from "the space between the molecules"—a place that is different from where emotions and conscious thoughts operate. Thom describes intuition and its role in Big Decisions as follows:

> Information reaches us through a variety of conduits: the senses, language, innuendo, body language and our intuition. The mind filters and interprets much of this information before we are aware we have received it. Sometimes, however, the mind does not succeed in putting everything it receives into a "rational" place. Then we're left with the troubling task of justifying how we know what we know through the intuition that got through. People have a hard time explaining where their intuition comes from because it bypasses the "rational mode" that does our explaining.
>
> The *Random House Dictionary* defines intuition as "the direct perception of truth or fact, independent of any reasoning processes" and "a keen and quick insight." Once we accept that we have intuitions that are not anchored in reason, and that intuition is a valid perception of truth or fact (albeit independent of the reasoning process), we can start to listen to intuition as one of the voices in a Big Decision.

When your intuition shows up, talk to it. *Why do I have this doubt? Why do I want to do this so much? Why do I keep coming back to this point? Did I look into this issue thoroughly enough? Why doesn't this feel right? Why am I so comfortable with this choice, but not with that choice? Why does this dream stick in my head? Why did I dream this just last night? Why does my heart tell me to go in a different direction? Why do I have a gut feeling this is going to be a disaster?* Pursue your intuitions until you understand them as best you can. Explore what your intuition is saying to you. When intuition doesn't show up, try to find it. Look "between the molecules."

Your doubts and intuitions won't always be correct. People you don't trust in the first meeting can prove themselves to be highly trustworthy. "Negative" proposals can grow on you. Worries can be baseless or pure neurosis. Intuition may be wrong. Intuition may be influenced by emotion and psychology. Sharon Thom, whose professional work depends on intuition, knows the limits of intuition:

> You should always listen to your intuition. That doesn't mean you always act on it. Intuition may be impractical. It may not be the best thing for you. You may intuit that "God loves me, and I know he doesn't want me to suffer. If I kill myself, I could rest, finally." That may be your intuition, but it's not put into the context of your life. The joy and pain connected with your life are not only yours. Suicide does not solve the problem of pain. It spreads it. Your action would cause pain to your loved ones for the rest of their lives. So, you see, intuition is not logical, pragmatic or societal. Listen to it, learn from it and understand what I call its "wild irrationality." Then, sometimes, step away from it.

Business-decision advisor David Fishman wants to know and understand the intuitions of an experienced client on a business decision. "Experience-based intuition is critical to understand," according to Fishman. "When the intuition of an experienced executive, who's proven herself, disagrees with what a decision process shows, we must understand the difference. We either conclude that the decision process had shortcomings or the intuition is wrong. Both outcomes provide huge learning. Either way, the team members involved become better at making decisions—something that everyone is certain to do again and again."

Bring intuitions into your conscious mind. Dig into the source of intuitions and understand them. Pursue your intuitions until you cannot find out any more about them. Most important, as Sharon Thom says, put your intuition into the context of all factors that bear on your decision and your life.

Make a Beautiful Big Decision

Intuition has an important role if, after you've gone through the process, your choice still is not clear. Let's say you've correctly identified the decision. You broke it down into nice little pieces and eliminated distractions. You investigated it to the hilt. You analyzed the probabilities, and you scrutinized your fact and opinion sources. The time is right. You took stock of the long-term consequences and will do what's best in the long term. You assessed the emotional factors and know how they are influencing you and the people around you. You understand the risks and have taken steps to reduce them in the event there's a bad outcome. Yet you still can't decide. You want to make the best choice for yourself and people who depend on you. There's no clearly "right" solution—it's "six of one, half dozen of the other." You want to make the Big Decision, but there are still two choices. Maybe three. Or four . . .

Take a walk. Or ride a bike. Or go to church. Or sleep on it one more night. Clear your head and take a few deep breaths. Maybe clean your desk (or deck). Take a final step back and let all of your deliberations blend. Ponder the options, and think about them and about who you are and your unique values. One of the choices soon will become more comfortable—more "you." Having gone through a thorough decision-making process, you've pierced many barriers to honesty with yourself. You're now in a position to say, "All things considered, this is what I *want* to do. It is what I *should* do. It is what I am *going* to do."

Architect R. Buckminster Fuller once said, "When I'm working on a problem, I never think about beauty. I think only how to solve the problem. But when I have finished, if the solution is not beautiful, I know it is wrong." A Big Decision is not always as "beautiful" as Fuller preferred his architectural solutions. While Life is Beautiful, life with a small "l" is a mixed bag. Disappointment, sorrow, frustration, pain, sacrifices and grief are inevitable. The only questions are when and how much you'll suffer. Some choices are tough because both alternatives hurt. The best alternative, even among good choices, is not always clear. Most of our choices are mired in ambiguity in the vast space between fabulous and awful, success and failure. Great decisions must be chiseled, sometimes crudely, from the choices that are presented, with whatever tools are available to us at the time.

A beautiful decision is one that moves you forward. It has costs and risks, but they are less than the costs and risks of standing still and allowing circumstances to control you. A beautiful decision has benefits, even if they are only benefits in comparison to a terrible alternative. It leaves some things more certain and others less certain, but to a degree you can accept. A beautiful decision is one that you make the right way—even if you don't make it right away. Whatever the outcome, you won't look back and say you handled it wrong. You did your best. You took control. You moved forward.

A wonderful benefit of approaching a decision correctly is that it will work out well most of the time. Life is not so random that good decisions normally lead to bad outcomes. With few exceptions, your good decisions will turn out far better than you ever imagined.

We close with a sampling of personal thoughts from people we interviewed illustrating the complex beauty and diversity of human decision-making:

- "At the end of the day, while the mechanical process may be somewhat different, after a person has looked at all of their lists, it still comes down to how they feel about the decision. I find it hard to believe that someone would think a list can make a decision."—Bill Pack, professional photographer

- "Coming from my heart, I just had to do it once I knew I would be the best candidate for the transplant. My gut feeling was 'do it'—no matter what it took. Was there a spiritual influence? Yes, I really believe there was in a lot of aspects."—Kenneth Anderson, who chose to donate a kidney to his brother

- "You end up using rationality to defend the decision you make based on your gut instinct. At least that's what I did. I could rationalize staying in San Francisco. I could rationalize moving; I could call it a career move to the East Coast to perform more. On occasions when I have not trusted my judgment, it has ended up badly. Often it's things you can't articulate."—Sharon Wayne, who moved across country for love without a marriage commitment

- "People who come into my office are unhappy, whether they're asking for the divorce or are on the other side. They're trying to free themselves of the unhappiness of their situation. Every issue is secondary to getting to a happier place. I constantly say to people that making the tough, painful decisions now will improve the long-term quality of their lives. You have to look beyond the mechanics of today's problem and find the power that is offered by a better future."—Andrew Ross, family lawyer

- "An analogy best describes where I come out on human judgment and experience-based intuition vs. a disciplined decision process. When I'm on an airplane, I want the pilot to have a lot of experience. I want him to have flown jets in the military and then flown commercially for twenty years. But I also want him to fly with instruments. I wouldn't want to travel on a plane without instruments. But then again I wouldn't take instruments without an experienced pilot. If push came to shove, would I rather have the instruments override the pilot or the pilot override the instruments? Even though you hear all these stories about human error, if push came to shove, I'd take the pilot over the instruments. But I'd want to make sure the pilot actively consulted the instruments. For a major decision, disciplined decision processes are your flight instruments."—David Fishman, managing director, Strategic Decisions Group

- "When it comes to decision-making, there is one thing you can count on: If you cannot or will not make a decision, one will be made for you."—Sharon Thom, spiritual practitioner, grief counselor and former CEO of Esalen Institute

Appendix A

A Guide to Finding and Managing Attorneys, Physicians and Other Expert Advisors

Court watchers marvel at the "battle of the experts" that often takes place at trial. Finding experts to testify and putting their advice to good use are critical tasks for trial attorneys on both sides of a case. A consumer or businessperson who needs expert advice must become involved in a similar process on the road to getting good input. While we were writing *Get Off the Fence!* we decided that an appendix by coauthor/trial attorney Jeffrey Makoff on the subject of hiring and managing expert advisors—including, of course, attorneys—would be valuable to our readers.

Yes, You May Have to Apply for an Expert

Hiring an expert can be an onerous task. Ask anyone who has tried to hire an attorney to handle a small case. You'll leave twenty messages before getting a return call from the lawyer's assistant. The assistant will inform you that her boss "doesn't practice that kind of law." Likewise, there are a lot of doctors in town, but not too many who will see you within a day (other than at an emergency room). If you are in pain but not dying, you'll make a lot of futile calls. When you find a doctor who will see you, there's a good chance you'll be referred to a specialist—who can't see you. Welcome to the world of finding an expert!

Let's start at square one—the first appointment. There are two categories of experts: those who will provide service to anyone (at least anyone who can pay for it), and those who must be persuaded to take your case. Most physicians fall within the first category. If you get an appointment, you will be treated if the physician is qualified. Most attorneys fall within the second category. The first appointment with an attorney is primarily to determine whether the lawyer will advise or represent you at all. In short, you need to apply for some experts, including an attorney, a business broker, a business advisor, and some bankers and money managers.

If you find yourself applying for an expert, such as when you need a lawyer, do some basic research so you understand what the expert seeks in a client. If you have a legal case and don't want to pay up front, how will a contingent-fee lawyer evaluate your case? If you want to sell a business, how will a business broker look at your business? With this approach, you avoid wasting time approaching experts you do not want and who do not want you. Do you need a generalist ("a business broker"), a specialist ("a small-business broker") or a subspecialist (for example, an "expert in selling one-hour photo labs in Manhattan")? What are the best directories and other sources for the expert you need? What are typical fees?

The Internet is a valuable research tool for background information about all kinds of experts. You can obtain much information from reputable Web sites of professional organizations, as well as opinions of people who have received advice from all types of experts.

How to Narrow the List

Once you've determined the type of expert you need and surveyed the field a little, you'll identify candidates. Two principles should govern this search: (1) start at the top and (2) let the experts help you do the work. There's no consistent way to determine who is "at the top" and who is not. In many professions, the established experts don't advertise heavily. Their clientele is longstanding and expands through word-of-mouth. Established experts may work at firms that promote themselves heavily, but not all members of the firm are equal. You still need to find *the* person. Scientific professionals (such as engineers) often belong to professional associations with rosters. Some associations are easy to join, however, and others are very selective. Determine whether the type of expert you need should be affiliated with a particular association or have a professional designation.

Take the field of real-estate appraisal, for example. The field roughly breaks down into MAI-designated experts and people who have not obtained the Member of the Appraisal Institute designation. MAI-designated experts have completed extensive training, passed a rigorous set of exams, obtained practical experience and are required to take continuing-education courses to stay up-to-date. The opinion of an MAI-designated appraiser carries great weight in matters of valuation, but an MAI appraiser may charge more. Don't ask a non-MAI appraiser whether you need an MAI appraiser. Work from the top down. Ask the MAI appraiser if it's overkill. The MAI appraiser has a bias, of course. If she says it's overkill, it probably is. If she says it's not overkill, consider an opinion from someone who uses appraisers but who is not in the business. For residential real-estate appraisals, the Appraisal Institute has a designation called Senior Residential Appraiser or SRA.

The Certified Financial Planner (CFP) designation is another example. A CFP has taken a series of financial-planning courses, passed an examination and fulfills continuing education requirements. While hiring a CFP alone is no guarantee that you will get a great financial advisor, the CFP designation is a big plus on the résumé of a financial advisor. Unlike law or medicine, in which licenses are required, a CFP generally is not required for a person to call himself a financial advisor or financial planner.

When you've narrowed the expert pool to some good prospects, you'll need to contact prospective experts and interview them. It's debatable whether you should make this initial contact by telephone or e-mail. The problem with e-mail is it's very easy to ignore. Moreover, some experts do not check their e-mail regularly, do not respond to unsolicited e-mail or don't appreciate e-mail from people to whom they did not provide their address. In the business world, where e-mail addresses are widely published, initial introductory contacts by e-mail are common. The benefit of e-mail is that you have a captive audience. You may never get past the expert's assistant on the telephone, but if you have a good e-mail address, the expert probably will see your note. Yet that may not improve your chances.

Whether you call or e-mail the expert, use the name of a friend or other person who referred you, if the referrer has a good relationship with the expert. Anything that gets you the benefit of the doubt is helpful. Experts (or their staffs) generally will screen you even more than you will screen them. When you've narrowed the list to a few prospective experts, focus on these questions: (1) Are the expert's professional skill and experience sufficient for your project? (2) What do other people who have worked with this expert think about his or her work? and (3) If this expert is not the right person for the job, can he or she recommend someone more suitable? The last point is the most important because the first calls you make probably will not be a perfect fit.

If the expert does not have references you can contact, something may be wrong with that expert. In our experience, even the most "confidential" advisors (attorneys, physicians, accountants, money managers) have clients who will recommend them. Indeed, happy clients are rather passionate about their favorite experts, and many will be willing to talk your ear off about how great their fifteen-year relationship has been with the expert. Ascertain how much work the expert has done for each reference, for how long and whether the work is sufficiently similar to what you need so a comparison is valid. If a reference says, "I use Jim for my personal taxes, but probably would not go to him for my company's taxes," take that qualification to heart. You are being told that Jim is not a great business accountant, which is that much more credible coming from a happy client.

You are not going to be pointed in the direction of the expert's disappointed clients, if there are some. Consider the bias that is inherent in the expert's reference list. The expert is trying to impress you. Talk to references, ask lots of questions, then ask follow-up questions. Ask a mixture of precise questions ("Does she bill her time fairly?" "Is she easy to reach?") and open-ended questions ("What is her style? How is she under time pressure?"). Also consider the identity of the references. Is this expert currently working with clients you respect—people who are unlikely to keep a bad advisor?[22]

Professional societies for practitioners in medicine, law, business and just about all other vocations are listed in reference directories or on the Internet. These groups can help you locate publications and professionals in the field you require. Local universities have experts in many areas. Universities, junior colleges and trade schools with adult-education programs have faculties in

---

[22] If an expert pulls out a client list with lots of impressive client names, find out how much work the expert actually has done with the big-name clients. Assume that client lists and other résumés cast the expert in the best light possible. Remember, it is marketing.

most practical areas of business and professional services. Move beyond the idea that experts are limited to doctors, dentists, lawyers, accountants, architects and the other traditional professional vocations. Did you know that experts are available to advise you in all of the following areas, among others?

- To help your child apply to college
- To improve your town's tourist attractions
- To set up a day-care center
- To advise you on starting a restaurant
- To show you how to get a local ballot measure adopted
- To help you write a book, song or screenplay
- To improve your wardrobe
- To help you prepare for a beauty pageant
- To train you in breast feeding
- To teach you (or your children) to have better manners
- To help with a pet psychology issue
- To help you choose and acquire a car

If an expert says he or she cannot help you with your precise issue, ask for a referral to another expert. A referral from an expert usually will be better than a referral from someone who is not in the field. Experts can appreciate fine distinctions between subjects within their areas—do you need a pediatrician or a neonatologist, a urologist or a nephrologist, a litigator or a trial lawyer? Professionals in large advisory firms keep track of qualified experts at smaller professional firms. In many cases, the list includes professionals who used to work at the large firm, but simply decided to open a smaller business for lifestyle reasons. Sometimes as you move from larger to smaller firms, the price goes down, but not always. When the price is lower, the smaller firm may not have the breadth or depth of talent. Your goal is to reduce the price of obtaining high-quality advice without reducing the quality of service too much. If you cannot find a suitable expert at the smaller firm, you may be able to find another referral. Keep moving down and around the referral chain until you find the expert you need and can afford. You may end up at the telephone book, but why start there?

The Qualifications and Qualities of an Expert

The qualifications and qualities of an expert are different. An expert's *qualifications* are, in essence, her credentials: What has she done that makes her eligible to call herself an expert, and contribute advice and opinions that will help you accomplish an objective? An expert's *qualities* are her other personal and professional characteristics. For a courtroom expert, this might include how well the expert speaks and responds to tough questions; how rigorous the expert's analysis is; and the expert's attitude toward billing, travel and preparation. Qualities also may include how the expert looks and dresses. While you can debate the relevance of a nattily dressed veterinarian for your puppy, an expert testifying on the witness stand should dress for success!

Use the following checklist to assess the qualifications and qualities of an expert advisor:

- Who is he or she? What is the expert's *relevant* education, *relevant* work experience, *relevant* background and other *relevant* qualifications? Is this a self-proclaimed expert, or does someone else recognize his talent? The expert's gold medal in swimming is great, *if* you need an expert in competitive swimming.
- What is the expert's track record? Has the expert accomplished something noteworthy or written notable pieces?
- Does the expert represent a certain school of thought, if there are divergent schools? You might have the world's foremost expert in primal-scream therapy, but if you require expertise

in another type of therapy, that won't help much!

- If the advisor claims to have published an article, where was it published? Peer-reviewed publications are more reliable than self-publications. Anyone can put advice on a personal Web site, self-publish a book or submit to journals with no peer review. Peer-reviewed journals only accept information for publication after it has been reviewed by a team of experts in that field who have spent a great deal of time studying the specific subject area of the publication. Before an article is published in a peer-reviewed publication, these expert editors ask the author to clarify to the publication points that do not meet the generally accepted analysis in the field, or to further justify points that are new or for which the data appear inadequate. By definition, peer-reviewed publications tend to be somewhat conservative (skeptical of new approaches that claim to "change everything"). When your health, money or future is on the line, the conservative view is not a bad place to start even if you end up taking more novel advice.

- If you are relying heavily on an article or other source, whether it was given to you by an expert candidate or is the product of your own research, are there sources that criticize the article? How credible are the critiques? In peer-reviewed articles, opposing views often are cited. You should read these other publications and data until you have a reasonable grasp of the controversy. In a field where controversy exists, a thorough expert will explain the varied opinions and why he or she holds a certain opinion. Be skeptical of experts who are too defensive, dismissive or insulting of contrary views, especially when the contrary views have credible support.

- There may be some connection between what an expert charges and the extent of his professional skill, although the correlation may not be perfect. Nonetheless, if you go out to find "the cheapest soil engineer in town," you may find a person who has been unable to build up a solid clientele after many years. The law of supply and demand applies to expert services.

- Do not choose an expert advisor based on stereotypes. A surprising number of people choose professionals based upon racial and religious stereotypes or age. After many years of dealing with all kinds of advisors, we can safely say that there are great and lousy practitioners from all backgrounds. While occasionally there are benefits to an expert who "has gray hair" (looks older), all in all it is what's under the hair that counts. You might be surprised to find that the gray-haired business lawyer you hired went back to school at age fifty-five and has been practicing law for only a year.

Be cautious of experts who do not treat you well. Do not assume that rudeness, insensitivity or poor communication skills are minor personality flaws that go with the expert's brilliance. If you cannot establish a rapport with the expert in the first couple of contacts, the situation will unlikely improve over time. Consider bailing out then and there.

Working with Your Experts

Depending on the subject, your relationship with an expert advisor may be short-lived or long. If you are about to buy a house, but are concerned with a geologic issue, you may hire a soil engineer. The engineer will come to your house, do a study, write a report and be gone. If you hire an accountant or attorney for advice and representation, you often will establish a long-term relationship. Many clients stay with their attorneys, accountants and physicians until the client or expert dies! To some extent, the expected length of the relationship will determine how much time and effort you spend hiring the expert. That is not to say that you always will give short shrift to temporary experts. You'd want to spend a lot of time to find the right brain surgeon to perform a single operation.

Whether the expert relationship will be short or long, keep the following in mind:

- Many professional advisors habitually give risk-averse advice. Their goal is to help you succeed—and if that doesn't work, to make sure you don't fail on their watch. Some people make risky decisions against professional advice because their own analysis tells them that a risk should be taken. While you certainly ignore expert advice at your own peril, peril also sometimes emerges in following an overly conservative path.

- You can and should question an expert about his conclusions and methods. Do not stay with the advisors who do not have time to explain themselves.

- Remember that experts make mistakes, some quite frequently. Never take your eye off your professional's work. Understand it as best you can. Do not just sign papers. If you have a court case, go to court with your lawyer—even to hearings that don't matter much. Listen to your doctor, but also listen to your body. If something's not right with your health, do not let anyone dismiss it. Nobel Prize–winning physicist Niels Bohr observed, "An expert is a man who has made all the mistakes which can be made, in a narrow field." What Bohr's comment omits is the fact that experts don't always learn from their mistakes. Expert knowledge is inherently limited by the complexity and increasing narrowness of professional fields. There are more than a hundred recognized medical specialties and subspecialties. Attorneys practice in dozens of distinct areas, and one who has loads of experience in one field may be incompetent in another.

- Try to figure out the hierarchy or other structure in which the expert operates and use it. If you are consulting a law firm, are you talking to a partner, associate or paralegal? Is it possible to seek a second opinion if the need arises from someone who is more senior or specialized at the firm?
- Change advisors if the advisor makes frequent or serious mistakes. Do not stay with an advisor just because it may be time-consuming to find another one. Don't be afraid of hurting the advisor's feelings by switching to someone more suitable for the job. You'd be amazed how often this is actually a factor!
- Make an acceptable financial deal with your expert up front, then do your part. If you don't pay your bill, service to you will not be high on the list when the expert has a choice (especially if the expert knows you can afford it). Taking an expert's time without paying for it is like telling the grocer that you'll pay for the vegetables when you get around to it. The only difference is that your life may be in the expert's hands.

Your Referral Source Is Important

When getting a referral—whether to a doctor, a lawyer, an accountant or a hairdresser—identify the best referral source, which often requires you to go beyond your usual network. If you live in a neighborhood where there are many lawyers, it may be easy to get a referral to a legal specialist from a neighbor who is an attorney. If you do not know any attorneys, find someone who does know attorneys. Seek a referral from a person who knows a number of people in a field. One person's experience with a single professional is anecdotal (see Step 5). A person with a terrible attorney, but a great case, can still win. It takes a good attorney to win a tough case. Likewise, an outstanding physician can fail to save a patient, while many people regain their health under the care of physicians who are prone to repeated incidents of malpractice. The professional reputation of an advisor is far more important than what a single client says.

Be creative when you look for a referral. Ask for help from people you might not normally approach. As discussed above, a famous physician may not have time to take you on as a patient, but may have a list of other physicians whom she respects. The same is true of attorneys. In some cases, the "Famous One" might even get on the phone with you. Professional practices tend to be part of informal referral networks—somewhat of a "you-scratch-my-back-and-I'll-scratch-yours" concept, to be blunt. The chance to send business to a colleague is often seen as an opportunity.

The same is true of business referrals. Many senior business-people operate in a world of business friends and contacts through neighborhoods, organizations and clubs. They pride themselves in knowing qualified people in many areas, often around the country or world. Just as it is with doctors and lawyers, the chance to send business to a contact is an opportunity. The chance to send "bad" business is not an opportunity, so prepare to be sized up when you go higher up for a referral. While you must be tactful when you request something from higher up, you rarely will be chastised. More often than not, the response from "Mr. Up" will be something like, "You know, one of my golfing friends is always talking about Cathy Smothers, who does exactly what you want for XYZ Corporation. Let me give you Cathy's number." If things work out with Cathy, report the success back to Mr. Up. If things don't work out (preferably not because of you!), consider reporting that back as well. After all, you don't want Mr. Up to be blindsided on the golf course with bad news.

It's hardly worth mentioning that self-referral is the weakest form of referral. The statements made in an expert's paid adver-tisements should be regarded with extreme caution. Most advertising publishers are just as happy to accept an ad from a charlatan as from the next oracle at Delphi. When you get to a pro-fessional through an advertisement, be sure to check qualifica-tions, track record and references if the consultation is on an extremely important issue.

Six Unfair Questions That Will Help You Manage Your Expert Advisors

For whatever reason, a lot of people are reluctant to put expert advisors on the spot. You are paying for the advisor's best advice. You will not benefit from the advisor's best advice unless you probe her thinking and understand as many of her assumptions and biases as possible. Some advisors would argue that the fol-lowing questions are unfair or misleading. We think they are great questions when asked properly, and be sure to follow up with more questions:

What would you do if you were me? This question is improper, right? The advisor is supposed to give you information and opin-ions, not run your life. You are supposed to make the Big Decision. Therefore, for all kinds of metaphysical reasons, asking your attorney whether he would plead guilty or your doctor whether he would have the surgery is not nice, right? Wrong. It's true that you should not make a decision based solely on what your advisor tells you he would do. Nonetheless, your advisor's response will tell you something about the advice, his or her feelings about your decision, and almost certainly will lead to further information that is valuable to your decision-making process.

Has this come up in your own life? What did you do? You'll hear some surprising responses to this one, especially from people in the medical field. When you ask your obstetrician whether you should get amniocentesis for your first baby if you are under thirty, you probably will be told, "No, it's only recommended if you're thirty-five or older unless you have genetic risk factors—otherwise it's not worth the risk and cost to do the procedure." If you ask whether his own wife had an amniocentesis at twenty-nine, you may find out that when it came to the physician's own family planning, a different rule applied. Likewise, a gastroenterologist may tell you not to start colon-cancer testing until age fifty if you have no special risk factors. That's the official position of the American Medical Association as of 2002. Would it change your view if you knew that your gastroenterologist started his own screening at forty? You may not get such contradictory results when you ask your own physician about his decisions, but shouldn't you know? It is appropriate to ask *relevant* personal questions of your physician. If your physician does not want to answer, she will let you know. Always do it nicely, respect the physician's privacy and thank the physician for sharing her own experience.

A certain number of professionals in every locale are the "doctors' doctors" and the "lawyers' lawyers." In other words, they are so respected in their field that the professionals themselves consult with these experts when an issue arises. If you have a serious problem, it may be worth your while to find out who the experts consider to be the expert. The "best" may not come cheaply, but may not be as expensive as you think. Without suggesting that the process should last forever, you may want to find out who the "doctor's doctor" or "lawyer's lawyer" sees when *he* needs a professional consultation!

Don't you have a conflict when you recommend that course of action? This question is touchy because the question will sound as if you are questioning the expert's integrity. Touchy or not, do it. "Isn't it true that I will pay you the same contingent fee if we settle right now or finish trying the case? . . . Why wouldn't you be telling me to settle?" "Isn't it in your interest to have your in-house medical lab do as many tests as possible on your patients?" The gist of the inquiry is totally legitimate. You are concerned that the incentives that govern your expert's advice may be skewed against your interests. Don't be intimidated, just ask nicely: "Are you sure this is the time to settle? I recognize that finishing the trial will be more work, especially for you, but I want to be sure I get a result I am happy about when I look back on this in two years." "Do you really think the test is necessary? I don't want to have an extra test even though it's very convenient." You'll get the point across, and a good professional will give you a reasoned answer.

What is your real view of the likely outcome, you know . . . not the view you have to give to protect yourself? This is a provocative question and should be delivered with a smile. When it is, you'll be surprised how often you actually get some new information! In medicine, the standard advice is often driven more by fear of malpractice suits than anything else. A good advisor will share some of the personal experience that makes him support or doubt the standard advice. The core of the advice will not likely change, but you will get some additional perspective and be able to make a more informed choice.

Have you ever handled a situation like this before? If not, are you the best person to do it? Many clients and patients are reluctant to ask questions that might bring a professional's skill or experience into question. It's hard to pinpoint why this is true—probably a combination of not wanting to disrespect the professional and desperately wanting the professional to be fully qualified to provide needed assistance. Nobody wants to feel that his expert is unqualified, and many people detest the process of searching for advisors and want to have found the right person for the job. Few professionals are resentful of this type of question. It is expected.

How much will this really cost me, now and down the road? The question not only goes to the expert's fees, although that certainly is something you want to understand. The expert's suggested course of action may have long-term cost implications that are highly relevant. When you are talking to a lawyer about filing a case, don't just talk about how much it will cost to get into the case. Talk about what it will cost for you to get out.

The quality of your Big Decisions will benefit greatly if you have the right team behind you. When you need an expert, take the time to find the right person for your needs. If the relationship doesn't work out, make a switch.

Appendix B

Thoughts on the Emotional Aspects of a Manager's Big Decision to Terminate an Employee

We want to offer a perspective on the emotional aspects of the employment relationship, especially a manager's decision to terminate an employee. Even the toughest businesspeople will tell you that the decision to terminate an employee can be among the most difficult management tasks. Here are common concerns:

- When an employee deserves to be terminated, as in a case of dishonesty, there is concern about the employee's reaction. Will he or she become hostile? Deny it and threaten litigation? Break down and cause an unpleasant scene at the workplace?
- When the termination results from economic circumstances, an employer may feel she has let down the employee. The economic problems were not caused by the employee, yet the employee (and possibly the employee's family) will suffer the most.
- When the termination results from an employee's poor performance or incompetence, the employer may be forced to tell the employee that he or she has failed—even if the employee tried hard. It's worse when the employee and supervisor are

friends. Many employees are loyal and put in enormous personal effort to do a good job. When it doesn't work out, and the relationship must end, plenty of personal disappointment is felt all around.

The trend in business is for employers in layoff situations to ease the pain through, for example, severance payments, outplacement benefits, references and other assistance. Many large employers offer early retirement or allow the employee to resign rather than be terminated as a way of putting the transition in a more favorable light. Although most U.S. employees are "at will" (an employer may terminate without any reason), some employers feel a moral need to justify a termination. Mergers, acquisitions and other major transitions frequently are used as an opportunity to clean out a backlog of employee terminations that could not be justified earlier.

For all these reasons, the termination of an employee frequently is a Big Decision for a manager. We have a few thoughts for managers who are faced with a termination decision. Employees (including all you managers!) may find these thoughts relevant as well:

- Your decision to terminate an employee probably will cause pain, both to you and to the employee. Your employee will suffer much more than you will, financially and emotionally. In many cases, neither of you deserves it. Do not tell the employee that the termination hurts you as much as it hurts him.

- Perpetuating dishonesty about where an employee stands damages the employee and your business. Keeping an employee until a business downturn forces your hand may put the employee in the job market at a poor time. Waiting until the employee "really screws up" may make *you* feel more justified when you terminate her, but it won't help the employee get another job. When things are not working out, you owe it to your employee to be "honest in real time" and put into motion a smooth transition.

- Explain to the employee clearly, honestly and tactfully why you made your decision.
- If you consider an employee to be your friend, treat him or her as a friend in a termination. Be honest. Provide support. Let your friend know that your friendship makes the situation extremely difficult. If the termination can be done without creating a worse problem, give your friend a "heads-up" when you know what's coming. In general, it is better for a terminated employee to know that a termination is coming, allowing the employee to find alternate work and start the emotional healing process while he or she is still employed.
- If you must terminate an employee because of a personality conflict, don't invent job performance reasons to avoid discussing the personality conflict. If you have to terminate an employee for job performance reasons, don't exacerbate personality issues just so you can feel better about the termination. You won't feel better, and the employee will feel worse.
- You owe it to your employee, unless the employee has done something very wrong, to handle a job transition compassionately and with the utmost respect for the employee.
- Try not to make termination decisions alone, even if you have the power to do so.

Nothing will make a termination decision easy. In most cases, a strong element of emotion will be present. The emotion should be acknowledged, respected and addressed head-on so everyone can move forward.

Index

About the Authors

Rhoda Makoff, Ph.D., is the retired chairman and CEO of R&D Laboratories, Inc., a specialty pharmaceutical company, and cofounder of the Crossroads School for Arts and Sciences in Los Angeles. Dr. Makoff received her B.A. in zoology from U.C.L.A. in 1958 and her Ph.D. in biochemistry from the U.C.L.A. School of Medicine in 1961. She was a U.S. Public Health Fellow, Department of Biochemistry, Harvard Medical School (1963–1966). She is presently the chairperson of the Board of Directors of the Los Angeles chapter of the U.S. Fund for UNICEF. Dr. Makoff is married and has four grown children and eight grandchildren.

Jeffrey Makoff, Esq., is the founding co-chairman and CEO of DigitalCustom Group, Inc., an international creative-services company, and an attorney licensed to practice in California and the District of Columbia. Mr. Makoff received his B.A. in political science from U.C.L.A. in 1981 and his law degree from University of California, Hastings College of the Law in 1985. Mr. Makoff practiced law at Skadden, Arps, Slate, Meagher & Flom before he and his wife, Charlotte Makoff, Esq., founded their San Francisco litigation and advisory firm in 1992. The firm handles a wide variety of matters, including media, antitrust, corporate, fiduciary, intellectual property and complex financial services cases. The Makoffs have two children.